Jesus Have I Loved,
but Paul?

Jesus Have I Loved, ***but Paul?***

A NARRATIVE APPROACH TO THE PROBLEM OF PAULINE CHRISTIANITY

J. R. DANIEL KIRK

Baker Academic
a division of Baker Publishing Group
Grand Rapids, Michigan

Published by Baker Academic
a division of Baker Publishing Group
P.O. Box 6287, Grand Rapids, MI 49516-6287
www.bakeracademic.com

Printed in the United States of America

Library of Congress Cataloging-in-Publication Data

Kirk, J. R. Daniel.
Jesus have I loved, but Paul? : a narrative approach to the problem of Pauline Christianity / J. R. Daniel Kirk.
p. cm.
Includes bibliographical references (p.) and index.
ISBN 978-0-8010-3910-2 (pbk.)
1. Bible. N.T. Epistles of Paul—Theology. 2. Jesus Christ—Teachings. 3. Narrative theology. I. Title.
BS2653.K57 2012
227′.066—dc23 2011028862

Unless otherwise noted, Scripture citations are the author's own translations.

11 12 13 14 15 16 17 7 6 5 4 3 2 1

For Opa

Contents

Acknowledgments

There are many people to thank, without whom this book either would not have come to fruition or else would be greatly impoverished.

I was aided and abetted by a veritable legion of readers. David Vinson faithfully read through the entire book, chapter by chapter, as it was being written, and thereby greatly improved both the content and the writing. Readers will never know how much in his debt they are. Other friends and colleagues have also provided invaluable feedback: Love Sechrest, Susie Flood, Pete Enns, Evan Curry, Alex Kirk, Brian White, Karyn Traphagen, and Mark Traphagen. Thank you all.

I want to thank John Franke, Scot McKnight, and Pete Enns for seeing the value in this project and connecting me with the folks at Baker Academic. And I wish to thank Bob Hosack for his encouragement on the project from day one. Special thanks go out to John Darnielle for permission to use the lyrics from "Love Love Love" that serve as the epigraph to chapter 9. Fuller Theological Seminary is my academic home, and I am thankful for its granting me a sabbatical in the fall of 2010 to complete work on this manuscript.

The energy to write the book has come from numerous conversations with people who love Jesus but have yet to meet a Paul who is largely in step with the Master. Thanks to all of you who have shared with me your intense and faithful wrestling with the biblical texts. In particular, thank you, Opa, for the conversations that gave me the passion to sit down and start writing. This book is for you.

Introduction

> In a deconstruction, our lives, our beliefs, and our practices are not destroyed but forced to reform and reconfigure—which is a risky business.
>
> —John D. Caputo, *What Would Jesus Deconstruct?*[1]

Problems with Paul?

"Now that Paul is out of your system," my grandfather said, "how about a book on Jesus, who actually got Christianity right, rather than writing about that rascal who mucked everything up?" I had just received a contract for my first book, a study of Paul's letter to the Romans. And though my grandfather's suggestion was playful, it also reflected genuine misgivings he harbors about Paul. Jesus preaches love of neighbor; Paul wants to expel the immoral brother. Jesus says, "Do unto others"; Paul is hung up on being a wretch.

My grandfather is not alone in these concerns. His consternation is likely due, in part, to the work of European New Testament scholarship from the early twentieth century trickling down from the ivory towers to the people on the streets. Scholars at that time gave more focused attention to Jesus and his proclamation of the kingdom of God. This led some experts on the New Testament to declare that a significant shift had occurred between Jesus and his followers. Although Jesus proclaimed the reign of God, Paul (and the early church more generally) proclaimed the reign of Jesus: "The proclaimer became the proclaimed."[2] This perspective took root outside the walls of the academy in the World War II generation of Europe and North America.

In our own day there is a resurgence of attention being paid to the Jesus of the Gospels, especially among Christians who were raised in evangelical churches. In these circles, Paul has traditionally served as the primary mouthpiece for the gospel. But this new generation is discovering afresh what scholars wrestled with a century ago: Jesus came proclaiming the reign of God, and if this is the gospel, then we need to reconsider a good deal of what we thought we knew. Why is the arrival on the scene of a wonder-working Jewish prophet good news? What does it mean for God to be at work in Jesus? Why is the life of Jesus before Calvary a gospel to be proclaimed? In the process of wrestling with Jesus, and falling in love with the figure we meet on the pages of the Gospels, many have simultaneously lost their affection for Paul.

The apostle might seem to fall short of the Master on any number of fronts. Paul seems unconcerned with the stories of Jesus's life. Related to this, some might see him as a thinker who spent too much time theologizing about Jesus's death. Others might be drawn to the activist ministry of Jesus over against a faith-alone heart religion.

Still another challenge grows out of the history of American (and Western European) Christianity. Paul gave voice to preservation of the status quo during the era of American slavery. When he is juxtaposed with the Jesus who proclaims liberty to the captive, the contrast between the early preachers is stark. Thus, particularly in scholarly circles, Paul has struggled to find a voice among some segments within African American Christianity.

The issues of race and slavery might also be seen as simply one subject under a larger umbrella of justice where Paul falls far short of Jesus. And now we are right up against the vexing issue of homosexuality, where many Christians who are affirming find an ally in Jesus that they do not find in Paul, who condemns such practice.

So if you are someone who follows Jesus but have at some point wrestled with Paul or felt some dissonance between Paul and Jesus, you are not alone. Some people find Paul lacking in comparison with the Master; others simply find Paul distasteful, offensive, oppressive, exclusive, confusing, arrogant, or just plain wrong. This book is, in part, for folks who at times find themselves resonating with the statement, "Jesus have I loved, but Paul have I hated." I have been there myself.

One of my earliest memories of reading the Pauline letters is a nettled encounter with 2 Corinthians 11–12. In these chapters, Paul is defending his work as an apostle, piling up language of boasting, through examples of acting foolishly, of glorying in disgraceful experiences, of weakness and visions of glory. As I read those chapters, Paul's litany of irony and boasting struck me as truly foolish and arrogant. When I first met Paul I simply did not like him.

Even when I began to appreciate Paul, however, he still caused me problems. In college I began investigating some of the classic theological questions, including the subject of predestination and issues of church government. Now, finally, the letters bearing Paul's name became my friends, because they addressed most directly the questions I was asking. But this new relationship was starting to cause discord in some of my old ones; specifically, my understanding of "the church" left little room for affirming my brother's "parachurch" ministry, and my zealous affirmation of male leadership disrupted relationships with many women in ministry, including my mother, who was ordained while I was in this stage in my theological pilgrimage. And so my relationship with the apostle continued to be uneasy.

In the process of going through graduate school in New Testament I began to read Paul differently. Though there are still some tensions between us, I not only find myself more at peace with him, but I also find the apostle to be a challenging and theologically generative partner along the way of following Jesus. This book is an invitation to join me along the present leg of my journey.

Moving toward a Storied Paul

My current reading of Paul has its roots in several complementary factors. I have spent much more time with Paul's letters and so have a broader understanding of those letters' purposes and arguments. This has enabled me to see more clearly that the questions I was bringing to the text were not usually the questions that the text was written to answer (even if the assumptions that broke through in the course of a Pauline argument might still pertain to the issues on which I was seeking guidance).

A second, related factor placed Paul on a broader canvas, where he made more sense. My seminary taught what it called "redemptive historical" readings of Scripture. Such an approach involves continually asking how the work of God in Christ is connected to the prior works of God in the Old Testament. I began to see that Paul was assessing the work of Jesus and the lives of Jesus's followers within a narrative that had its roots in Adam and Abraham, Moses and David. In this sense, even Paul's didactic arguments evoke an indispensable narrative dynamic.

Such a positioning of Paul within the larger narrative sweep of Israel's story prepared me for a third factor in how my reading of Paul has changed, and it is this facet of Paul's letters that frames the invitation to rediscover the apostle on the following pages. This third element is a recognition that Paul's letters themselves contain narrative dynamics: the story of Christ creates a controlling narrative in which Paul sees himself, the church, Israel, and ultimately the entire cosmos participating. In arguing for a more storied reading of Paul, New Testament scholars have undoubtedly been participating in cultural trends that tend toward a deeper appreciation of the role and value of narrative—and, I will argue, they have provided a lens for reading Paul that has tremendous potential to answer some of the most pressing questions brought to Paul by his postmodern readers.

Because in my own journey I have moved from taking offense at Paul, to relishing Paul as Reformed theological ammunition, to delighting in Paul the storyteller, I find that I have something to say to my fellow followers of Jesus who want to keep Paul at arm's length. I have discovered through conversation with numerous Christians during the past several years that the Paul I now love is not usually the Paul others cannot abide. Measured against the portraits of Paul that have been carefully crafted by the past generation of New Testament scholars, many common images of Paul prove, on closer inspection, to be distortions. Some of these common images include:

- Paul the angry Reformed theologian, who delights in the God who takes pleasure in sending huge numbers of people to hell
- Paul the promoter of internalized Christianity, who leaves saved individuals with little motivation for faithful work or life in community
- Paul the Neoplatonist, who despises embodied life and the good things of the earth
- Paul the exclusivist, who undermines Jesus's missional ministry of indiscriminate embrace
- Paul the oppressor, who lends his apostolic credentials to narratives of enslavement and domination
- Paul the judge, whose whole life is lived in contradiction to Jesus's admonition against judging articulated in the Sermon on the Mount
- Paul the chauvinist, who doesn't want anything to do with women—especially not in the ministry of the church and, preferably, not in sexual relationships either
- Paul the imposer of order, who effectively squelched the Spirit-led worship and life that had characterized Jesus's first followers

In all, such assessments might be summarized as an abandonment of the sweeping vision for discipleship articulated in Jesus's proclamation of the kingdom of God. In response I would suggest that many followers of Jesus need a healthy deconstruction of their understanding of Paul.

A Storied Paul for Postmodernity

At a conference in 2007, John Caputo articulated a winsome vision of the philosophical concept "deconstruction." Deconstruction is not destruction, at least not destruction for destruction's sake. Rather, deconstruction is an attempt to break through hardened structures and traditions for the purpose of reengaging the stimulating, life-giving substance that gave rise to the now-encrusted traditions.[3] In this spirit of deconstruction as a punching through the rocks in order to open up a well from which to draw life-giving waters, this book is about deconstructing Paul. I am suggesting here not that Paul needs to be deconstructed in order for postmodern followers of Jesus to appreciate him but that our understandings of Paul need to be deconstructed for that purpose. This will begin, as the pages that follow will show in greater detail, with an appreciation for the narrative dynamics of Paul's letters.

Having invoked the words *postmodern* and *deconstruction* in the previous paragraph, I should say a little more about why I am embracing these labels. I use the word *postmodern* as a description of the multicultural ethos one finds in places such as Western Europe, North America, Australia, and New Zealand in the early years of the twenty-first century. Characteristic of these cultures are ways of knowing, of defining one's values, and of defining one's community that depend on networks of relationships and other contextual factors rather than what previous generations would have seen as the implications of supposedly objective criteria.

To my mind, the advent of postmodernity as a social reality in North America is marked by the release of the film *Pulp Fiction* in 1994. The movie teems with questions about how we know, about our own roles in shaping knowledge, about our society's place in shaping the meaning of words and actions. You can't refer to a sandwich as a "Quarter Pounder" in a country with the metric system. A man giving a woman a foot massage means something, even if we act like it doesn't.

The world of evangelical Christianity provides its own numerous illustrations of the cultural shift from modernity to postmodernity. A prominent example is evangelicals' assessment of the Bible. In an earlier era, modern culture strengthened evangelicals' confidence in what could be known through metaphors of construction, what philosophy refers to as "foundationalism." Building from the ground up, so the image goes, the strength of any piece of knowledge is dependent on the strength of prior, more foundational pieces of knowledge on which it is built. In such a world, evangelical Christianity insisted that the Bible is the foundational source of all our knowledge about the work God has done for us. Therefore, it must be true in all that it says if people are to be expected to believe its message of salvation. Without the foundation of an inerrant Bible, so the argument goes, the edifice of Christianity would soon come crashing down.

I take it as a sign of the significant cultural shift to postmodernity that innumerable evangelicals are holding on to their core evangelical convictions (including the Bible as the Word of God) without feeling the compulsion to embrace the notion of the inerrancy of Scripture. Part of what contemporary Christians have acquired is the ability to step back and recognize that their own commitment to following Jesus was not, in fact, built on a prior theology of the Bible. They see the witness of Scripture being directed primarily to something other than itself: the work of God in Christ. And the Bible is but one part of a larger whole. The person who shared the faith with them is another such witness, as is the community of believers that embodies for them the truth of the message they heard. They meet with God in song and prayer and liturgy and sacrament. For this generation (in which I include myself), a network of relationships and experiences fills the primary role of confirmation of our beliefs that earlier evangelicals would have located primarily in "objective" truths such as the inerrancy of Scripture or, to take another example, proofs of the resurrection.

Both modernity and postmodernity have the power to reach back into the history of the church and highlight aspects of the old that deeply resonate with their respective cultures. The concerns of modernity find deep resonance with the desire to "prove" Christianity found in the early church's apologists and with the argumentative power of Augustine, Aquinas, and Anselm. And Paul is adept at building logical and complex arguments in his letters.

But what moderns too easily lost sight of was the way that all knowledge is received and assessed within complex webs of relationships that help people know what is true. If modernity's metaphor was "building," postmodernity's metaphor is "story." The impact of this is not only to cause a reassessment of how or why someone knows something to be true. In Christian circles it has also begun to generate considerable reflection on how the narratives of Scripture function, *as stories*, to define the respective identities of God, Jesus, and Christian communities.[4]

How well can Paul possibly fare in such a context? Paul writes letters rather than stories. To make matters worse, the argumentative nature of his letters has caused Paul to be a favorite biblical source for theologians of earlier generations whom postmodern readers no longer find compelling.

Despite such setbacks, however, the postmodern attention to story has generated an important stream of scholarship that is now highlighting the narrative dynamics of Paul's letters. In this book I am going to mine the storied texture of Paul's writing to show how it offers a compelling reading strategy for making sense of the apostle. Moreover, I hope that the result will be a more attractive picture of his theology for those who have been put off by caricatures of Paul such as the ones I listed above. So what sort of story does Paul have to tell? And how does this mesh with the stories of Jesus we discover in the Gospels?

1

Jesus Stories in the Gospels and Paul

> The only "system" in Holy Scripture and proclamation is revelation, i.e., Jesus Christ.
>
> —Karl Barth, *Church Dogmatics*[1]

To understand the Jesus story that awaits us when we turn to the New Testament, we must be attuned to it as a climactic scene in the larger story of Israel. This is how both the Gospel writers and Paul invite us to make sense of the significance of Jesus. What Christians refer to as the "Old Testament," what for Paul and Jesus were simply the Writings or "the Law and the Prophets," contains a narrative awaiting a dramatic conclusion. The story that holds together the Gospels and Paul might be summarized like this: the God of Israel acted decisively in the person of Jesus to restore God's rule and reconcile the whole world to himself. If this sounds to your ears more like a scene than a fully developed plot, then you begin to see the importance of locating Jesus within the larger narrative sweep of which his life is a part.

The God of Israel

Growing up in church circles, I observed that the adults around me talked about God using all-encompassing adjectives such as *omniscient*, *omnipotent*, and *omnipresent*. To such a list of somewhat abstract traits we might also add the claim that "God is good." The importance of naming such descriptors was to help introduce us to the God we serve. To understand God was to know which attributes applied.

But there was a surprise awaiting me when I turned to study the Bible a bit more closely. Though such apparently timeless, abstract categories are not entirely absent from the Bible, the key ways of naming God describe him as someone who is at work within and even bound to the story of Israel. God in the Scriptures is "the God of Abraham, Isaac, and Jacob"; "the God of the Hebrews"; "the God who brought us up out of the land of Egypt, out of the house of bondage." The point here is simply to signal that we fall into a trap if we think we have identified God by simply stating *what* God is (eternal, infinite, unchangeable) without showing *who* God is.

The God we are talking about when we talk about the God who is at work in Jesus is the God who has bound himself to the story of Israel. This means both that the God who is worthy of our worship has acted to save Israel from countless enemies past (the story of the Old Testament) and that this God is bound by a promise to bring about one more climactic act of deliverance. This new act of redemption would fully restore God's people to the glory he had promised. In other words, to read the Scriptures of Israel is to discover not only that God has a past, with a complex relationship to one particular people, but also that God has a future, in which all those relational complications will be resolved. Both the Gospels and Paul claim that this is the God at work in their gospel message, and both claim that Israel's long-anticipated deliverance is the purpose of Jesus's life, death, and resurrection.

The opening verses of each Gospel (Matthew, Mark, Luke, and John) issue invitations to read the ensuing stories as ones in which the God of Israel is once again at work. The God of Abraham, Isaac, and Jacob is bringing the narrative of Israel to its long-awaited conclusion. To take but one example, Mark begins like this: "The beginning of the gospel of Jesus Christ, the Son of God. As it is written in Isaiah the prophet, 'Behold! I am sending my messenger before of you, who will prepare your way'" (Mark 1:1–2).[2] The good news about Jesus begins with God acting to fulfill what the prophets spoke long before. The God who is at work here, to send John the Baptist and then Jesus after him, is the God who spoke by Israel's prophets. Isaiah's (and the Old Testament's) long-awaited future is Jesus's present. God is the main character of the biblical narrative, and the Jesus stories of the Gospels claim to be God's long-anticipated return to bring the narrative to its definitive resolution.

Turn to Paul and you find an identical claim. Paul introduces Romans with an indication that the letter is read aright only when we see how it proclaims the great, climactic work of the God of Israel to bring the story of the Hebrews to its promised conclusion.[3] Here is how the letter begins: "Paul, a slave of Christ Jesus, called to be an apostle, set apart for the gospel of God that God promised beforehand, in the holy Scriptures, concerning his Son" (Rom. 1:1–3). The similarities with Mark are striking. The gospel message is about God's Son. That message comes in fulfillment of the promises spoken in the Scriptures of Israel. And this message about the Son is simultaneously the story where God is at work (this last point becomes more clear as one moves through the letter). Jesus is the embodiment of God's making good on the ancient promise to bring Israel's story to a saving end.

Both the Gospels and Paul intend to show us that Jesus's story is God's story. Depending on where you come from, this might be obvious to the point of being trite, or it might be the key to unlocking the whole mystery of the relationship between Jesus and Paul. For now, I simply draw our attention to the fact that Paul couches his narrative of the saving Christ in terms almost identical to Mark's. As our study unfolds, it will become increasingly apparent that God, precisely as the God of Israel, holds the story together from start to finish in both the Gospels and the letters of Paul.

Israel

Getting Israel firmly on the table is crucial for a couple of reasons. First, it helps to ensure that when we talk about God we know which

God we are talking about: the God of Israel. Thus, this discussion is very closely tied to the previous section. It also draws our attention to the story within which Jesus's and Paul's missions both make sense. As both Paul and the four Gospels depict the Jesus story, we discover that Jesus simultaneously meets and transforms the expectations of ancient Israel. We need to recognize why Israel's good news is good news for the rest of us as well.

From early on, the story of Israel is one of a scandalous particularity: God elects one nation from all the peoples of the earth. And yet it is a particularity in service of a worldwide vision: God elects Israel to mediate God's presence and blessing to the world. This is something we have to allow to sink deep into our minds and hearts if we are to sing out in response to what the New Testament so often depicts as the "good news." Simply put, because the God who created all things has chosen to be the God of Israel, salvation must therefore come through this particular people, in accordance with the promises that God spoke through Israel's prophets.

Israel as New Creation

Reaching back to the beginning of all things, Israel told the story of the world, and of people in it, as the prelude to its own story. In fact, Israel's unfolding drama reads as the story of one nation that God has chosen to play the role that God had first assigned to humanity as a whole. Hints of this come as the creation narrative is echoed in later stories. At the beginning, God blesses humanity with the mandate to be fruitful and multiply (Gen. 1:28). Later, when God establishes covenants with Abraham, Isaac, and Jacob, he promises to make them fruitful and multiply them (Gen. 16:10; 17:6, 20; 22:17; 26:4, 24; 28:3; 35:11; 48:4). The original blessing of creation is focused on the forefathers of Israel.

We also read in Genesis 1:26–27 that God creates people with one particular function: to rule the world on God's behalf. And we then find a promise to Abraham that from his line kings will arise (Gen. 17:6). Humanity's calling to rule the world on God's behalf will be fulfilled by the kings of Israel who perform precisely this function. The story of Israel is the story of God's refusal to give up on humanity.

It is the story of God re-creating humanity through this one people, Israel, to whom God has chosen to bind himself.

The reason God chooses to focus humanity's purpose in Israel is not for Israel's sake alone. Rather, Israel will be the protagonist who works good for the sake of the world. And so the forefather of Israel, Abraham, is promised more. Yes, he will be fruitful and multiply, and yes, kings will come from him. But God also tells Abraham that he will be the conduit for God's blessing to the nations of the earth: "I will bless those who bless you, those who curse you I will curse, and all the families of the earth will bless themselves by your name" (Gen. 12:3). If God is the source of Abraham's blessing, Abraham is the source of the world's blessing. This means that the only way for the world to be blessed is for God to bless Israel first. And this is why the story of Jesus, in both the Gospels and in Paul, is the story of Israel brought to its God-ordained climax.[4] God is making good on the promise to Abraham to bless the entire world through Israel.

Israel's Future

The story of Israel becomes, over the course of the biblical narrative, a tale of unrequited love leading to national disaster. Israel's failure to live up to God's calling to be the obedient, faithful representatives of humanity lands the people in exile. A people who had been promised a land was carted off to another country. A people who had been promised abundant descendants was decimated in war. A people who had been promised a king was living in subjection to foreign overlords. A people who had been promised the presence of God had its temple destroyed. A people who had been promised prosperity had been plundered.

Israel's prophets were unflinching in their prognostications of exile, but they were even more expansive in their hopes for restoration. Among the many promises for the future were the following: there would be a new king from the line of David who would rule God's people faithfully and thereby lead God's people into faithfulness (e.g., Ezek. 34:23–24; 37:24–28); God would pour out his own spirit so that people would be transformed, given new hearts, and thereby made able to obey God for the first time (e.g., Isa. 44:1–5; Jer. 31:31–34); the people would be on the land, free from foreign overlords, and the land would produce for them in abundance (Jer. 31; Ezek. 34, 37); the temple would be gloriously restored, greater than before, and God would fill the temple with his presence (e.g., Ezek. 40–47; Hag. 2:6–9). All this glorification of Israel would, in turn, glorify the God of Israel in the sight of all the nations so that they, looking on the transformed, restored people of God would be drawn to worship Israel's God (Isa. 56:1–8; 60:1–22).

When the Old Testament draws to a close, this vision of glory is all in the future tense. The people had, in fact, come back from exile, but they were not yet free on their own land. They had no king, being subjected still to the rule of the nations. There was a rebuilt temple, but it was pitiful compared to the old. There was no glory of Israel with which to draw the nations to glorify Israel's God.

The Gospels as Israel's Future

So when we pick up the Gospels and read about the generations from Abraham to David to the exile to Jesus (Matt. 1:1–17), or the declaration from Mark, cited above, that the subsequent story is what is spoken in the prophets, we need to pause to consider two things. First, each Gospel narrates the claim that the prophets' future tense has now become present reality with the life, death, and resurrection of Jesus. Second, it is *only* by completing the story of Israel that salvation can go out to the nations.

Luke's Gospel provides a striking example of how the Jesus story provides the resolution to Israel's previously unfinished drama. The angel announcing Jesus's birth to his mother, Mary, says that Jesus will be given the throne of David and will rule over the house of Jacob (Luke 1:32–33). In her own song celebrating Jesus's coming birth, Mary anticipates that a new reign will be established and old kings deposed because God is going to fulfill the promise spoken to Abraham and his descendants (Luke 1:52–55). And in a song that weaves an elaborate tapestry from the threads of Old Testament promises, Zechariah, the father of John the Baptist, sings about God redeeming his people; about God raising up a king in David's line who will save; about fulfilled prophecies of deliverance from enemies; about God remembering and acting on the covenants sworn to Abraham, Isaac, and Jacob, creating a people who can serve God righteously; and about all of this as God's salvation to the people of Israel (Luke 1:68–79).

Luke certainly intends for us to see Jesus's story bringing the story of Israel to its climactic resolution. But there is a surprise in store as well, something so shocking that his disciples could not believe it even when Jesus told them plainly. The means by which all these great promises of redemption and restoration would come to pass would be through the Messiah's death, resurrection, and exaltation. And so Luke concludes the story of the Gospel with the resurrected Jesus appearing to his disciples and telling them what the Scriptures say about the Messiah (that is, about him).

> He said to them, "These are my words which I spoke to you while I was still with you: It is necessary for all that is written about me in the law of Moses and in the Prophets and in the Psalms to be fulfilled!" Then he opened their minds to understand the Scriptures and said to them, "Thus is it is written that the Messiah has to die and rise from the dead on the third day, and that repentance leading to forgiveness of sins has to be proclaimed in his name to all the nations, beginning from Jerusalem." (Luke 24:44–47)

The fulfillment of Scripture's expectations about the Messiah who would rule the world on God's behalf comes to pointed realization with the crucifixion and resurrection. This is how Israel is going to know the forgiveness that can lead to its restoration; this is the light that will enlighten the nations. Shortly thereafter (Luke 24:49) Jesus promises the Spirit to the disciples, providing them another clue as to how Jesus's death and resurrection form the fulcrum point on which Israel's story turns.

We will wrestle with several implications of this story in more detail as we work our way through the various issues that confront us in Jesus's ministry. For now the important takeaway is that Jesus as we meet him on the pages of the Gospels is not living out a self-contained story. He is acting out a final, climactic scene in the ongoing drama of Israel that stretches back to creation and comes to its promised resolution with his death and resurrection. And we see the same claim in Paul.

Paul's Churches and Israel's Future

The Corinthian correspondence is a treasure trove of indications that Paul reads the story of Jesus as the continuation and climax of the story of Israel. Once we have our minds tuned to the frequency of Paul's storytelling, we can receive how he wants his non-Jewish (gentile) churches to reconceive their own identities. They have been scripted into the story of Israel. Israel's God is their God. Israel's people is their people. Israel's hopes are their reality. To help us get hold of this, we will look at one indication that the Corinthians share in Israel's past and one indication that they are participating in Israel's hoped-for future.

Paul wants the Corinthians to know that Israel's past has become the church's story as well. In 1 Corinthians 10 he draws on stories from the exodus narrative and the book of Numbers to encourage the church to faithful perseverance. He begins, "For I do not want you to be unaware, brothers and sisters, that our fathers were all under the cloud and all passed through the sea" (1 Cor. 10:1). As is so often the case, Paul addresses the church in familial terms: "brothers and sisters." As such, he beckons them to look back on their common ancestry: our fathers were all under the cloud of God's presence. But the church that Paul is addressing is made up completely of gentiles, while the "fathers" in the exodus story are all Jewish. Paul has written his gentile converts so thoroughly into the Jewish story that they, no less than Jews physically descended from Abraham, Isaac, and Jacob, can look back to the trials of the exodus generation and see in those forebears their own fathers and mothers.[5] They have a new story. We begin to understand Paul only when we see that his is a narrative theology in which the story of Israel plays a determinative role in forming the identity of the people of God.

Not only is Israel's past the past of the church, Israel's hoped-for future has begun in the church's present. Recall in our summary of Israel's story that we mentioned how Israel was to be a blessing to the nations. In particular, Israel as a glorified people, among whom God's presence is clearly manifest, was to be the means by which the nations would be drawn to glorify Israel's God.

One verse that anticipates the nations in such a posture of glorifying Israel's God is Isaiah 45:14, where the gentiles proclaim, "God is with you alone, and there is no other" (NRSV).[6] Paul picks up this verse and inserts it into his discussion of spiritual gifts in 1 Corinthians 14. How is it that God's glory is so made known among the nations that they fall on their faces, glorifying God, declaring that God is certainly among the people? It is by God's pouring out the Spirit on the church, the body of Christ, so that by the Spirit's power the people may prophesy. Israel's role of drawing the nations to worship Yahweh has now become the calling of the church. The church not only adopts the story of Israel's past; it also becomes the story of Israel's hoped-for future.

The upshot of all this is that the story of the church is intelligible only as the continuation of the story of Israel. Paul is not merely making arguments in his letters; he is narrating the story of Israel with his gentile churches as full participants in that drama. Paul also understands that we not only interpret stories but also are interpreted by them. And so we discover that Paul is a narrative theologian, striving to help his churches understand a new past, present, and future that are all-determinative for their identity, now that they are followers of Jesus. To understand who they are in Christ, Paul's gentile churches, no less than we, require a comprehensive reframing of their story, what Richard Hays refers to as a "conversion of the imagination."[7]

Jesus Restores God's Rule

If the gospel story is the story of Israel's God, it is still an open question what role this God might assign to the principal New Testament protagonist, and how such a character will relate to God and the people within whose story he is operating. To probe the ministry of Jesus as it relates to the God of Israel is to bring us face-to-face with the greatest challenge of reconciling Jesus and Paul: what does Jesus's proclamation of the reign of God have to do with Paul's proclamation of Jesus as the crucified and risen Lord?

Jesus the King of the Kingdom

In the Gospel narratives, Jesus proclaimed, inaugurated, embodied, and enacted the kingdom or dominion of God.[8] Someone reading through the Gospels from a traditional Christian perspective might be surprised to discover what many contemporary Jesus followers have seen, that the major theme of Jesus's teaching is the dominion of God rather than the dominion of Jesus or the dominion of the Messiah more generally. Jesus begins his public ministry in Mark's Gospel by crying out, "The time is fulfilled and the dominion of God has come near." He tells mysterious stories that shroud the nature of the dominion of God—but these mysteries Jesus reveals to his inner circle (Mark 4:11). The dominion of God is depicted as the quintessential destination: a realm of salvation entered into by children but nearly always shut up to the rich (Mark 10:13–31). In teaching about God's dominion, Jesus seems to be entirely focused on drawing attention away from himself as God's Messenger and to the God who reigns as the object of his and his followers' devotion.

However, the story of the Gospels is not so simple. If it is faithful to the Gospels to say that Jesus proclaims God, it is equally true to say that in these same Gospels God proclaims Jesus. There are only two or three times in the Gospels when God's voice literally sounds from heaven, and in each the heavenly witness is testifying to Jesus's identity as God's Son. The readers of Mark are privy to this divine interpretation of Jesus's identity at the beginning of his ministry, when Jesus goes out to be baptized by John the Baptizer. "You are my beloved Son," the voice from heaven declares (Mark 1:10–11). Later, just after the pivotal moment of Peter's confessing Jesus to be the Messiah (Mark 8:29), the voice of God speaks from a cloud on a mountain. While Jesus becomes gleaming white before his disciples' eyes, the heavenly testimony again proclaims Jesus to be the Son of God: "This is my beloved Son. Listen to him!" (Mark 9:2–8).[9] The point is made for us as readers as well as for the characters in the story. To know God's plan for the salvation of humanity is to watch and listen to Jesus as he embodies that plan in the unfolding Gospel story.

How, then, is Jesus related to the dominion of God? The Gospels depict Jesus filling the role of the king who rules in God's kingdom, the one through whom God is exercising God's reign. Many of the stories of Jesus's miracles and exorcisms are told to make just this point. When Jesus calms a deadly storm on the Sea of Galilee, his disciples respond in amazement: "Who then is this that even the wind and sea obey him?" (Mark 4:41). Jesus, as one given dominion over the order of creation, is the point of the story. The Son of Man has authority over all the earth.

We see a similar emphasis when Jesus casts out demons. When Jesus is first confronted by a person with an "unclean spirit," the demonic voice and the response of the people both draw attention to the person and power of Jesus, which are the point of the narrative. A spirit asks Jesus if he intends to destroy them, a capability that Jesus has because he is "the Holy One of God" (Mark 1:24). People wonder about Jesus and his teaching because they contain so much power that even unclean spirits obey. Jesus is putting on display not only the dominion of the God whom he proclaims but also his own role as one given unique authority to see that dominion realized on earth. The story of the Gospels is the story of God, to be sure, but of God at work in a uniquely powerful way in Jesus. Jesus is the Messiah, the King of Israel who represents God's rule to the world. And in doing this, Jesus plays the role of the first humans, a role later assigned to Israel, to rule the world on God's behalf (Gen. 1:26).

The Resurrected Lord

As we will see in more detail in chapter 2, Paul assigns to the resurrected Jesus what the Gospels ascribe to his life on earth. When Paul tells the story of the cosmos, one great determinative event is the resurrection of Jesus, which made him Lord over all things. There is a hint of this in the titles Paul assigns Jesus. "Lord Jesus Christ" means that Jesus is Israel's promised Messiah who is therefore the sovereign over all the earth. "Christ" and "Messiah" represent the Greek and Hebrew words that mean "anointed person." In Israel's Scriptures this is a king, a priest, or a prophet. And to call Jesus "Lord" is not to issue an invitation but to make a statement about who is in charge of the entire cosmos. Jesus, the Messiah, is the Lord over all.

The story of the man Jesus becoming Lord over all things is told at several points in Paul's letters. One of these is Philippians 2:5–11. This passage speaks of Jesus, who, as a human, humbled himself to become obedient to death on a cross (v. 8). Therefore, God exalted him and gave him the highest name, such that everyone will confess, "Jesus

Christ is Lord," to the glory of God the Father (Phil. 2:11). Whereas the Gospels give us a voice from heaven as proof that God bears witness to Jesus, Paul gives us the resurrection. Whereas the Gospels show us Jesus on earth acting like the one empowered by God to rule the world on God's behalf, Paul's letters proclaim that this power is bestowed when Jesus is enthroned to God's right hand at the resurrection.

From time to time I hear of people whose struggle with Paul is that he seems to think that the world and embodied life in it are bad, or that what he thinks is truly real and weighty is the heavenly world we hope to escape to when we die. Some version of this was in the mind of someone who told me that he could not read Paul without seeing Plato's philosophy all over the place. But escape from this world is not the story Paul tells about the resurrection of Jesus. Resurrection is not about flight from creation but about new creation.

Paul does not make his claims about Jesus as the exalted ruler of the earth because Jesus has escaped his life of embodied humanity. To the contrary, he issues his claims because Jesus, as embodied and resurrected, is the quintessential human, the one who fulfills the role God intended for people at the first: to rule the world on God's behalf (Gen. 1:26–27). When Paul works out his theology of Jesus as resurrected Lord, he evokes Genesis 1–3 by drawing an extended analogy with the first man, Adam (1 Cor. 15; see also Rom. 5). As Second Adam, the One who now represents humanity in the presence of God, Christ must reign until the whole world is put in order (1 Cor. 15:24). This is Paul's theology of the kingdom of God: Christ is the resurrected human who is reigning, now, over the kingdom that is God's. The dominion that the Gospels depict Jesus inaugurating during his ministry on earth is the kingdom over which Paul sees Jesus enthroned at God's right hand. And Paul's perspective, we might add, is shared by Matthew, who has the resurrected Jesus proclaim, "All authority in heaven and on earth has been given to me" (Matt. 28:18). It is also shared by Luke, who has Peter declare at Pentecost that at the resurrection God made Jesus Lord and Messiah (Acts 2:32–36).

How do we understand Jesus's story as Paul tells it? We must understand it as the story of the man who, as Israel's king and therefore representative of all humanity before God, rules the world on God's behalf. There are sweeping implications for this: if God has chosen to save the world by a human, to enthrone a human over God's kingdom, to see humanity's creation-order role restored, then we are not reading a story of a God who has given up on the created world. We are reading the story of a God who is going to see the creation of his hands renewed and restored from top to bottom. Our journey through Paul's story will show us that the restoration is as vast as the cosmos and as deep as the human heart, and that in between it seeks to restore not only humanity's relationship with God but also humans' relationships with one another and with the whole created order.

The story Paul tells is one in which the God who made all things maintained an unshaken commitment to his beloved creation. It is not a story of escape from a fallen world on which God has given up. It is a story of God restoring the world and winning a victory over the powers that had supplanted his rule. Paul's letters should be read as an attempt to help the young Christian communities of the ancient Mediterranean world figure out how to live under the reign of the resurrected Christ, which is to say, guiding them in how to take hold of the future of the redeemed world and bring it to bear on the present. Jesus is raised to restore the rule of God, and the churches are the entry points for this restoration project.

Jesus Reconciles God's World

Both the Gospel writers and Paul proclaim the good news that the story of Israel's God is being brought to its consummation as Jesus restores God's reign on the earth. But if Jesus's life entails inaugurating the reign of God, and Paul sees the reign embodied by the resurrected Christ, what about the cross that falls in between? Why does Jesus have to die in the Gospel narratives if his life on earth is, itself, the good news? And how does Paul's "word of the cross" fit into his proclamation of the resurrected Lord?

Mark's Crucified King

The first thing to say about the Gospels is that the story of Jesus the King is the story of the crucified King. An overview of Mark will help drive this home.

I have already mentioned that God bears witness to Jesus in Mark, revealing to the reader that Jesus is "God's Son." As Christian readers, we are often quick to fill this phrase with the idea of divinity; we think, "preexistent Son," something more or less equivalent to "Second Person of the eternal Trinity." But in the story of Israel "son of God" means something else. It refers to the king who rules the world on God's behalf.

Psalm 2 is a perfect example of this. It is a song about the king of Israel being enthroned. Yahweh says, "I have set my king on Zion" (Ps. 2:6). When the king is enthroned, he becomes God's son. The king's voice speaks, "I will tell of the decree of Yahweh! He said to me, 'You are my son, today I have begotten you.'" To be the king of Israel is to be the son of God. This is exactly what God promises David in 2 Samuel 7:14: God will be a father to the Davidic king, and the king will be a son to Yahweh. And this is nothing less than a claim that the king of Israel fulfills the role of Adam, who was created in God's image and likeness (i.e., a son of God; cf. Gen. 5:1–3) for the purpose of ruling the world on God's behalf. In the drama of the cosmos, humanity rules for God as son of God, and Israel enacts that story in the enthronement of its king.

Thus, when we come to the very beginning of Jesus's ministry in Mark and the divine voice tells him, "You are my beloved Son," we are entering a story about Jesus as King. What, then, does this have to do with the crucifixion?

The book of Mark is structured by three direct revelations that Jesus is the "Son of God"; this happens twice by divine voice, at the beginning and the middle/turning point, and once by a human at the end. Jesus's ministry begins with one of these divine proclamations as he comes up out of the waters at his baptism. In the ensuing story, we catch a glimpse of how it is true that Jesus is the Son and therefore the King: Jesus exercises authority over demons, bodies, sins, laws, nature, and social systems. And so when the disciples are asked, at the turning point of the book, "Who do you say that I am," and Peter answers, "You are the Messiah!" (Mark 8:29) we have seen good reason for this confession. Jesus is anointed by God to rule the world on God's behalf. He is the Son of God, the Messiah.

But then Jesus's conversation with Peter, and the Gospel story as a whole, takes an abrupt shift. Jesus says that the culmination of his messiahship will come in rejection, death, and resurrection (Mark 8:31). This Peter cannot accept, and he begins to rebuke Jesus.

Here is the point: if the first half of Mark's Gospel is devoted to creating a plausible case that Jesus is, in fact, the Messiah chosen by God to rule the world on God's behalf, the second half is devoted to showing us that the way that Jesus comes to his throne is not by armed rebellion but by suffering, death, and resurrection. Jesus in the Gospels is like David in 1 Samuel: the anointed king who has not yet taken his throne. The story of Jesus's death is the story of Jesus's path to the coronation. Peter had seen enough to get the title right (Jesus is, in fact, the Messiah, the Son of God), but he could not believe what that title implied for the content of Jesus's ministry. Jesus would have to die to fully come into his reign.

This episode, and its teaching about the necessity of the cross, is followed by Jesus taking three of his disciples up on a mountain, where God bears witness to Jesus for the second time. This time, however, the divine proclamation is directed to the disciples—and comes with an imperative: "This is my beloved Son, listen to him!" (Mark 9:7). In the flow of the narrative the implication is clear: "Yes, Jesus is the Messiah, and he knows better than you disciples what it means for him to fulfill his calling. Without the crucifixion, there is no enthronement." This second divine affirmation of Jesus as King comes after Jesus's proclamation that to be king of Israel means to suffer and die. The gospel narrative is a storied claim that without the crucifixion Jesus would have gone down in Jewish history as simply another great wonder-working prophet.

Revelation of this cruciform (cross-shaped) messiahship, together with its divine affirmation, forms the turning point in the narrative. Jesus now turns south, to Jerusalem, en route to his death. Along the way he will predict his death twice more; both times he will tie this death to the life of self-giving discipleship to which his followers are called; and both times his disciples will give clear indication that they do not understand (Mark 9:30–37; 10:32–45). They understand that Jesus came to fulfill the promise of a coming Messiah; they cannot understand how Jesus is transforming that category from a military victor to a suffering servant.

The third time Jesus's identity is acknowledged as "Son of God" (by someone other than a demon) is at the crucifixion. The crucifixion scene drips with irony. Jesus is mocked as "King of the Jews," and the crucifixion is supposed to be Rome's way of saying that he is no sort of king at all. All this is summed up in the sign over Jesus's head, delineating the charge on which he was convicted: "The King of the Jews." But we, the readers, know that the charge rightly interprets the story for those with eyes to see: this is how Jesus comes to take his throne as Son of God and King of Israel. The only character who seems to realize this is the centurion guarding the cross. When he sees the way in which Jesus dies he declares, "Surely this man was a son of God" (Mark 15:39). Jesus makes good on his kingly calling precisely by going to the cross.

The task for us is to find a way to hold the whole of Jesus's story together. What I would suggest is something along the following lines. Through his death on the cross, Jesus finally comes into the kingship whose authority he exercises proleptically (that is, in anticipation of the future) during his time on earth. In the same way, the redemption he enacts in his earthly ministry is only fully accomplished by his crucifixion and resurrection.

Throughout his ministry on earth, Jesus brings about deliverance that is real and yet anticipatory of a more extensive and permanent freedom. He delivers from demons, and yet his victory over Satan's powerful emissaries awaits a future day when Jesus enacts a more permanent destruction (see Mark 1:24; 5:7). Jesus raises people from death and heals them from sickness, and yet final redemption awaits the future day of resurrection.

And so, when Mark gives us hints about how to interpret Jesus's death, we should see these as indications that the death secures the final and ultimate realization of what Jesus begins during his time on earth. "The Son of Man did not come to be served but to serve and to give his life as a ransom for many," Mark 10:45 tells us. The idea of being bought out of slavery (ransomed) highlights that the ways Jesus has freed people from demons, sickness, sin, death, hunger, and fear are anticipations of what will arrive more fully after Jesus has secured such liberation through his death. When Jesus is eating the Last Supper and reinterprets the Passover meal around himself, he makes a similar claim. The Passover meal reenacts the ransom of Israel from slavery to Pharaoh. Now Jesus, in his own person, is ransoming the people of God through his body and blood.

In the mystery of the economy of God, the story of the victorious King is not brought about by a mighty battle in which the armies of Israel's enemies are slaughtered on the battlefield. Instead, the victory is won in a peculiar act of obedience that sends the eventual victor to his own slaughter, there and in that act to win the promised crown. The second exodus of Israel's great story is realized by Israel's would-be king doing what neither Adam nor Israel nor David had been able to do before: faithfully obey, without grasping after God-like power, in self-giving service on behalf of the world God had created. The Jesus stories of the Gospels demand the way of the cross—both for Jesus and for Jesus's followers. This is how God scripts the surprising climax of Israel's story.

Paul's Story of the Cross

For Paul, also, the cross takes center stage. The story of the cross as the act of God to fulfill his purposes for the world through Israel is one of the core points at which we see Paul leaning into his narrative theology.[10]

Second Corinthians 5:11–21 brings together a number of the elements I have discussed already. First, the story of Jesus's death and resurrection is clearly a story about God's action. Christ is the center of that work, but Christ's work is the doing of Israel's God. "All this is from God . . . God was reconciling the world . . . God is making his appeal through us. . . . He made Christ to be sin for us" (2 Cor. 5:18–21). We must never fall into the trap of thinking that the purpose of Jesus's mission was to subvert the purposes of an otherwise hostile God. God is the one who provides Jesus as the means for reconciling the world to himself.

Moreover, this is all unfolding within the narrative of Israel, and its king, as humanity's representative before God. "The love of the Messiah compels us, having concluded this: that one died for all, therefore all died" (2 Cor. 5:14). The reason Jesus can represent humanity before God is that God has chosen Israel and Israel's king to play precisely that role of representative in the drama of redemption. Israel's Messiah has loved us, and that love propels us out into the world, both proclaiming and embodying a new reality that has come to pass.

We must not miss the expansive nature of this new creation. Jesus, in his death and resurrection, has not only opened up the possibility that people might find forgiveness of sins. This much is true. But when Paul later says, "If anyone is in Christ—new creation!" (2 Cor. 5:17) the further point is that God's plan for the cosmos has now been fulfilled. The King of Israel has arrived and is gathering a people to himself, for the purpose of restoring humanity to its intended, blessed state. The story of Jesus is not just about new relationship; it is also about new creation. It is not merely about Jesus as Lord of my heart; it is also about Jesus, the King of Israel, as Lord of the cosmos.

What, then, was needed in order for God to bring this narrative to its conclusion? We see in these verses that humanity needed to be fundamentally changed in its disposition toward God. A people who had lived in rebellion against God needed to have a new representative to create a new alliance with God. In the death of Jesus, God was creating a way to look on humanity without counting its acts of rebellion against it. On the cross Christ was "made sin," but that sin died and was put out of sight with the burial of Jesus. The resurrected Christ is the first of a new humanity that stands as a people faithfully serving God, reconciled. The death of Jesus opens up the possibility for being truly human, which is to say, being the kind of people depicted in the creation narratives: at peace with God in a world of life, harmony, and plenty. No longer must we be in rebellion against God. We can belong to a reconciled humanity. Jesus's death accomplishes this.

And, in parallel with what we see in the Gospels, this is not just about making new people or freeing people from an old way of life. It is a far-reaching transformation. The newness Jesus brings about is "new creation." Not only are there new creatures, but also "the old *things* have passed away. Behold! New *things* have come!" (2 Cor. 5:17). As we go through our study of Paul, we are going to see just how far new creation reaches. We will find him looking for a new cosmos, for the overturning of old power structures, for the implementation of a new community, for a new ethics. And in all this his invitation is going to be for his audience to participate more fully in the narrative that is now theirs in Christ.

That phrase "in Christ" means, among other things, that the story of Jesus becomes the story of God's people. This means that we participate both in the reconciling death of the Jesus and in the reconciled new creation. And we are called to start realizing and implementing in the present the things that lie ahead. "Jesus is not merely a good moral example," Richard Hays summarizes; "rather, his story absorbs and transforms the world."[11] The narrative of a reconciled, new creation is our narrative, and its inauguration in the death and resurrection of Jesus becomes the role that we are called to play as God's people.

A Storied Paul for the Twenty-First Century

Once we recognize the narrative backbone of Paul's theology, we are in a position to do two things. One of these is to begin seeing Paul's Jesus story and the Gospels' Jesus stories in much closer relation than we might otherwise. As we have already seen, drawing their stories together will mean giving a good deal of reconsideration to not only how we think about the content of Paul's letters but also how we read the Gospels. Thus, this book will unfold as an introduction to the stories of both, even as it keeps its eye on reclaiming Paul for followers of Jesus.

We are also now in a position to begin reconceiving the content of Paul's letters. Paul was not a systematic theologian in the Christian tradition of that enterprise. He was a missionary whose pastoral letters strove to help churches faithfully play the roles God had assigned them in the drama of Israel as that drama was being brought to its head in Christ. He was a director, cuing the understudies to imitate the Master Actor's performance. He was a narrative theologian, writing letters to churches to help them see more clearly how God had written them into the cosmic story of salvation. The upshot of all this is that we are being the most faithful stewards of the Pauline correspondence if we use these letters to help us narrate our own communities' participation in the Jesus story. That is the goal this book strives toward.

Having now laid out a basic narrative approach to Paul, we will turn in chapter 2 to the question of whether Paul has an answer to Jesus's sweeping proclamation of the kingdom of God. Paul's category of "new creation" will give us a point of comparison, enabling us to see that Paul cares about much more than the salvation of our souls.

From that broad category of creation we will then narrow our focus, in chapter 3, to the question of community: does Paul have an adequate answer to the Gospels' depiction of a community gathered for the purpose of following Jesus together? Living in community is one crucial component of faithfully embodying the narrative of God's work in Christ, but so too is the calling for each person to live faithfully as one bearing the name of Christ in the world. And so chapter 4 will answer the challenges created by the idea of salvation by faith alone: Are we not called to work? Are we not called to participate in the inauguration of the reign of God on the earth?

After sketching these considerations, ranging from the narrative approach itself through cosmic, corporate, and individual expressions of Christian discipleship, we will turn our attention to particular issues: What kind of universalism and embrace of everyone do we find on offer in Jesus and in Paul (chap. 5)? What role do women play in the communities living out these cosmic narratives (chap. 6)? How can we read Paul after his letters have been used to perpetuate slavery and oppression when we care deeply about freedom and social justice (chap. 7)? Does this narrative approach to Paul shed any light on the issues of sexuality that are currently confronting the church (chap. 8), and the question of homosexuality in particular (chap. 9)? Finally, we will offer some concluding reflections on how our study speaks to the challenges raised by the realization that, as a function of being human, we are always interpreting the world, and that Scripture contains sweeping reinterpretations of the world based on Jesus's and Paul's convictions (chap. 10). If we are always interpreting the world, our communities, and our own lives based on our own deeply contextualized understanding of how the world works, does Paul's project of reinterpreting the world on the basis of Jesus's story provide us with an example to follow in our own Christian contexts?

Is Paul Worth It?

I am advocating something that, for many readers, will amount to a wholesale reinterpretation of Paul. Is it worth all the time and mental, spiritual, and emotional energy it will take to rehabilitate and reconceptualize him? I believe so. First, I am convinced that if we learn to embrace and articulate a narrative theology, we will be speaking a language that more readily resonates with people both inside the church and beyond its walls. People in postmodern cultures are increasingly aware of the powerful role that story plays in our understanding of reality, and our theology needs to catch up with this fundamental insight.

Mark Turner, a cognitive scientist, articulates the importance of stories like this: "*Story* is a basic principle of mind. Most of our experience, our knowledge, and our thinking is organized as stories. . . . Narrative imagining is our fundamental form of predicting [and our] fundamental cognitive instrument for explanation."[12] We know, we predict the future, and we explain the past all by means of stories—and so when we find a way to articulate a narrated gospel and to call people to living into the story of God's work in Christ, we are not only being more faithful to Paul but also employing a wiser, more effective medium of communication. But of course, what we think (and what we might get others to think) about Paul is much less important than our understanding of Jesus. Paul's goal all along is to draw his audience into a more faithful narration of Jesus's story so that their lives, like his, might truly reflect the love and glory of God that people were created for.

Paul's insistence that true believers are swept up into the story of Jesus provides a way forward for Christians who want to faithfully follow Jesus in the twenty-first century. How will we know when our communities are faithfully embodying the story? Earlier readings of Paul have pressed him into the service of an agenda of theological correctness: we know we are being faithful if our theology is on target. But the idea of an all-embracing narrative pulls us to answer a more profound set of questions:

- Is our community one in which the means of power and prestige offered in our society (e.g., money, education, physical attractiveness, certain careers, powerful rhetorical skills) continue to be the measures of a person's capability to lead? Or does our community illustrate a narrative whose most powerful moment comes when God turns the economy of the world on its head?

- Is our community one in which knowledge and theological subtlety are given pride of place? Or do we give voice to the less articulate and learned who are more faithfully giving themselves in service of the kingdom of God? That is to say, do we honor, learn from, and follow people whose lives are illustrating the gospel?
- Does our community give evidence of participating in a narrative in which the Jesus whom we are following is the Lord who now sits enthroned over all things? Do we give weight to personal growth in holiness, growth as a community, environmental advocacy, social justice, evangelism, expressions of Christian oneness, and reconciliation of differences with those outside the bounds of Christianity (to name a few)?
- Perhaps most centrally of all: Are our communities embodiments of the self-giving faith, hope, and love that lie at the heart of the Christian story? Are we, in other words, living out in our life together the cruciform narrative that makes us Christian?[13]

Part of the power of a narrative theology is its dynamic character. Our calling is not simply to recite agreed-on points of doctrine. Rather, our calling is to freshly discover with the communities we are part of what it means for us to live out the narrative of Christ crucified. This is the summons not only of Jesus as we find him portrayed in the Gospels but also of Paul as we hear him in his letters. We learn this once we grasp the fact that the story is the thing. And we turn now to see how sweeping that story is.

2

New Creation and the Kingdom of God

> And we beasts remember, even if Dwarfs forget, that Narnia was never right except when a son of Adam was king.
>
> —Trufflehunter the Beaver in *Prince Caspian*[1]

For many of us who grew up in churched worlds of Sunday school, youth group, retreats, and summer camps, the gospel narratives into which we were enculturated focused on what we might call individualistic and escapist visions of the work of Jesus. In these depictions, the gospel is about my soul's salvation, offering me a chance to get to heaven when I die. And for many of us, the primary promoter of such a vision was none other than the apostle Paul. Schooled on the Romans Road to Salvation, we walk from "all sinned" (That's me!), to "the wages of sin is death" (I've got a problem!), to "while we were yet sinners Christ died for us" (God's done something about my problem!), to "confess Jesus is Lord and believe he's been raised and you will be saved" (Yes! I get to go to heaven when I die if I only make Jesus Lord of my heart!). While such a telling communicates some important facets of the gospel story, many of us have found that Scripture itself generates questions that destabilize such me-centered, escapist systems.

Different parts of the Bible's story don't seem to fit into that narrative. Perhaps we begin to wonder, Why bother with Jesus's resurrection? The gospel presentation I know really needs only Jesus's death. At other times we might ask, What about Jesus's life in the Gospels? Apart from the crucifixion, Matthew, Mark, and Luke add precious little to the message of salvation I've heard. To put this issue differently, How is the "kingdom of God" the gospel? Then, for some, the question begins to arise, Is the phrase "Jesus is Lord" really an invitation I issue, a request that Jesus come to live in my heart? We begin to be gripped with a far more expansive vision of Jesus's lordship as a state of affairs that we are called to align ourselves to. Tugging on any of these threads will begin to unravel the fabric of an individualistic and escapist gospel tapestry.

We have already seen that the Jesus narratives in both the Gospels and Paul are intertwined with the story of Israel. In the next chapter we will deal with the problem of individualism and community. But we now turn our attention to the way that the narrative of Jesus is inseparable from the narrative of creation, which is to say inseparable from every facet of this world in both its beauty and its brokenness. It is a message for body and soul, for persons and communities, for peoples and systems, for the world and all that is in it. By the end, I hope to have shown that Jesus's enacting of the dominion of God and Paul's vision of new creation in the resurrected Christ are complementary visions of a holistically restored cosmos. This is the gospel we sing about as we take the words of "Joy to the World" to our lips: "He comes to make his blessings flow / far as the curse is found."

A Good World Gone Wrong . . . and Restored

Follow Jesus through the early steps of his ministry in Mark's Gospel, and this is what you find him doing: teaching, creating a community of followers and coworkers, exorcizing demons, healing innumerable sick people, restoring a leper to physical health and to life in community, restoring a paralytic's body as proof of the forgiveness of his sins, including tax collectors and sinners socially by means of a shared meal. When set next to the gospel presentations many of us learned as part of our evangelical upbringing, this story is as enigmatic and mysterious to us as it apparently was to Jesus's contemporaries. What role does this story play in atoning for our sins? The gospel proclamations that formed so many of us in church youth groups and campus ministries have no need for the story of Jesus's life. This glaring omission should set off alarm bells for us, alerting us to how the gospel we learned is, at the very least, far too small. Jesus's story is pushing us to reassess what we thought we knew.

In this vein, I want to suggest that these Gospel stories, taken together, disclose to us a summary of what it means for Jesus to be not only announcing but also inaugurating the dominion of God. And this arriving reign of God is itself the good news, the "gospel" that Jesus proclaims. The story is the thing. But what does this story mean?

Creation Kingdom and Its Undoing

Once again, Israel's story is where we need to start. And we need to go back to the beginning, to the creation narratives of Genesis 1–3. In both Genesis 1 and Genesis 2–3 we get pictures of a rightly ordered cosmos. The striking thing about these stories is that each in its own way insists that a rightly ordered, "very good" world entails a special place for humanity as the mediator of God's rule over or care for the earth. The very purpose of humanity, according to Genesis 1, is to exercise dominion over the world on God's behalf (Gen. 1:26–28). This is a primal vision of the "kingdom of God": a world subject to the reign of God by means of God's appointed agents—humans who represent God's loving and authoritative dominion by acting as vicegerents, ruling the world in God's stead.[2] In fact, being "created in the image of God" carries two related ideas: (1) humans are created with the vocation to rule the world on God's behalf, and (2) at the start, without need for adoption or any sort of overcoming of the distance between God and people, humans are in relationship with God as his sons and daughters (compare the image-and-likeness language in Gen. 5:1–3). To bear the image of God is to be the son or daughter who reigns on earth under God. In Genesis 2, we similarly see Adam and Eve entrusted with the care and keeping of God's creation, though in this case it is the cultivated garden to which they turn their attention, not the creation as a whole. And so the first thing we should keep in view as we mine the Gospels for a richer understanding of the dominion of God is that the biblical narrative itself begins with a picture of such a reign. The story of the kingdom of God is one in which humanity rules a world that is, in its entirety, subject to God through the faithful work of God's people. One can read not only the creation narratives but also the entire Old Testament as an exhibition of the dominion of God, noting how the stories of Abraham, the exodus, the conquest, the rise of the Davidic kings, and the expectations of exile and return all envision a world that has been set to rights by means of a faithful human agent representing God's rule to the earth.

Just as instructive as these kingdom visions, however, is the anti-kingdom narrative of what goes wrong as that story is told in Genesis 3. This is the story that strives to explain the world as we meet it.

The problems begin when the man and the woman cede their position as those who represent and speak for God, choosing instead to listen to the serpent. The snake questions God's instructions ("Did God really say you must not eat?"), twisting God's words and offering an alternative prediction for what will happen if God's instruction is disobeyed ("You will not surely die, but you will become like God"). This not only puts the serpent in the role of God as the one whose counsel people heed, it also places the serpent in the role of humanity as the one who is exercising dominion in God's garden. The reign of God is undone.

The results of this abdication are nothing less than catastrophic. We discover, first, that humanity's relationship with God has been marred, as the man and woman hide themselves from the presence of God (3:8–10). The relational fracturing is also horizontal, as Adam turns to blame his wife for what transpired, thus indicating a breach of relationships among people (3:12). The woman, in turn, blames the serpent, indicating a breach between humanity and the creatures over which people were given authority (3:13). The curses issued by God underscore the wholesale disintegration of the harmony of the world: enmity is placed between the serpent and the woman's seed, the relationship between man and woman will be disordered by desire and power, and the man is implicated in the extension of the curse as it envelops not only living beings but also the very dirt itself: "cursed is the ground because of you; you will eat of it in toil; it will produce thorns and thistles for you" (3:17–19).

Ramifications of disobedience are not merely to be found in a ruptured relationship with God. That much is true. But if the problems extend as high as heaven, they also descend as low as the dirt itself. And they encompass everything in between: our fractured relationships with other people, our subjection to would-be ruling powers, our unjust and life-sapping social relationships, our disharmony with the animal kingdom, the failure we experience in both caring for and cultivating the earth. Each of these is a facet of the world gone wrong in the biblical narrative that begins in Genesis. And Jesus comes into just such a story of the world off-kilter to reestablish the reign of God, which will entail a restoration of the entire created order.

Genesis 1–3 creates the narrative tensions that drive the remainder of the biblical story. What will happen to God's very good creation? Will it be forever handed over to the rule of alien powers? Will God's co-laborers ever rejoin God in the work of ruling the world for him and with him? Will God have to give up on this world and simply take people out of it? Will God find some way for his originally chosen agent (humanity) to play the lead in restoring God's originally chosen order (a world in which humanity rules on God's behalf)? As the story unfolds, Abraham, and later Israel, are called to play the role God had originally given to Adam: a people who stand in for God, representing God as rulers and caretakers of the earth. Later, this task is located more specifically in the hands of the kings, themselves understood to be the sons of God (Ps. 2; 2 Sam. 7). But the tensions created in Genesis 1–3 will be resolved only when the biblical story's chief protagonist comes on the scene.

Kingdom and Re-Creation: Holistic Narratives of Redemption

With the stage now set, let's return to Jesus's ministry in Mark 1–2. We find first of all that he was teaching—proclaiming the reign of God (Mark 1:15). Interestingly, Mark has little by way of extended examples of the content of Jesus's teaching. At several points in the story, including here, readers are invited to see that the teaching and the actions of Jesus interpret each other. In other words, we have a series of stories under this broad heading of "proclaiming the dominion of God," precisely because Jesus's actions in such stories reveal what that reign entails.

Jesus begins by calling people to follow him. This is an early hint, which we will see played out in more detail as the Gospel goes on, that Jesus is redefining the people of God around himself. Jesus calls followers so that they may be sent out: "Follow me," he says, "and I will make you fishers of people" (Mark 1:16–20). At its heart, the mission of Jesus, the mission of God, is active and participatory. Jesus, as the leader of this band, and those called to follow him are all active agents in bringing the reign of God to expression on earth. These workers, this group of people, are the ones putting on display the nature of citizenship in God's kingdom.

After Jesus has called a few initial followers, his first miraculous deed is directly tied to his teaching ministry (Mark 1:21–28). The people are amazed at Jesus's teaching because Jesus is teaching on his own authority, not under the authority of inherited tradition. By this same authority, we are told, Jesus casts out a demon (Mark 1:27). In light of the sketch above concerning what we learn about the "problem" of the world from Genesis 1–3, we do well to see that the reign of God is being manifested here by Jesus playing the role, given to him by God, of the man who mediates God's rule to the world.

In this exorcism story Jesus restores order to the world in two ways. First, he teaches the Word of God on no one else's authority. As Adam was charged directly by God and should have spoken for God in response to the serpent, so Jesus is depicted as speaking the Word of God as one who has immediate authority to do so. It is surely no accident, then, that this reclaiming of authority for rendering the Word of God is directly tied to Jesus's dislodging of spiritual forces from their seat of control over humanity. In both the teaching and the exorcism, Jesus is recovering the function of rule that Adam ceded to the serpent. A human once again has the power to rule the earth for God. The advent of the kingdom of God is the renewal of creation. God is bringing the story of creation to its climax, and we see that God is unwilling to give up on either the creation or his image-bearers' place in it.

If stories of exorcism demonstrate the end of demonic thrall, the narratives of table fellowship and of the healing of a leper indicate a holy upheaval of social systems of exclusion. Here, we are a bit removed from direct resonance with the garden of Eden, but we are watching Jesus combat an extension of the primordial disintegration of human relations: social systems contain elements of evil that are larger than the sum of persons' sinful acts. In the case of the leper, his skin malady has excluded him from both the worship of God in the temple and an integrated life in society. Thus, Jesus's curing of his ailment not only enables him to reenter the sanctioned place of worship but also restores the man to a condition in which it is possible to function as an integrated member of society. In a striking twist, the consequence of Jesus's healing of the leprous man, who would not have been allowed to enter densely populated hubs of activity, is that Jesus is no longer able to enter cities but stays outside them in the desert places (Mark 1:45). Jesus has surrendered his own place in society in order to bring societal restoration to a man with leprosy.

Similar restorative concerns are in play when Jesus has a dinner party with all the wrong people: notorious sinners and tax collectors (likely seen as colluders with Rome, and hence emblematic of how God is not reigning over Israel). As was the case with the leper, so here also the exclusion of these people from the mainstream Jewish faithful is being regulated by the guardians of orthodoxy (or orthopraxy, "right practice," as the case may be). The scribes and Pharisees want to know why Jesus is embracing such sordid company, and he indicates that these people are included for the very reason that they are coming to him for healing restoration. A transformation must take place—these "sick" come to a "doctor" after all (2:17)—but the result is membership in this new community that is subjecting itself to the coming reign of God. As the Jesus story unfolds, the reign of God works its way through the people in such a manner that social exclusion is undone by acts of healing. And in this movement the societal disorder inaugurated in Genesis 3, formalized in the law, and extended in later Judaism, is being displaced in favor of a new, healed social space that Jesus's own hands are creating.

A final story will have to suffice for this foray into Mark's creation-restoring picture of the kingdom of God. The healing of the paralytic as told in the Gospels (Mark 2:1–12) is a multilayered story that holds together elements of the community of faith (Jesus heals when he sees the faith of those who bring the paralyzed man to him), the physical brokenness of the world (Jesus heals the man's body), and the spiritual needs of people in a fallen world (Jesus forgives the man's sins). Three points merit special attention for our purposes. First, the "traditional" articulation of the problem with the world, as many of us learned it growing up in church, is correct even if incomplete. Individual people as well as humanity in general are alienated from God due to our sin, and we need Jesus to forgive us our sins (or we need the work of Jesus so that God will forgive us our sins). When highlighting that there is more to the story than this, we must not fall into the trap of thinking that forgiveness is eliminated or of lesser importance. Second, the healing of the broken body (in comparison with the exorcism in an earlier story) is inherently intertwined with the forgiveness of sins. The two problems Jesus addresses are inseparable components of being in a fallen world where human bodies get weak and sick and die, and where people are separated from God due to sin. But if the problems are inherently connected, so is their solution. Third, the solution is found in Jesus, who as "Son of Man" has authority on earth to forgive sins.

Scholars will debate what the phrase "Son of Man" means until this "Son of Man" returns on the clouds of heaven. Notwithstanding, here is a modest proposal: Jesus is drawing on language from Daniel 7, which uses imagery from the creation narratives to speak of the world being rightly ordered. In Daniel, this right ordering occurs as God's people, Israel, fulfill the role of Adam by ruling the world on God's behalf. What in Daniel 7 is a story of new creation through Israel ruling the nations becomes, in the Gospels, a story of new creation through Jesus playing the role of Israel by inaugurating a reign that will extend to the entire cosmos.

In other words, Jesus is the agent of the reign of God because he is the human being entrusted by God with the task of restoring humanity's God-subjected and God-ordained rule to the world. This means that the dominion of God entails newly creating not only humanity's relationship with God but also humanity's broken bodies, broken social systems, enslaved existence under ruling powers—every facet of the world gone wrong, from our relationship with God above to our standing vis-à-vis plants, dirt, and water below.

What, then, does the reign of God look like? It looks like Jesus rectifying all that is not good with the world that God created "very good." The kingdom of God is deeply entrenched in this world, to the point where I am tempted to say that it is at core a world-affirming reign. And yet to say this might be to betray the transforming work of Jesus that he brings to the world as he embraces it. Because for all these deeds of power we see performed by Jesus, Mark's Gospel is still headed toward the cross. There is an element of judgment that overshadows this ministry of the kingdom—that not only overshadows it but gives the ministry its very character. Jesus redefines what it means to play the part of the Messiah, God's anointed representative of God's rule on the earth, around the cross. Self-giving and even a word of judgment are inherent to Jesus's message of the dominion of God.

But this does not mean, either, that this ministry is creation-condemning. The notion that Jesus's ministry is simply one of judgment gives rise to a version of sub-Christian hope that looks forward to flight out of this world and into another—a "hope" that is insufficiently biblical. Neither naively creation-affirming nor hopelessly creation-condemning, the kingdom of God is a ministry of creation's restoration. It is creation-redeeming and creation-healing. Only such a ministry can bring the biblical narrative to a triumphant climax without either ceding defeat to the intruding powers (the creation-condemning mistake) or ignoring that the powers of sin, death, injustice, and brokenness hold God's creatures in thrall (the creation-affirming mistake). The kingdom of God is at hand in the undoing of all the sin and death and brokenness and disorder that mar the very good world of God.

The snapshot of Jesus's ministry we have just seen indicates that the gospel of the Gospels is the story of God's redeeming the world through the all-encompassing work of Jesus. This is the story of the coming reign of God. As the story unfolds, we see that, yes, forgiveness of sins (individual as well as corporate) is a necessary component of this work. But we also find that such forgiveness is located within a narrative in which God is, in Christ, making all things new.

New Creation in the Resurrected Christ

So far we've had a chance to look at the story behind the story, observing that the kingdom of God, as depicted in the Genesis creation narratives, consists of a human agent (or humanity in general) faithfully ruling the world on behalf of God. The Gospel stories show how the two elements of a human ruler and a rightly ordered creation are joined in the ministry of Jesus: as God's representative King, Jesus restores every element of a sinful and broken world. What I want to add as we turn now to Paul is that Paul drank deeply of the same creation stories. He also narrates a climax to the drama of Israel's history that portrays Christ as the one in whom humanity has been restored to its rightful sovereignty over the earth, and through whom this world as a whole is being set to rights.

Jesus the Lord

Jesus the resurrected Lord restores humanity to its primordial vocation, and this lordship is inseparable from what Paul refers to as "new creation." For Paul, no less than for Genesis and Jesus, being fully human is about much more than an individual's standing before God. All three affirm that, in order for humanity to be fully participating in God's best intentions for people, the world will have to be transformed; not only do hearts need renovation but so also does the entire context in which we live and move and have our being. For Paul no less than for Jesus, newness of life before God unites speaking and acting for God, both creating communities that undermine mores of social exclusion and restoring the natural order.

On the surface of it, claiming that the Gospels and Paul tell the same story at this point appears counterintuitive. The great unifying theme of "the dominion of God" is almost absent in Paul's letters, and Paul's letters do not allude to Jesus's life of wonder-working and community formation. A helpful bridge at this point is to remember what we noted in chapter 1. Both Matthew and Luke depict the resurrected Jesus as the one who has now been fully imbued with the authority he put on display in the course of his earthly life. At the resurrection Jesus fully receives the authority that is proleptically given to him at his baptism and that he exercises in nascent form throughout the time of his earthly ministry. And for Paul, it is the resurrection itself that carries the implications of lordship and new creation that drive him to affirm with the Gospels that Jesus comes to make all things new.

For many of us, when we start talking about the implications of resurrection we find ourselves on unfamiliar ground. I remember being struck by my own ignorance about resurrection just before Easter during my senior year in college. What was my problem? The story of salvation as I understood it did not need the resurrection in order for the narrative to come to its climactic conclusion. All it needed was the cross. So long as Jesus died for me, my soul could be in personal relationship with God. The resurrection was, at best, a tack-on, perhaps an empirical validation that God had accepted Jesus's sacrifice.

But for Paul, as for the other early Christians, the resurrection was pivotal to the whole story. It meant that Jesus had become Lord, and it meant not only that God was going to renew the whole creation but also that the renewal of creation had already begun.

I started this chapter with some discussion of humanity's place in the world: God created the world and placed humans in it to rule the world on God's behalf. In the biblical narrative, the abdication of that rule introduces spiritual, physical, relational, social, agricultural, and other failures that mark the world we experience day by day. This provides the framework within which we can understand why, for Paul, the idea of Jesus as Lord is inseparable from the idea of a new creation. When Jesus is raised, he is enthroned as Lord over all things. Jesus's resurrection is itself a crucial component of the restoration of humanity, Jesus's assuming the mantle of a new Adam who reigns over the earth (1 Cor. 15). This return of humanity to its primal calling (ruling the world on God's behalf) means a full-scale restoration of every aspect of the cosmos gone wrong.

We'll start by exploring some of the implications of Jesus being the resurrected Lord. Two passages in Romans draw together the ideas of resurrection and lordship. One is the verse often cited from chapter 10 about what is necessary for salvation: "If you confess with your mouth, 'Jesus is Lord,' and believe in your heart that God raised him from the dead, you will be saved" (Rom. 10:9). But if we want to know why and how resurrection and lordship are connected, we have to go back to Romans 1.

In Romans 1:3–4 Paul says something so surprising that most of our Bible translations refuse to print it. A literal translation reads as follows: the gospel promised by God "concerns his Son, who was born of the seed of David according to the flesh, who *was appointed Son of God* with power, according to the Spirit of holiness, by the resurrection from among the dead, Jesus Christ our Lord." When Paul says Jesus "was appointed Son of God," he means to say that Jesus became something that he was not before. Without denying Christ's preexistence, this passage asserts that something happens to the human Jesus when he is raised from the dead. Like the kings of Israel, Jesus becomes a son of God when he is enthroned to rule the world on God's behalf (see Ps. 2 and 2 Sam. 7). Jesus's adoption and enthronement come at his resurrection.

The resurrection of Jesus functions for Paul much like the baptism of Jesus functions for the Gospels. In both, the Spirit that comes upon and empowers Jesus is a Spirit that anoints him "Son of God." This spiritual endowment marks the beginning of the new work that God is doing in him. And in both the Gospel narratives and Paul's letters this reception of the Spirit empowers Jesus to execute the reign of God. And so it is not surprising to discover that Jesus's lordship, as depicted in Paul, overlaps considerably with the picture of God's kingdom we painted above. Jesus, as Lord, exercises dominion over the spiritual realms, entrusts such authority to his followers, empowers them by the Spirit to restore broken bodies and to speak for God, and creates new communities where social injustice and disintegration are undone. The earthly Jesus's ministry of the kingdom that we read about in the Gospels echoes through the ministry of Jesus the resurrected Lord as depicted in Paul's letters.

Through their depictions of exorcisms, the Gospels acknowledge that the evil in this world is greater than the sum of individual human actions—and that freedom from such forces is integral to the mission of Jesus. What these stories show in Jesus's interactions with individuals, Paul depicts of the entire cosmos.

In Galatians Paul speaks of elementary principles, spirits that enslave humanity. In Romans he more particularly delineates such forces as the powers of sin and of death. Note that sin here is not simply lack of conformity to God's rules. In Romans 5 sin, along with death, is depicted as an enslaving power. But Paul's point throughout is to show that with the death and resurrection of Jesus the dominion of sin is brought to an end.

On an individual level, this conquest of hostile powers means that people are liberated and thus able to obey God. The resurrection life of Jesus means both that people will be raised like him in the future and that the future resurrection life intrudes on the present. In Romans 6 it is as though Paul is telling Christians to take hold of their future and bring it to bear on the present. Look at how resurrection opens a possibility for new life here and now: "Do not present your members as weapons of unrighteousness to sin, but present yourselves to God as those alive from the dead, and your members as weapons of righteousness to God, for sin shall not be lord over you" (Rom. 6:13–14). People who have been joined to Jesus through baptism have entered a new realm, the realm defined by the freedom, power, lordship, and resurrection life of Jesus. The kingdom of God has come near.

In the Gospels, such authority over the spiritual realm comes hand in hand with Jesus's own calling to speak for God, thus representing God to the world in both words and deeds of power. A very similar dynamic is found in Paul's discussions of "spiritual gifts." Too often we fail to note the inseparable connection of these gifts with Jesus. When Paul says, "You are the body of Christ," he is thinking of the church as those who are "in Christ," who are therefore the continuing presence of Jesus on earth.

It is because Jesus is the Spirit-raised Lord of all things that those who receive the gift of the Spirit have the sorts of gifts Paul delineates in 1 Corinthians 12. As Jesus on earth reclaimed humanity's vocation to speak to the world for God, so the church as Jesus's continuing presence on earth is gifted with apostles, prophets, and teachers (1 Cor. 12:28) who speak for God. It is not incidental that Paul tells the Corinthian church in this chapter on spiritual gifts that words can be motivated by many different kinds of spirits, and that it is only God's own Spirit who leads a person to confess that "Jesus is Lord." Speaking for God, by God's Spirit, as something that overcomes speaking against the work or Word of God, is an essential component of the restoration of the world at work through Jesus's resurrection. To speak for God is to reclaim what was ceded to the serpent. It is to continue what was begun when Jesus taught with an authority that even the spirits were subject to.

Beyond gifts of speaking, 1 Corinthians 12 and other passages indicate that the body of the resurrected Lord Jesus will do other things that Jesus began to do on earth: healing, helping, leading, and showing hospitality and mercy. In such lists of gifts we see ways that Paul envisions the continuing work of the Lord Jesus as reordering the entire world: enslaved spirits, captive words, broken bodies, disordered communities—all are signals of a world gone awry, and Jesus presides over a community where all are being rectified.

Expanding a bit on the corporate implications of Jesus's lordship, we find Paul insisting that it promotes the very sort of communities of embrace that Jesus instituted while on earth. We see this clearly in Romans 14. Remember that Jesus's ministry was within the people of Israel, which is to say that it took place among and for Jews, whereas Paul's ministry goes beyond Israel such that his communities are largely comprised of non-Jews (gentiles). The challenge that Paul faced as he took his message beyond the nation of Israel was the extent to which gentiles were going to have to adopt the particular practices that separated Jews from non-Jews. The answer Paul gives is the same that Jesus gave: coming to Jesus is the one requirement for inclusion in the people of God.

In Romans 14, the issues confronting the Jew-gentile mixed community in Rome are two of the three practices that set Jewish people apart from their neighbors: dietary laws and holidays (the other practice was circumcision). Paul insists that for followers of Jesus, keeping the Jewish laws is one viable way of life and that not keeping them is an equally acceptable course of action. The reason behind this ambivalence is that Jesus is the Lord whom each person is serving through that choice (esp. Rom. 14:8–9). Paul embraces a plurality of worship and lifestyle practices because he believes that God is honored in each through people's service to Jesus as Lord.

In fact, it may be that this does not state matters strongly enough. It is not merely that persons from either group equally honor God. At the heart of Paul's vision of the worldwide family of God created by Christ is that God is most honored when people of different ethnicities, defined by a whole host of socially defining practices, come together in their worship of the God who raised Jesus from the dead, the God who seated him as Lord over all things (see Rom. 15:7–12). From such a vision of the ethnicity-affirming character of the worldwide family of God, Paul makes the radical deduction that even the biblically required markers of Jewish ethnic identity are not to be required of all God's people. Jesus overturns the requirements to become Jewish through his death and resurrection. His death and resurrection make him Lord over both the dead and the living (Rom. 14:9). The story of God's people has been reconfigured by the resurrection-lordship of the crucified Christ, such that even the biblically mandated identity markers found throughout the pages of the Old Testament Scriptures no longer apply to everyone. Paul continues Jesus's practices of overturning social exclusion that tied the identity of the people of God to one social and ethnic group defined by the biblical law.

New Creation

Throughout the discussion of Jesus's lordship we have seen hints that Jesus's occupying a position over the world entails something much more comprehensive than persons in a restored relationship with God, that something more on the order of a new creation is in view. Paul uses the phrase "new creation" to describe the effects of Jesus's resurrection and suggests that this itself is the world that Christians inhabit and are called to bring into existence (2 Cor. 5:17; Gal. 6:15).

The idea that new creation begins with Jesus's resurrection is tied, in part, to the fact that the resurrected Jesus has a body. The life that Jesus lives now is embodied; the hope that Jesus's resurrection therefore holds out for his followers is an embodied life. This itself spells the beginning of the end for stereotypical views of salvation as our souls' going to heaven when we die. No, our ultimate hope for salvation is to live a re-embodied life on a new earth.

Few passages offer more generative material for thinking through the implications of new creation than Romans 8. This chapter, though, as much as any other, has been victimized by distracting theological debates. The presence of the language of "predestination" in 8:29 has made the passage a perennial area of theological argument. But our task is to come at the chapter with a different set of questions. How does this chapter fit into the story of the God who created the earth? How does this chapter fit into the story of the Jesus who inaugurated the reign of God by making all things new? Having our ears tuned by the biblical narrative, we find in Romans 8 a climactic scene in which a newly re-created humanity, representing God on the earth, plays the role of our first parents by holding the fate of the world in its hands. Only this time, the scene is one of redemptive faithfulness resulting in the renewal of all things.

Paul invites us to read this chapter in conversation with the creation narratives. Not only does he talk about the whole created order (we'll come back to this shortly), but he also invokes the language of "image bearing" that we find in Genesis 1:26. As we mentioned earlier, to bear the image of God means two related things. First, it is a relational term that has connotations of being God's child. Second, this relationship itself is then defined by a vocation to rule the world on God's behalf. In Romans 8 we discover that Paul's statement earlier in the letter, that Jesus was appointed Son of God by the resurrection from the dead (Rom. 1:4), is a declaration that God has appointed a new image-bearing Adam who will determine the fate of the world for good, even as the first Adam determined the fate of the world for ill.

If the first Adam was created as God's image-bearing, ruling son, Jesus as the Second Adam is raised from the dead to be God's image-bearing, ruling Son. Because of this new creation, Jesus's resurrection creates a sort of cosmic space, a realm that has been reconciled to God. As the Gospels also do, Paul's letters maintain that humanity has a problem, that our own sinful actions and inclinations separate us from God—and that Jesus acts on God's behalf to create a reconciled people around himself. We will delve into this in more detail below when we talk about community.

For both Jesus and Paul the "reconciled people" is a new family. In Mark we hear Jesus affirm that those attending to his words are his mothers, sisters, and brothers (Mark 3:34–35). In Romans we read that Jesus's resurrection-sonship is the identity marker of the family of God, a marker given to us when we receive the Spirit of adoption as children, the Spirit who raised Jesus to resurrection-sonship, the Spirit by whom we cry out, "Abba, Father" (Rom. 8:11, 14–17). Because Jesus is raised up by the Spirit to be the image-bearing Son of God, the destiny of those who love God is to be "conformed to the image of his Son so that he might be the firstborn among many brothers and sisters" (Rom. 8:29). The beginning of "new creation" is the creation of a new humanity: Jesus as God's Son, and us as partakers in the image of God as it is borne by Jesus.

What does it mean to be God's children, wrapped up in Jesus's resurrection-sonship? First, it means that we have a secure future. Resurrection is about what happens when God makes all things new: a new creation with new bodies—it is inherently tied to the future. Since that future is determined already by Jesus's resurrection, Paul can insist that "all things work together for good" for God's family. Since we know the ending of the story we participate in, we have hope.

What, then, is the content of this secure future? The second point is that we will at last receive our own "adoption as God's children" when we receive new, resurrected bodies (Rom. 8:23). Jesus's fate is our fate. And Jesus's fate is tied to much more than a new individual body. As God's Son, Jesus is also the heir of all that belongs to his Father. The consummation of history comes when God gives the entire created order to his most prized creation, his beloved children. With Christ, we will inherit all things. The future, with the hope entailed in it, is crucial.

But one of the most important dynamics of the story Paul tells is that our future intrudes on the present. Yes, we will be adopted as God's children when we are raised from the dead, even as Jesus was. But this future is, in part, ours already by the Spirit. We have already received the Spirit who both raised Jesus to eternal sonship and makes us children of God in the present. By that Spirit of the resurrected Christ (Rom. 8:11) we are already participating in our future identity. Our future resurrection life bursts backward into our present so that even now we are children of God (Rom. 8:16). This means that new creation is not simply something that we look forward to; it is something in which we already participate. The culmination of the story is exerting a sort of backward force, such that the future, by the power of the life-giving Spirit, is intruding on the present and transforming it.

I want us to keep this backward-moving force of the future in mind as we look at how the fate of humans continues to determine the fate of the rest of creation. In Romans 8 Paul ties together God's redeemed humanity and the created order in both the present and the future. Right now, Paul says, those who are united to Christ "groan," an image of pain, for sure, but the sort of pain associated with giving birth. We groan, but new life is right around the corner. Similarly, Paul says, "the whole creation groans." The labor pains of this age, giving birth to the age to come, are shared by all. But creation will not be redeemed by some entirely separate act of God. Creation will be restored when God's children are made fully known (Rom. 8:19). In other words, when we consummate our identity as God's image-bearing children by receiving our resurrection bodies, then the whole created order will go the way of this new humanity and participate in our restoration. Genesis 3 shows the dire consequences of creation going the way of a human ruler who rebels against God and abdicates his vocation to rule the world on God's behalf. Romans 8 shows the hope entailed for creation in having its fate tied to a faithful, obedient humanity.

Like the Jesus narratives of the Gospels, Paul's articulation of the good news insists that the only way for us to be truly restored in our relationship with God is for God to bring about a work of salvation that embraces every aspect of this broken and disordered world. Scot McKnight puts it like this:

> The cross addresses not only *my* problem as sinner but *our* problem as sinners gathered together in what is best called systemic injustice and evil. Which means that the cross addresses *the problem of evil*. We are not being fair to the Pauline texts on the cross if we narrow them simply and woodenly to resolution of *my* sin problem. The cross addresses *our* sin problem—"our" in the sense of yours and mine and the Western world's and the Eastern world's and the northern and southern hemispheres' problems. It addresses *the world's captivity by evil.*[3]

Not only are we embodied beings, but these bodies of ours reside in a world that bears all the marks of futility that our own "spiritual" lives manifest. For Jesus's lordship to be something that truly sets us free, it must be a rule that he manifests throughout the entirety of this good but fallen world.

The World's Future and Our Present

The question this raises for us, then, is how we should relate to this world in the present given that God has a glorious plan drawn up for its future. Although Paul is silent on this point, he has provided us with a narrative dynamic by which we can fill in the gaps of his silence. Let me work out how I see the story functioning with us as individuals and as Christian communities in order to set the stage for talking about our posture toward the created order.

The way the story is working itself out is that Jesus's own death and resurrection are definitive for both our present and our future. Our future resurrection life intrudes on the present as we walk in newness of life and participate proleptically in our identity as God's children. What theologians sometimes refer to as "sanctification" is nothing less than a present realization of our future identity as God's purified, renewed children. Pursuing holiness and obedience is tantamount to an active posture of taking hold of our future life and bringing it to expression in the present.

Similarly, when we pursue Christian community, we are taking hold of our future identity as God's children and manifesting it in the present. We will be God's children, raised up and conformed to the image of our firstborn elder brother. But inasmuch as we participate in that future identity even now, we gather with our brothers and sisters, those who have also received the Spirit of adoption as God's children, serving one another through the gifts that this same Spirit gives for the building up of Christ's body. This too is an active intruding of the future on the present, wrought by the hands of those who follow Jesus. New creation, with its new humanity, entails a new identity for God's image-bearing children, and we live into that identity when we engage in acts of self-giving love that express our kinship with those to whom we are united by the Spirit.

So when we come to the created order itself, both the animate and the inanimate facets of the nonhuman creation, I believe that the calling before us is to prayerfully discern what it might mean to grasp the future that God has in store for creation and draw it into the present. Although some have suggested that the Judeo-Christian insistence on humanity's place as subruler of creation is the cause of our exploitation of the environment, I want to suggest that recognizing our vocation to be faithful vicegerents, ushering the creation into a redeemed future, should put us on exactly the opposite path.

The Christian calling toward the environment is one of cultivating and sustaining. Far from being a story of exploitation, the narrative dynamic by which Paul envisions us moving from sin and failure to freedom and glory is one in which self-giving love is the road to redemption. Jesus's own resurrection comes by way of the cross, the Spirit of sonship is validated by our own suffering with Jesus in order to be glorified with him (Rom. 8:17), and so we can anticipate that the means by which we will serve as re-creators of the environment will be a path of self-sacrifice.

The story of salvation as Paul tells it moves from creation, via the resurrected Christ, to new creation. This is as dramatic and sweeping a gospel narrative as one could hope for. It is not a vision of individual souls being swept up to heaven. It is not a simplistic story of a legal transaction setting people judicially right with God. In Paul's story the resurrection of Jesus creates a realm of reconciliation where individuals have their relationship with God rectified, for sure, but only as that relationship with God is part of an ever-expanding series of contexts that extend from the "soul" to the body to the communities we live in to the food we eat to the ground that provides the food to the powers of slavery and injustice that continually twist it all. To confess with our mouths that "Jesus is Lord" is to be drawn by the Spirit of God into the realm where Jesus is reigning over all things in God's name and thereby making all things new. Paul's narrative of salvation is nothing less than the proclamation and embodiment here and now of the coming dominion of God.

Redeemed Humans and a Redeemed World

What does it mean for us to join in the task of proclaiming the good news of Jesus Christ? We cannot answer that question without knowing what sort of story it is we're telling. If our story is only the story of sinners whose souls are alienated from God, then preaching the gospel is nothing more, and nothing less, than urging people to put their faith in Jesus's death on their behalf. Such a story has one conflict to resolve: the conflict of guilt as it stands in the way of the relationship the story holds out for its two great protagonists, God and humanity. And if that is the extent of our story, we are left with a rather perplexing collection of Christian artifacts known as "the Gospels," which do not actually contain much of the gospel at all.

The key, as so many are discovering, is to recognize that such a gospel is too small. The story of salvation depicts the coming reign of God which sets to right not only persons' standing before God but also every other disordered element of the creation that was once "very good" but now shows pervasive marks of disintegration. A story that depicts the entire created order being restored is not adequately told when it is reduced to one of its elements, even so important an element as the narrative of guilt and forgiveness.

One of the most important realizations we come to when we see that the story enfolds all creation is that the story cannot be adequately told with words. Because it is a story of cosmic transformation, the story has to be embodied and lived or it will be falsified. For Jesus, to proclaim the reign of God is to heal, forgive, restore, exorcize, and speak. For Paul, to proclaim the reign of the resurrected Christ is to heal, forgive, embrace, restore, exorcize, and speak. Both Jesus and Paul declare a coming future that breaks in on every aspect of life in the present, and both envision the communities formed by their messages to be the continuing agents of the coming new creation that is the dominion of God. Both call would-be disciples of Jesus to continue the ministry of Jesus, to embody the identity of Jesus to every corner of the world that God claims as his own.

The Jesus narratives of both the Gospels and Paul are stories of new creation. They draw deeply from the well of Israel's creation traditions and present Jesus as the solution to the problem of a world gone wrong. That story was set in motion by God placing humans at the pinnacle of creation, charged with representing God's reign to the earth. They were stories of the kingdom of God. What we have, at times, too quickly glossed over is that the so-called gospel story that envisions our salvation as deliverance from the earth is a story that concedes defeat to the powers that oppose God. Put simply, if our hope is flight from this earth, evil wins. New creation is absolutely essential to God's fulfilling of his purposes in creation.

But if new creation is the indispensable goal in general, then the accomplishment of such a creation by means of human agency is just as imperative. The means God ordained for reigning over the earth was a human vicegerent, and if no human could ever fulfill that calling, then God would have to concede defeat to the powers that oppose God. In other words, if God has to save directly, without human mediation, evil wins. Human agency is absolutely essential to God's fulfilling his purposes in creation.

And so, when we look to the Jesus narratives, we begin to realize more and more that he inaugurates the reign of God and sits enthroned as Lord precisely because God has appointed him as the human who bears God's authority over the earth. Jesus is the manifestation, in human form, of the restorative grace of the God who desires to make all things new, once again. Jesus is Lord because he is the first person to live his life as a true human: perfectly in submission to God and perfectly faithful in bringing the Word and reign of God to bear on the earth.

What it means, then, for us to be followers of Jesus is to live into the full potential of our God-given humanness. Or, put differently, we come more and more to bear the image of God that is the image of our older brother, Jesus. And this means that, like him, we will be agents of God's reign. We will anticipate that not only our hearts but also our bodies, our communities, our justice systems, and our use of the earth will all become increasingly conformed to the pictures of self-giving, restorative love by which God has made himself known to the world in Christ. For Paul no less than for the Gospels, the fact that Jesus is the new picture of what it means to be truly human carries with it the implication that we who participate in this new humanity must carry on every facet of his work. As those who bear the name of Jesus, as those who are "in Christ," we are the agents through whom Jesus makes his blessings flow far as the curse is found.

3

Christianity as Community

> The mission of God is to establish a community of people that transcends every human division. . . . It is the vocational calling of human beings created in the image of God to anticipate this community.
>
> —John R. Franke, *Manifold Witness*[1]

My heart. My life. My relationship with God. My alienation from God. My repentance. My faith. My allegiance. My Lord. My justification. My sanctification. My membership added to the church. My quiet time. My closed-eye self-examination at communion. My route to heaven. My escape from the coming conflagration. My soul with Jesus forever. The gospel story as so often told over the past century has relentlessly hammered away on the individual's need to get right with God, the individual's need to repent and believe, the individual's need to have a personal relationship with Jesus. In what is perhaps a caricature of historical Protestantism, which distanced itself from the Roman Catholic insistence that the church is the place of salvation, contemporary evangelicalism sometimes insists that neither institutions nor other humans have anything to do with our relationship with God. All that matters is my own faith as I stand before the Creator.

Is there an advantage to such a focus? Without a doubt. In an era in which personal responsibility is shirked in favor of a posture of entitlement, a call to take account of one's own standing before God issues a healthy corrective. And even when a sense of accountability is not lacking—when, for example, a person is struggling with a profound sense of guilt—this focus on the individual underscores that the Christian narrative tells the story of a God who desires intimate connection with each person and of a Savior who makes possible such fulfilling relationship.

But there are downsides to an individualistic gospel story. In the previous chapter we explored the cosmic dimensions of the Jesus narrative that are missed when we focus overmuch on getting individuals into relationship with God. God's work in Christ entails a full-orbed restoration of every aspect of the created order. In this chapter we are going to narrow our focus from the cosmic context of human life to its communal dimension.

Even in our individualistic Western world, people are increasingly coming to realize that our personal identity is never separable from our corporate identity. Or to put it in somewhat more dynamic terms, our identity is always part of, and shaped by, a larger narrative we find ourselves in. To be in a relationship with God is not, and can never be, solely about my own personal relationship. Scot McKnight puts it this way: "Eikons [McKnight's word for people created in God's image] can't eikon alone. Eikons are made for *relationship* and to give Eikons a life without relationships, without dependence, and without love will diminish them."[2] This is the story of both Jesus and Paul. My relationship with God is always, and must ever be, about how I am participating in the narrative of God's people.

Being in relationship to God is a "storied" affair in the old sense of that adjective: it involves one in a narrative. The story of our relationship with God is a family story. And our family history is the true tale of a Father who has acted to make us his beloved children through the act of our firstborn elder brother. Because this is a family story, it is one in which we who participate discover a new corporate identity. Because it is God's story, it is a story of grace and forgiveness. And because it is Christ's story, it is a story of embrace and unity that glories in difference and diversity. The good news as proclaimed and lived by both Jesus and Paul is not merely the promise of power to make us new persons. It is also the promise of a new people. This new family comes into being in particular communities here and now.

We have already looked at the foundational narrative of the world gone wrong from Genesis 3. It depicts human rule being ceded to the serpent and the subsequent disintegration of the natural world. Dysfunction in human relationships is another aspect of that story. After their act of disobedience, Adam and Eve find themselves confronted by God. "Have you eaten from the tree?" God asks. "The woman," the man replies, "she gave me fruit from the tree" (Gen. 3:11–12). In this story, whose purpose is to explain life in a fallen world, blame-shifting and finger-pointing mar the intimate relationship of man and wife. We see in Adam's response to God's question one of the fundamental dynamics of the economy of this world: we pursue life for ourselves even at the expense of the lives of others. But we discover in the cross of Christ that the economy of God's kingdom is precisely the opposite: it is a giving up of our own lives in order that others might live. And, paradoxically, we learn that this is the way to life.

We will explore the upside-down economy of God's kingdom more in depth in the next chapter. For now, we need to note that in the narrative of a world thrown off balance by disobedience to God, interpersonal relationships are one of the first casualties. We must therefore anticipate that when God acts to redeem the world, the restoration of human-to-human relationships will be part of God's all-encompassing agenda.

How deep does this fracture between humans run? We get a hint when God predicts the couple's future. Addressing the woman he says, "Your desire shall be for your husband, and he shall rule over you" (Gen. 3:16 NRSV). Such is a picture of disordered relationship and misdirected power. A relationship that began with woman as a coequal helper is now one marked by desire, rule, and servanthood.

As if to underscore that fissured human relationships lie at the heart of the sin and brokenness that typify life after Eden, the next episode in the story is one of anger, jealousy, and murder. The sons of Adam and Eve, Cain and Abel, are the characters in this intrafamilial squabble. When Cain's vegetable sacrifice finds less favor in the divine nostrils than Abel's animal sacrifice, Cain is stirred to rage and kills his brother (Gen. 4:1–8).

These early scenes in the biblical drama clearly show that brokenness and sinfulness in human relationships are central components of the world's reality that the biblical narrative promises to resolve. If the gospel is truly to be good news for those of us who live in such a reality, it will have to include the creation of communities where such brokenness is healed, where such self-serving defensiveness is replaced by self-denying service, and where oppressive power relations are undone in favor of coequal relationships. If the biblical narrative is to resolve the problems articulated at its beginning, then creation of harmonious community will be an integral part of the gospel. And this is what we find.

Communities of Grace: Disciples and Churches

If Jesus had come simply to call individuals to follow him, his message would have been incomprehensible to first-century Jews, and God's promises to Israel would have failed. When Jesus comes on the scene, the Jewish people are expectant. In the early chapters of Luke's Gospel we meet people such as Simeon, who was waiting expectantly for God to "comfort Israel" (2:25). We meet Anna the prophetess, who gave voice to those waiting for the redemption of Israel (2:36–38). God had promised that he would restore a people, gather those who had been scattered, reign over them, and pour out the Spirit on all of them, transforming them into a people who would reflect his glory to the world. For all the ways that Jesus's ministry is a genuine surprise to his audience, he upholds the collective character of these promises. Jesus comes to create the kind of community that will be a light to the world, a (re)new(ed) family of God.

In one early story we catch a glimpse of the surprising way that Jesus is redefining the people of God. When his family comes to see him but cannot get through because of a crowd, Jesus looks to those who are sitting around him and says, "Here are my mother and brothers; whoever does the will of God is my brother and sister and mother" (Mark 3:34–35). He is renarrating the identity of the people of God. Anyone in Jesus's Jewish audience would have agreed that doing God's will makes one part of God's family; however, Jesus has displaced other measures of doing God's will (such as keeping the law that God gave to Israel) and has placed himself in that position. It is those who are following Jesus, attending to his words, who are doing the will of God. The significance of this claim is fully seen only once one realizes that Jesus is providing an alternative reading of Israel's narrative, one in which he takes to himself the role previously assigned to Torah as the defining marker of the faithful people of God.

Perhaps some of the collective force of Jesus's words and actions is lost on us because standard written English does not have a plural form of the word "you." Had we the wisdom to more broadly adopt the Southernism "y'all," we would be confronted with proclamations such as this one from the Sermon on the Mount: "Y'all are the light of the world. . . . Let y'all's light so shine before people that they will see y'all's good works and glorify y'all's Father who is in heaven" (Matt. 5:14, 16). For those whose imaginations had been formed by biblical imagery, such words would likely evoke the promise of Israel's glorification. In the prophecy of Isaiah 60:1–5, the people of God shine because God has shone on them and so the nations are drawn into the presence of God. What does it mean to be a follower of Jesus? Following Jesus means being part of the people who are living into the promises of restoration, the people through whom God is on mission to the nations.[3] Each of us as an individual can claim this vocation for ourselves only if we belong to the people about whom it is true. To be a disciple of Jesus is, inherently, to be part of a community. Better: to be a disciple of Jesus is, inherently, to be part of a family.

Jesus invokes familial language in the Sermon on the Mount, telling those gathered to hear his proclamation that God is their Father; they are God's children. This reinforces the idea of the familial redefinition we saw above from Mark 3. Through his words and actions, Jesus communicates that those who follow him have a new collective identity as the family of God, and that only those who follow him can claim such kinship.

In the next chapter we will delve more deeply into the actions that define such communities, after which we will wrestle with issues of inclusion, exclusion, and universalism. For now, I want to draw attention to two important dimensions of communities that are defined by the Christian story. First, since they are communities living into the story of the God of the Bible whom we call Father, these groups must reflect the character of this God by acting like this God. And second, since this God was acting definitively in Christ, we know what it is to act like God by looking to the narrative of how God has acted through Jesus. Or as a friend of mine likes to say, "God is a verb that acts like Jesus."

Acting like God

On the more general point of acting like God, the Sermon on the Mount has this to say: "Love your enemies and pray for those who persecute you [= y'all] so that you may be children of your Father who is in heaven; for he causes the sun to rise on the evil and the good, and he sends rain on the righteous and the unrighteous. . . . Be perfect, therefore, as your [= y'all's] heavenly Father is perfect" (Matt. 5:44–45, 48). What it means to be like God cannot be dissociated from the mission of God in Christ. This call to love one's enemies, to be agents of blessing to them, sits in a potentially awkward tension with Jesus's earlier allusion to Isaiah 60 and its vision for restoration. Such visions in the Old Testament often entail indications of military victory, of defeating Israel's enemies as though they are God's own adversaries. And yet Jesus invites us to see that the story of the world, and the story of God's actions in Christ to save a people to himself, depicts God as one who repays insult with blessing, offense with forgiveness, persecution with prayer.

What types of actions might typify a community that is generating the sort of light that would cause onlookers to see their good works and glorify their Father in heaven? To take but one specific example, to be like this grace-extending God is to be a community of forgiveness. In the next major section of the Sermon on the Mount, we find instructions on how to pray, including the so-called Lord's Prayer. There we find God's forgiveness of us and our forgiveness of other people in tightest possible connection: "forgive us our debts as we also forgive our debtors" (Matt. 6:12). Wittingly or no, whenever we pray this prayer together in Christian communities we are inviting God to measure our own posture of forgiveness against his own character as a forgiving God. Even starker than mere comparison, however, is Jesus's word of warning and promise. To a community that is to be defined as a forgiven people, Jesus proclaims that our ability to receive God's forgiveness is contingent on our own ability to extend such forgiveness to others. If we are not imitating the heavenly Father, then we are not his children: "For if you [= y'all] forgive people their transgressions, your heavenly Father will also forgive you [= y'all]; but if you [= y'all] do not forgive people their transgressions, neither will your Father forgive your [= y'all's] transgressions" (Matt. 6:14–15).

Extending forgiveness to one another is so central to the community's vocation to enact the story of God that Jesus calls us to be agents of forgiveness even when we are not the ones who need to extend this grace but the ones who need to receive it. This is the startling message of Jesus's warning against anger (Matt. 5:21–26). He begins by saying that anger, not merely murder, makes one liable to judgment, and that acting on anger by name-calling brings one to the brink of judgment in hellfire (Matt. 5:22).

Jesus follows this admonition, however, by telling people not how to deal with their own anger but how to mollify the anger of someone who has taken offense at them: "And so, if you're offering your gift and remember that your brother or sister has something against you . . ." (Matt. 5:23).

Notice the familial language, "your brother or sister." Jesus is concerned about the kinds of relationships that typify the family of God's children, the family that he is reforming around himself. This is a family that does not live by principles of self-interest, as though the only thing that really matters is seeing oneself preserved from judgment. On the contrary, this family is driven to pursue the good of one another, even leaving one's own worship of God behind to see that the family is embodying the forgiveness that God offers us. The most striking thing of all is that this is not an abandonment of worship driven by the realization that one's own heart is not right with a brother or sister; rather, it is a forsaking of personal communion with God driven by the realization that we are the burden on someone else's heart.

The call to leave the gift at the altar and be reconciled with our siblings is offered as an illustration of Jesus's teaching against anger. The upshot is that the family of God is so aware of the dangers of anger that we are called to forsake the worship of God in order to ensure that none of us is keeping another from experiencing the forgiveness of God. We are called to pursue reconciliation, not for our good but for the good of our sister or brother. This is what it means to be a family that lives out its identity as children of the God of grace and forgiveness. And what we should never lose sight of is that this type of community derives its identity from the gospel narrative itself. This is the story of Jesus, who comes to save his people from their sins (Matt. 1:21) and pursues their reconciliation even at the cost of his own life.

Acting like Jesus

Although each Gospel offers a unique portrait of Jesus, they are in agreement that the ministry of Jesus is to be embodied by Jesus's followers. The community he forms around himself is the continuation of Jesus's presence on earth. In the previous chapter we noted how Jesus's mission to teach and thereby make disciples is entrusted to his own disciples at the resurrection: "All authority in heaven and on earth has been given to me. Therefore, go and make disciples . . ." (Matt. 28:18–19). Jesus was a disciple-making teacher, and his disciples are to continue that mission. Similarly, we see nearly one-to-one overlap between Jesus's mission and the mission on which he sends his disciples during his life. After showing us a Jesus who gathers people to himself, preaches, and exercises authority over demons, Mark tells us that Jesus calls twelve to himself in order to be with him, preach, and have authority to cast out demons (Mark 3:13–15).

Of course there is one thing Jesus did for us that we could never do for one another: he died on the cross for us. But in a calling that is just as surprising to us as it was to his first disciples, Jesus summoned his disciples to embrace even this narrative of the cross, the most unrepeatable act of his ministry, as the hallmark of life in Christian community.

As the story goes, a dispute arises among Jesus's disciples concerning greatness in the kingdom of God; specifically, this is a debate about which of them is greater. We can safely assume that they are not humbly exalting each other to the positions of greatness. And so Jesus demands that their understanding of greatness be turned on its head. The greatness in his community of followers is not the greatness of the world. Out there, among the nations, those who are great lord it over others and wield their power as a sign of greatness, "but among you, it shall not be so" (Mark 10:42–43). What will be the difference in Jesus's community? The upside-down nature of the dominion of God is put on display in the person of Jesus: "Whoever wants to be first among you must become servant of all, just as the Son of Man came not to be served but to serve and to give his life as a ransom for many" (Mark 10:44–45). This community is to shine its light by continuing Jesus's vocation of giving himself so that others might live.

The stories and teachings of Jesus show us not only how he formed a family during his lifetime but also ways in which his ministry will be extended through the communities that continue to follow him after his death and resurrection. Matthew, in particular, anticipates a community called "the church" (Matt. 16:18; 18:17). And each Gospel depicts a community that bears the title of God's family, brothers and sisters who find their oneness in a God whom they call Father; its identity is shaped by the story of what this God is doing and has done in Christ to gather a people to himself. With these pieces in place I want us to turn our attention to Paul's letters, where we will see that his vision of the people of God is no less a matter of participation in community than the Gospels'.

Reassigned to Israel's Drama

Paul's story of a community of Jesus followers contains many of the same narrative dynamics as the Gospels, though with two particular points of difference. These differences are, first, that though Paul tells the story of discipleship as one of being part of the people of Israel, his churches are comprised not of Jews but mostly of non-Jews (gentiles). The other major difference has to do with how Paul depicts the church as the continuing presence of Jesus in the world: it is Jesus's own body. As Paul reflects on the story of Israel that preceded Jesus, and reflects more deeply on the church story that comes afterward, he walks a wide, common ground with Jesus in calling for an imitation of God through an imitation of Christ.

Children of Abraham, Family of God

Stories from the Scriptures of Israel form the well that Paul draws from as his letters narrate the life and identity of his communities. Israel's story becomes the story of the church. It is precisely God's commitment to a corporate people, Israel, that causes Paul to articulate salvation in an inherently communal manner. To be part of the church is to belong to a community whose identity is being molded into the shape of that people of God whose story is written on the pages of the Old Testament. And that story, in turn, is being shaped by Paul's convictions about Jesus as the crucified and risen Messiah.

When we turn to Paul to probe his writings for indications of Christian identity, we must always remember that he is writing first and foremost to churches. What narrative do these communities locate their identity in? First, it is a story of God's promises. When we read the Gospel narratives, we find them easily referring back to God's vows to make Abraham into a numerous people with a territory for its own possession. In Mary's song in Luke 2, the birth of Jesus is anticipated as the fulfillment of the promise to Abraham and his descendants (Luke 1:55). The identity of those who will be saved by the work of Christ is the seed of Abraham whom God has helped.

But here Paul, the missionary to the gentiles, has a problem. (And we discover in Romans that this is God's problem too, though that is a story for another day.)[4] His converts are not physically descended from Abraham and do not bear the mark of the covenant people—they are not circumcised. And so, in one of Paul's most daring moves, he renarrates the story of Abraham so that it will include his gentile converts as well. The story of Abraham is one of the most formative narratives for Jewish identity, and Paul tells it in such a way that non-Jews can become part of the family.

Paul renarrates the Abraham story in two places: Galatians 3 and Romans 4. And here we are about to walk over ground that has been well trod during the past five hundred years but that we need to reassess using our narrative framework. These are the places in Paul where he tackles the issue of "justification by faith" head-on. But what may seem strange to anyone with experiences of Paul influenced by Protestant churches in the modern West is that these passages, which have fomented so much debate and division, were written for the purpose of defining all the followers of Jesus as one unified people.

The question of unity will concern us more directly in chapter 7. Here we will lay the groundwork by taking stock of how Paul's treatment of Abraham reveals that the church has a narratively constructed communal identity: we are the people of God, which is to say that we are the children of Abraham, which is also to say that we are the children of God and brothers and sisters of one another.

Paul presents two visions for how it is that we become Abraham's children. What this tells us, in part, is that the core conviction is that all Christians are part of this family and therefore recipients of God's promise, and there are many possible ways to conceive of how and why this is true.

The first time Paul tackles this issue is in Galatians. In chapter 3 of that epistle, we find Paul capitalizing on the specific language of God's promise to Abraham in Genesis 17:7. There, God tells the patriarch that the covenant is not just between himself and Abraham but between God, Abraham, and Abraham's seed. "Seed" in this case is an image for descendants.

In Galatians, Paul exploits the singular form of the noun *seed* and finds in it a hint that the covenant promise is going to be established through one person: Christ. The covenant is between God and Abraham and Christ. Therefore, the way for anyone else to be part of this promise, to be the "seed" of Abraham, is to be part of the one seed—to be "in Christ." As Paul works it out here, Christ defines the family of God, and everyone who is "in Christ" is a child of God, a recipient of the promise to Abraham.

If the God of Israel has acted to redeem a people for himself, this action must be read as the story set in motion when God bound himself to Abraham, Isaac, and Jacob. And yet God has also done something new and unexpected: he has poured out the promised Spirit on uncircumcised gentiles.

When we keep the issue of circumcision on the table, we catch our best glimpse of why Paul makes the somewhat strange argument he puts forth and the brilliance of his rereading of Genesis 17, which states in no uncertain terms that circumcision is absolutely necessary to be part of the covenant people of God. Circumcision itself is the covenant: "This is my covenant with you and your seed, the covenant that you are to keep: Every male among you shall be circumcised" (Gen. 17:10). And as if to underscore the point, God goes on to say that those who are not circumcised will be cut off from the people (Gen. 17:14). The passage that promises a seed, that ensures the covenant promise will pass to the seed, makes circumcision the indispensable marker of the people of God.

Paul, though, insists that gentiles are participating in the story without being circumcised, without becoming Jewish. In order to both affirm the story and write his gentile converts into it as gentiles, he rereads the story in light of what God has done: God has sent Christ as the fulfillment of the promise—he is the one seed.

But if the seed is *only* Christ, where does that leave us? It places everyone on the same ground: needing to be joined to Christ in order to participate in the covenant promises. Paul says: "You are all God's children, in Christ, through faith" (Gal. 3:26). To be a follower of Jesus is to be "in Christ" and therefore to be part of this family of God that has Abraham as its father. This is precisely how Paul concludes the chapter: "If you are Christ's then you are Abraham's seed and heirs according to the promise" (3:29).

The story of God's family is the story of Abraham. Paul retells this story, insisting that belonging to Christ makes us part of that community because he understands not only that communal stories determine our individual identities but also that this particular story is the one story that God has wrought salvation with. To follow Jesus is to be written into the story of the one worldwide family of God.

With this reorientation of gentile identity on the table, making gentiles part of the story of Israel without making them become Jews, we can begin to understand other passing comments. Recall our discussion from chapter 1: gentiles are being written into the story of Israel. In writing to the church at Corinth, Paul recalls part of the Old Testament exodus narrative, insisting that the story is "ours," a story that holds currency for both him and his non-Jewish coverts. When he begins to recall this piece of Israel's Scripture, he writes, "I do not want you to be unaware, brothers and sisters, that our fathers were all under a cloud, and all passed through the sea" (1 Cor. 10:1). "Our forefathers." Paul does not say, "The Jewish people." He does not say, "Their forefathers." He calls the gentiles his siblings and calls their attention to their common ancestral lineage. The gentiles have been written into the story of Israel.[5]

Christ's Body, No Longer Gentiles

We have looked now at how people's union with Christ writes them into the story of Israel: they are Christ's and therefore the story of

Abraham and his seed is their own. Throughout, we have been using the term *gentiles* (i.e., non-Jews) to speak of Paul's churches. We discover in 1 Corinthians that this might not make the apostle entirely happy. Paul sees the transformation of identity as being so complete that he can refer to his converts as "gentiles" in the past tense.

Leading into the famous chapter on spiritual gifts, Paul says, "You know that when you were gentiles you were led astray to mute idols" (1 Cor. 12:2). Christian community is a certain kind of community. Other kinds of communities, with other kinds of practices and identity markers, stand at odds with it. At the heart of this antithesis is whether one worships the true and living God of Israel or, instead, the idols that are not gods. The living God is the God who is not mute but speaks, and who not only speaks but also gives the gift of speech. The community that the true God has set apart for himself is defined by a common confession ("Jesus is Lord") that indicates a larger reality: the members of the community are recipients of the Spirit. These are some of the layers Paul puts in place as he tells the Corinthians that their identity is inherently corporate: by the Spirit they are united to and become the body of Christ. And so the word *gentile*, which used to characterize them as lying beyond the pale of the people of God, no longer applies.

As we saw when we reflected on Jesus's selection and sending of his disciples, the church, as a body and as a community, is the continuing story of Christ. In a passage famous for its discussion of spiritual gifts, Paul appeals to Jesus as the answer to the church's struggles against self-aggrandizement.

Divisions and self-promotion deny the story of salvation. In 1 Corinthians 1 Paul had condemned such factionalism by asking rhetorically, "Has Christ been divided? Paul was not crucified for you, was he? Or were you baptized in the name of Paul?" No, the Christian story is one of incorporation into Christ, not Paul, and the lives of believers are to dramatize that reality.

And so when we read in 1 Corinthians 12 about the "body of Christ," we need to pause and absorb the magnitude of what Paul is claiming. Although other passages in Paul will speak of the church as those charged to represent and speak for Christ where Christ cannot be physically present, that is not the image here. Although other passages speak of the church as a body in closest relationship to Jesus such as that of a husband and wife, that is not the image here. When Paul talks about the church as the body of Christ in 1 Corinthians 12, he speaks of the people being related to Christ in the same way that my ear is related to me. The members of the church make up Christ's body in the same way that my eyes, ears, fingers, legs, and other parts make up my body. This might be putting it even too mildly: Christ *is* the body that is made up of the parts. "Just as the body is one yet has many members, but all the members of the body, though many, are one body, so also is Christ" (1 Cor. 12:12).

Jesus is a body with many members. And we are those parts. By the Spirit, through baptism and the Lord's Supper, we are joined to Jesus's body and thereby become "the many" that comprise "the one." This is the mystery behind Paul's insistence that we are many and varied while at the same time one and therefore bound to use our gifting in service of one another.

When exploring our corporate identity, Paul first focuses on the notion that if we are to be a fully functioning community we must be different from one another (1 Cor. 12:14–19). If each person were the same, we would be deprived of sight or sound, of touch or smell. There is no room for a false humility whereby a member would see himself or herself as useless due to that member's apparently less important role. More important, because our identity is found in community, we must anticipate that God will bless this group with diversity. The one person who has everything that the church needs for life and health is Christ, and we are the members who embody those needful things. Diversity expressed within community is both inherent to our identity and essential for our health.

And so Paul goes on to explore the flip side of his claim. Not only do we need diversity, but we also need to recognize our oneness as well. In 1 Corinthians 12:20–26 he countermands our tendency to see certain members of the community as less important and therefore dispensable. The high calling not only to endure one another but to participate fully with one another in the use of gifts, in life's joys and sorrows, is a narrative we are called to live based on the part we play together in God's story. To paraphrase 1 Corinthians 12:27, "As a group you are Christ's body, and individually you are its members." Because of his focus on Jesus, Paul's gospel is inherently communal.

No Soloists

This communality is one of the most significant points about which postmodern cultures have prepared us to better read, understand, and appreciate Paul's vision of the Christian life. Of course, to claim that Christianity is inherently communal is not a "postmodern" claim at all, and those of us in Protestant contexts could have learned this much earlier had we listened more carefully to our Roman Catholic brothers and sisters. But the Reformation's insistence that salvation is not tied to one particular church, coupled with the individualistic quest for knowledge that typified the Enlightenment, eventually bore fruit in a self-centered understanding of salvation: all that matters is who I am in my heart before God. But this vision is not Paul's (nor was it the Reformers', though that is another discussion for another day).

Let's stick with the "spiritual gifts" discussion in 1 Corinthians 12 for just a moment longer. An overarching question of this book is whether the Paul we have previously encountered is a faithful depiction of the Paul we find on the pages of the Bible. How have we met the Paul who speaks of "spiritual gifts"? In one of the most profound ironies of my own experience, talk of such gifts has usually been part of a larger vision of self-discovery. We take inventories to see what gifts each one of us has. We sit down with a list of tasks wherein we might find ourselves well employed within our gifting. In the process, what for Paul was an inherent part of life in community is co-opted by our individualistic Christianity as a means to self-fulfillment.

When I speak with people who have struggled with Paul, many of them have a strong sense of the place of community in their lives, especially in their vocation to follow Jesus. As we approach Paul from various angles, we are going to see again and again that he shares this concern for community. To be saved is to be "in Christ," and to be "in Christ" is to be in his body, the church, a community of people who need one another not only to thrive but even to live. The story that determines my identity has as its fountainhead that I am inscribed in the story of Christ and thereby written into the story of the people of God.

So far we've explored ways that the narrative of Israel is determinative for our corporate identity, and some ways that the story of our reception of the Spirit and incorporation into Christ determines our corporate identity. If the former brings Paul's converts to an even playing field with Jesus's Jewish audiences, the idea of incorporation into Christ's body seems to take us away from the story as Jesus told it. Do we find in Paul what we saw in the Gospels, that the stories of a gracious Father and of a self-giving Messiah are themselves determinative narratives for Christian identity?

The Family Story

As God's family, we are called to live out the family story. For both Jesus and Paul this means imitating our Father, who receives us with welcome and forgiveness. As we saw with Jesus's calls to forgiveness, we also see in Paul that God's reception and forgiveness of each of us calls forth a way of life that puts community before self. And this imitation of God involves us also in embodying the story of Jesus.

Romans 15:1–13 lays out the options that confront a church standing face-to-face with a possible split along ethnic and cultural lines. The tendency to trumpet our own position, to pursue our own agenda for spiritual formation and obedience to God, is confronted with the cross of Christ. Paul insists that we are not to please ourselves and calls each of us to look to our neighbor, to act to please the other and to build others up (15:2). Such a call beckons the community to continually reenact the narrative that formed it.

The first part of the narrative that Paul alludes to is the crucifixion. Paul reads Psalm 69:9 with Jesus as the speaker: "The reproaches of those who reproach you have fallen on me." In bearing the scorn heaped on another, in his death on the cross, Jesus models the self-effacing humility that is to characterize the family of God. Because we are written into the story of Christ, his own self-humiliation for the good of the other becomes our model—the scriptural injunction applies to us, propelling us forward and granting us hope. We have hope because Jesus's fulfillment of the Scripture resulted in his resurrection from the dead. We can therefore be sure that when our communities enact the self-giving narrative of the cross, we too will be given new life by God (both here and now and in the hereafter).

A surprise awaits us as we start delving more deeply into Paul's call that we imitate Christ's self-giving. The psalm Jesus "recites" in Romans 15, Psalm 69, is a song of a righteous sufferer, a song addressed to God: "The reproaches of those who reproach you, *God*, have fallen on me." In Romans 15 the reproaches that fall on Christ do not refer to the sins we humans should have borne. Instead, they introduce the mockery heaped on the God of Israel.

When Paul calls us to dramatize the story of Jesus in our community, he is not calling us to look at ourselves as the savior and our brothers and sisters as sinners who need us to deliver them. Yes, Paul calls us to play the role of Christ. And yes, he calls us to see the fellow members of our community playing the role of the ones scorned in the psalm. But recognizing the divine audience in the psalm, Paul profoundly implies that he wants us also to bear ridicule directed at God, and that God, in turn, is known as he indwells his earthly family.

Paul summons us to bear with one another because when we look at the faces of our brothers and sisters we see in them the image of God. They represent God on earth. We view them as though their future were realized in the present, "perfect as our heavenly Father is perfect." We imitate Christ, who bore the reproaches of those who ridiculed God. I seek my sister's good, I seek my brother's good, rather than my own because in so doing I live into my family's story, the story of the elder brother who died for the honor of the Father. When I set aside my own desires and seek to please my siblings, I also am giving up myself for the honor of my Father, whose likeness I see in them.

As so often in Paul, the path of faithful Christian living ultimately leads to the worship of God. The purpose of our communal harmony is so that as one people, with one voice, we may glorify the God and Father of our Lord Jesus Christ (Rom. 15:6). When we so accept one another, and give ourselves for one another, the result is not merely the absence of discord but the production of a chorus of voices joined in harmonious praise to God. Once again, community is essential. More than this, Paul is intent to show us that such a God-glorifying community is the reversal of humanity's primal failure to glorify God (Rom. 1:21; 3:23). The story of the fall as it highlights our failure to worship God is undone only when God acts in Christ to overcome the effects of the fall as it has marred our relationships with one another. Worship is not simply about my heart before God or my voice being lifted up—it is about my heart as part of a community, my voice as part of our song. Like Jesus calling us to leave the gift at the altar if someone else needs to extend us forgiveness and then come back to worship, Paul calls us to submit ourselves to our brothers and sisters so that as one unified body we might offer our collective praise to God.

In the second paragraph of Romans 15, verses 7–13, we discover something as profound about God's identity as we discovered about our sisters' and brothers' identity in the first paragraph. If our siblings' identity is most truly known in God's identification with them, it is also true to say that God is most truly and fully known in his identification with us. Here, we are not talking about the incarnation of Jesus, though that event makes the same point in a different way. Romans 15 tells us that the existence of a unified community, specifically one that brings together Jews and gentiles, confirms the truth of God (Rom. 15:8).

God is known in such a community because God has chosen to bind himself to, and write himself into, the story of Israel. God's promises to Israel are confirmed when God embraces them in the embrace of Christ, but in order to truly show itself as the work of the true and living God, the community must be a unified group that embraces gentiles as well. Our existence as a unified yet diverse people shows that God is alive, that God is at work, and that this living, working God is a God who can be trusted to write the story of the world so as to redeem every part of its sinfulness and brokenness.

To the surprise of many of us who grew up thinking of God in abstract categories such as *omnipotent*, *omniscient*, *infinite*, and *unchangeable*, the God of the Bible has written himself into the story of a particular people and has linked his fate with theirs. God's identity is narrated for us in the story of Israel, and especially in the death and resurrection of Jesus, which bring this story to its climax. But God has not only staked his character on the one-off work of Jesus on our behalf; he has also joined his reputation to the community that is formed by being united to Christ.

Where we are tempted to say that Jesus's death on the cross itself is the reason for God to be praised, Paul says that it is the risen Christ's acceptance of us that results in glory to God. While our default mode is to say that Jesus's death and resurrection show us that God is faithful and true, Paul here says that the community formed by this service, a community of Jews and gentiles together, affirms "the truth of God and confirms the promises given to our forefathers" (Rom. 15:8–9).

Community could not be of any more vital importance to Paul. Not only is our life together an imitation or reenactment of the story of Christ, but the continuing narrative of the church continues to show (or call into question) the very character of God as one who embraces, loves, forgives, and keeps his promises. And so Richard Hays is right to conclude that Jesus's death and resurrection function, in part, to point beyond themselves, signifying "God's eschatological intention to create a messianic *community* of those who know themselves summoned to welcome one another, as the Messiah has welcomed them, for the glory of God."[6]

What Is Our Life Together?

Christian identity is inherently communal. Followers of Jesus are the family of God, brothers and sisters of one another. The postmodern current that places a high premium on community as shared life, shared spaces, recognizing the ways that these shape us and therefore carry us along in our efforts to create sustainable and vibrant webs of social interaction, finds ready allies in both Jesus and Paul. But where Jesus and Paul might call us to repentance is in the self-seeking tendencies that underlie even many of our endeavors toward community.

Above I mentioned the irony of investigating spiritual gifts as a path to self-fulfillment. Similar narcissistic tendencies might underlie other efforts at community. To take but one example: what sorts of communities are formed through social networking? As someone with a blog and LinkedIn, Twitter, and Facebook accounts, I have found tremendous value in connecting over the internet. But more often than not, these media are incapable of hosting truly Christian community because it is rarely possible in such contexts to enact our vocation of setting down our own lives so that others might live. Most often, the currency of such tools is that of self-promotion. Again, this is not always bad. Telling people our stories; allowing them to see that we possess the gifts of wit, irony, and sarcasm; and sharing our reflections on the world can cultivate relationships that blossom into true community.

But true community begins when I stop telling you what I think and begin to help you live out the fullness of what you believe (this is the point of Rom. 15). True community begins when I stop obsessing about myself long enough to help you walk the road you have before you. Christian community is recognizable in a oneness of purpose and worship that brings glory to God. I have even seen such acts of love and worship occur on the internet—worship united in the wake of a Twitter friend's suicide, oneness of purpose to give and pray in the aftermath of an earthquake in Haiti, and evidence of a church that knows no boundaries based on race, gender, nationality, language, or skin color. But we must not assume that being "connected" means that we are in community any more than we may assume that our belonging to a church means that ours is a healthy family. Even there we may be called to leave our worship aside in pursuit of our calling to be a people who, corporately, live into the forgiveness that God has extended to us in Christ.

What is Christian community? It is a family formed around Jesus. It is a family that has a certain look. Like a human family where unique persons bear a common family resemblance, so the family of God is comprised of an unmitigated diversity of people who are called to look like their Father, which means, in turn, to look like their brother Jesus. As a people we are called into a community. As a forgiven people we are called to be agents of forgiveness. As a Christian people we are called to continue the work of Christ in embracing one another so that our light will shine, giving glory to God or, in the words of Paul, so that with one accord we might with one voice glorify our God and Father.

Many of us living in the postmodern Western world are becoming increasingly aware that community is an inherent part of our story and that community is good. But community at arm's length is not enough. Simply being connected must not be confused with faithfully playing our roles as the engaged, committed, and invested family of God, the body of Christ. People looking on must be able to see the family resemblance, to see a people imitating God our Father by living the story of Christ our brother. This communal identity plays itself out in myriad decisions that we might speak of under the umbrella term of *ethics* or, perhaps, *spirituality*. This is where we must turn next.

4

Living Out the Jesus Narrative

When Christ calls a man, he bids him come and die.

—Dietrich Bonhoeffer,
The Cost of Discipleship[1]

Over the past couple of chapters we have been progressively tightening our focus. From the importance of storytelling we moved to the cosmic story of the dominion of God and new creation. Narrowing our focus in the previous chapter, we zeroed in on the communal narrative of the church as the family of God. From cosmic and corporate understanding of our salvation story, we turn now to the life that each of us is called to live.

Does the Pauline story of salvation, of Christians being written into the family of God by being united to Christ, have something to say to us about how we are called to live as individuals before the face of God, as those carrying the name of Christ with us while we go out into the world? This, I expect, is a very real question for some readers of this book. The Paul many of us have been introduced to is the Paul of "justification by faith alone." This sometimes carries with it an implicit or even explicit corollary that God does not expect us to do anything. At times, we might even hear that any attempt to act on God's behalf, or to act in faithful response to the gospel, is a denial of the good news. And small wonder—we tell stories about beginnings in large part to shape our understanding of our identity in the present. If faith alone is the beginning of our story, should it not be the story's continuing text?

I expect that such a reading of Paul is not unrelated to a deconversion testimony I heard while I was in college. An Asian woman in my Biblical Hebrew course wore a yarmulke to class, a surprising testimony to her Jewish faith. As the year wore on, she eventually shared her story: she had converted from Christianity to Judaism because she liked having something to do.

One could imagine any number of possible responses to her from within Christianity itself: living with a rhythm of rituals is a vital part of daily life for many Christian communities; the New Testament itself calls us to significant engagement in social issues; and the like. But I suspect that many of us whose communities or denominations walk in theological trajectories set by Reformation readings of Paul need to hear this story as a warning, and to ask whether we have gotten our own story straight.

For a "people of the book," how we read the Bible (in this case, the stories of Jesus and the letters of Paul) is inseparable from our self-understanding, which, in turn, is intimately bound to how we live our lives. There is an ethic entailed in Jesus's and Paul's storied theologies, the ethics of a people who are living into the narrative of a crucified and risen Jesus.

Responding to the Message: Following Jesus

The Gospels are stories. They have no choice but to show us action at every turn. Jesus goes, heals, teaches, feeds, and exorcises demons. To be like Jesus, so it would seem, is an inherently active affair.

When people are called to follow Jesus, he calls them to a new way of life. As we read through the Gospel of Mark, we discover that the call to follow Jesus is an invitation to participate in Jesus's own mission of inaugurating the kingdom of God. People's lives are transformed—and they are called, sent, or driven to do things they would never have done before. But those who will not answer this costly summons find themselves standing, dangerously, against the rushing tide of the coming reign of God.

Kingdom Ethics

The ethics of discipleship in the Gospels can be summarized as continuing Jesus's mission of bringing near the reign of God. This means both participating in the actions that gather a people to God through preaching, healing, and exorcism and, perhaps more centrally, embodying the cruciform means by which the kingdom ultimately comes.

From the first, Jesus's call is a summons to participate in his ministry of inaugurating the reign of God. The first call to Galilean fishermen is "Come, follow me, and I will make you fishers of people" (Mark 1:16–20). They are called to live out the narrative of God's regathering of his scattered people.

After the disciples have followed and watched the work of Jesus in and around his home base of Capernaum (see Mark 2:1), he summons a group of twelve to himself (Mark 3:13–19). As scholars have often noted, this gathering of twelve is itself emblematic of the reconstitution, the regathering, of scattered Israel. This connection with the tribes of Israel dovetails with Jesus's original call to his followers in Mark 1:16–20. They are called to be for Israel (and then for the world) what Jesus is for them: the one who gathers them in fulfillment of God's covenant promises.

The idea that the disciples are to extend the ministry of Jesus is reinforced in numerous ways, including three key scenes from the first half of Mark's Gospel. In Mark 3:13–15, when Jesus calls the twelve, we learn that their role is to be with Jesus, preach, and cast out demons. Jesus is the source of their new life, and this passage perhaps nods toward the contemporary church's concern to promote intimacy with God and Christ. They are called to be with Jesus.

But the purpose of their calling is not only to be but also to do. They are to continue and extend what Jesus has been actively engaged in: proclaiming and demonstrating that God's reign has been brought near.

Later in the story we read that Jesus sends the disciples out two by two in order to engage in just this sort of ministry. In Mark 6 the disciples go out preaching repentance, casting out demons, anointing the sick with oil, and healing (Mark 6:7–13). Jesus's ministry is both the one-time, unique set of deeds that inaugurates the coming reign of God and the script for the ongoing life of the church.

The ethics of the kingdom consist, in part, in continuing the proclamation and embodiment of the power of God that ushers people into a transformed world. As the subsequent story in Mark makes clear, the Christian life is the kind of thing that makes the kings of the earth nervous—not because it encounters them with force of arms, but because it testifies to a power that not even death can contain.

And so we find that the disciples' ministry makes Herod anxious. Why can they do such marvelous things in Jesus's name? Herod begins to speculate: "John the Baptizer has been raised from among the dead, and this is why the powers are at work in him" (Mark 6:14). Notice that the work of the disciples causes Herod (and others) to speculate on where *Jesus* gets his power. Later, when Jesus asks the disciples who people say that he is, they answer with a litany of dead people: John the Baptist, Elijah, or one of the prophets. The kind of power at work in Jesus and Jesus's followers is so great that it is as if death itself has been overcome. Now the question for us: if such power was available to the disciples before being empowered by the resurrected Christ, how much more should today's church be putting on display such divine, life-giving, restorative power?

The disciples imitate and replicate Jesus's ministry. Jesus's call to follow is not a vague call to be nice. It is a summons to play the part of understudy as the Master Actor performs the script and to step in to perform it when he is absent from the stage. The story of God's faithful people on the earth is perfectly interpreted in his words and deeds. At times we see a careful rehearsal: Jesus gives stage directions to go, to preach, to heal; Jesus not only blesses and distributes bread but also places it into the hands of his disciples to distribute. The story of the kingdom finds its fulfillment as it is told and embodied, and this is the life to which Jesus's followers are called.

Cruciform Ethics

But to say that we are called to continue Jesus's mission of inaugurating the reign of God is not yet to have all the pieces in place for articulating a Christian ethic. As the Bonhoeffer quote at the beginning of this chapter suggests, Christ's summons to follow takes the shape of his own enthronement procession: the way of the cross.

In the second half of Mark we see how shocking Jesus's mission is to even his closest followers, and the equally shocking indications that the way of the cross is the disciples' as well as the Master's.

In Caesarea Philippi, Jesus probes his disciples concerning people's ideas about his identity (Mark 8:27–38). As we read this story, we should be attuned not only to the words but also to the actions of the characters. After Peter confesses Jesus to be the Messiah, Jesus begins to define what it means for him to fill that role. How will Jesus finally stand in the place of Adam, the man who represents God's rule to the world? "It is necessary for the Son of Man to suffer many things and to be rejected by the elders and high priests and scribes and to be killed and after three days to rise." Suffering. Rejection. Death. Resurrection. Such is the destiny of the Messiah.

This is too much for Peter. He abandons his position. The one who is called to follow instead leads Jesus aside (Mark 8:32) and attempts to lead him astray. The staging tells us that Peter has misstepped: he is no longer in the role of follower.

The other disciples have held their ground—they are behind Jesus, illustrating their call to be his followers. Jesus turns and looks at those who are behind him (Mark 8:33), occupying their rightful place as his followers, and commands Peter to return there as well: "Get behind me." The question of whether Peter will follow Jesus is concentrated precisely at this point: the moment of discovery that the pathway that Jesus must walk along is the way of death.

To say that someone is the Messiah, the King of Israel, is not necessarily to answer the question of how that throne will be taken. In other Gospels, we see that Satan confronts Jesus with the temptation to come to this throne by bowing before him. Satan attempts to raise doubts in Jesus's mind about whether and how it is that Jesus will be King of Israel, the Son of God. Here in Caesarea Philippi, Peter forsakes his calling to be a "little Christ," an extension of the reign of God, and instead plays the role of Satan—the one who would undo Jesus's messiahship by having him pursue it along some path other than death.

What, then, does all this have to do with Christian ethics? As the passage goes on to demonstrate, what we confess to be true about the calling of Jesus we simultaneously confess to be the true character of

Christian discipleship. To follow Jesus is to walk behind him—as he goes on his long walk to Calvary.

Having rebuked Peter, Jesus calls the crowd to himself and describes both his own calling and that of his followers in cruciform terms. "If anyone desires to follow behind me, let that person deny himself, take up his cross, and follow me" (Mark 8:34). The story of Jesus, as that story goes to Calvary, is the story that scripts the narrative for the lives of Jesus's followers.

Jesus's life turns the economy of the world on its head. Into a world full of people who scrape together life for themselves at the expense of the lives of others, Jesus comes and reveals the power of God by giving his own life so that others might live. Richard Hays summarizes the ethic of Mark's Gospel this way: "The disciples are summoned to follow, and the single fundamental norm is laid down in the narrative of Jesus' own death on the cross. Unlike Paul and John, Mark nowhere explicitly interprets Jesus' death as an act of 'love.' The way of the cross is simply the way of obedience to the will of God, and discipleship requires following that way regardless of cost or consequences."[2]

Jesus calls his followers to a life that enacts the saving reign of God and brings it to greater realization on earth—in both doing kingdom deeds and doing them in step with the cruciform ministry Jesus embodies. Such a call to action means that people who live in the family of God are marked by an ethic of life by means of self-giving sacrifice. And, conversely, it means that those who reject either the deeds or the cruciform means find themselves at odds with Christ.

Love

But what about love? Can we not just say, in echo of Jesus, that the Christian ethic is simply about loving God and loving others (Mark 12:28–31)? We can, indeed, say that the Christian ethic is one of love—but the question then becomes, how do we know love when we see it? Or, better, what does love look like when it is shaped by the particular story of Jesus's life, death, and resurrection?

Jesus answers this question in the Gospel of John. Yes, the one command Jesus gives is a command to love. Throughout Jesus's last conversation with his disciples (John 13–16) he reiterates this.

But here we must not stop short. Jesus does not leave his disciples wondering what sort of love is the Christian love that enacts his story for the world. "I am giving you a new command, that you love one another, just as I have loved you in order that you also might love one another. By this all the world will know that you are my disciples, if you have love for one another" (John 13:34–35). Love is indispensable not merely to keep the family together (the concerns of our previous chapter) but to make manifest to the world that this community is a community of Jesus's followers.

John 13 also provides a hint as to what kind of love Jesus is talking about. His own love for the disciples enables them to be a community of love, and his love defines the community as his followers. These indications point to an idea of love that is different from the love that one might find elsewhere. There is a "Jesus love" that shows the world that a community consists of his followers. Such suggestions prove true, as Jesus elaborates at the beginning of chapter 15.

In this section of Jesus's final speech to his friends, he invites them to share in his life, to "abide in" him. The particular abiding that Jesus has in mind is an abiding in love. To love is to obey: Jesus loves and obeys the Father by loving the disciples; the disciples are to love and obey Jesus by loving one another.

The words of chapter 13 are echoed here: "This is my commandment, that you love one another, just as I have loved you" (John 15:12). But then Jesus goes on to spell out exactly what such love looks like: "Greater love has no one than this, that someone lay down his life for his friends" (John 15:13). The love of a Christian community is none other than the continuing embodiment of the self-giving love of Jesus.

The ethic of Jesus is comprised of a self-giving life of love, the giving up of self so that the other might live. And, in the surprise that is known only to the eyes of faith, such self-giving love is itself the path to glory. The community that is formed around the Messiah who inaugurates the reign of God with power, but takes his throne by obediently going to death on the cross, is the community that must faithfully enact its vocation of cruciform love. Jesus's ministry demands a response—the Christian faith is an active, living faith. And the life to which Jesus calls us is defined by his own. Can we say the same for Paul?

The Narrative Structure of Pauline Ethics: Cruciformity

The story of Paul's theology is the story of the God of Israel, at work in the death and resurrection of Jesus, to draw a people to himself and thereby bring his purposes for the world to fruition. Although it might seem obvious that no single one of these elements could be removed from the story without the story's being unrecognizably marred, the church has not always succeeded in making its life a living narration of the story of the crucified Christ.

Such is the life that Paul calls us to live. Yes, in a few pages we'll have to get to the question of faith versus works. But I want to step into Paul's letters not by tearing down our old structures but instead by exploring the one that Paul has constructed.

The death and resurrection of Jesus provide the form and content for Paul's ethics. We have mentioned several times that the basic model for salvation that we find in his letters is one of union with Christ, or being "in Christ." For Paul, this is not about a mystical experience, fleeing the body in order to enter into a few moments with a heavenly spirit. No, to be in Christ is to be joined to the earthly narrative of a crucified Messiah who found enthronement in heaven precisely because of his obedience unto death (Phil. 2:6–11).

The first thing this means is that ethics for Paul is not primarily about doing a set list of good things. Nor is it even about imitation of Jesus as though we were looking on him from afar. Instead, by being united with him in his death and resurrection we are freed from an old way of life and given divine power to live out God's desires for human life. Or to put it in Paul's words, "it is God who is at work in [us] both to will and to work for his good pleasure" (Phil. 2:13). We perform the story of Christ, to whom and to which we have been united. Put differently, to live "authentically" as a Christian is to become a living embodiment of the story of Jesus's death and resurrection, a person who enacts his or her true, God-given identity as God's child.

Spirit and Flesh

One of Paul's most famous depictions of life in Christ is his description of the fruit of the Spirit in Galatians 5: "But the fruit of the

Spirit is love, joy, peace, patience, kindness, goodness, faithfulness, gentleness, and self-control." What does such a list of virtuous dispositions have to do with the story of Jesus? Everything.

In getting some perspective on this fruit, we first need to see that it is set in contrast with the works of the flesh: sexual immorality, impurity, idolatry, witchcraft, divisions, drunkenness, and the like (Gal. 5:19–21). The contrast Paul has drawn here is not between "spirit," as in some pure, internal part of us, and "flesh," which means our bodies. No, the flesh-versus-spirit distinction is tied to the larger idea of, on the one hand, the world that stands in need of redemption and, on the other hand, the power of God's Holy Spirit as the agent of new creation. The framework for understanding this dichotomy is what scholars sometimes call an "apocalyptic" framework: the recognition that a new age has dawned with the work of Christ and faithful Christian living means participation now in this coming age.

But the idea of bearing the fruit of the Spirit is even more closely tied to the death of Jesus. Paul insists both that living by the Spirit is what we should expect of ourselves as Christians and that such a life is impossible without being crucified with Christ. He goes on, after listing the fruit, to say, "Those who are Christ's have crucified the flesh with its passions and desires" (Gal. 5:24).

In the battle between the flesh and the spirit, the decisive victory has already been won—on the cross. Living ethically is a matter of living into our identity as those who have been crucified with him. Because of the power of his death and of the life-giving Spirit, we can be marked as those who possess what Paul calls the one thing that matters: "faith working through love" (Gal. 5:6). Christian faith is faith at work.

True Servanthood

If the Christian life in general is to be marked by co-crucifixion with Christ, then leading God's people demands an even clearer, ongoing display of Jesus's death. This is the burden of much of Paul's two letters to Corinth. In these, Paul is constantly contrasting his ministry with the work of some who have come behind him and attempted to undermine his authority. The validity of his message is to be found not only in the content of his words but also in the life that illustrates the Christ he proclaims—the crucified and risen Jesus.

In 1 Corinthians, Paul must contend with the Corinthians' idea that ministers who are more rhetorically polished or socially well established better embody what one might hope for in a Christian speaker and leader. Rather than argue that his version of Christianity can also perform well by the standards of the world (which seems to be the default mode of many Christians today), Paul insists that the economy of the cross undermines the worldly standards altogether.

What does it mean to know Christ crucified according to 1 Corinthians, particularly as a minister of the gospel? As Michael Gorman summarizes it, "to live like criminals awaiting the death penalty or prisoners of war paraded in public (4:9); to be foolish and weak rather than wise and strong (4:10); to suffer physically, whether by circumstances or choice (4:11–12a); to bless and endure when mistreated (4:12b–13, echoing the teaching of Jesus preserved in Matthew's Sermon on the Mount); to be treated like so much garbage (4:13)."[3] The gospel story contains an inherent irony: wisdom and power are revealed by means of folly and weakness.

Therefore, Paul claims repeatedly, the truly Christian life is not one that can be assessed by the world and found to live up to its standards. What is true of the Corinthians is true of all followers of Christ: the stories they inherit from their society, stories of wisdom and power, need to be "deconstructed and reconstructed—reshaped by the story of Christ crucified. In this sense 1 Corinthians is . . . *subversive*—subversive to the status quo even within the church."[4]

The Corinthians are misassessing Paul's ministry because they have failed to have their understanding of the world's story retooled by the story of God's acting for us in the crucified Christ. To misconstrue the gospel story is to misconstrue the work of a servant of that story and is to further misconstrue the life we are called to live within that narrative.

The upside-down nature of the gospel story is the key to getting our minds around 2 Corinthians as well. Throughout this letter, Paul's and his companions' suffering becomes a living illustration of the gospel. This begins in chapter 1 of the letter with Paul's reflection on a near-death experience in Ephesus: "We had within ourselves the sentence of death in order that we might not trust in ourselves but in God who raises the dead" (2 Cor. 1:9). The death and resurrection of Jesus are not only the story Paul proclaims; they also give definition to God ("the God who raises the dead") and provide the interpretive framework for making sense of Paul's own story.

Indeed, this connection between the gospel message, God, and Paul's ministry provides the narrative matrix for understanding Paul's famous claim that we carry the treasure of the gospel in earthenware vessels: "We have this treasure in earthenware vessels in order that the surpassing greatness of the power might be of God and not of ourselves: afflicted in every way, but not crushed, perplexed but not despairing . . . always carrying around in the body the dying of Jesus in order that the life of Jesus also may be manifest in the body" (2 Cor. 4:7–10). Paul carries the gospel by literally embodying the message of the crucified Christ. What does it mean to be an ethical apostle, minister, or Christian leader? It means giving up one's own life so that others might live. Or, closer to Paul's own words, to have death be put on display in our own lives so that Jesus's life might be realized in the lives of others (2 Cor. 4:12, 15).

Realizing that the gospel itself, the story of Jesus's death and resurrection, is Paul's rule of life has been the key for me in overcoming my early antipathy toward him (that, and my ever-developing appreciation for sarcasm). As I mentioned in the introduction, I remember reading 2 Corinthians 11–12, the "boasting" chapters, and being turned off by Paul's arrogance. Paul is, of course, making significant claims for himself and underscoring how his own life validates him as a minister of the gospel. Such self-defense easily lends itself to the sorts of accusations of self-aggrandizement that I made when I first encountered the text.

But turning now to those passages with an eye for the inherent conjunction between the story of Jesus and the story of those who claim to follow him, what once looked like madness now becomes its own picture of the good news. And I find myself wishing that more contemporary Christian leaders would take their cues from Paul's standards of self-assessment.

At one point in his rant, Paul begins to compare himself with the "super apostles" who came behind him to Corinth: "Are they Hebrews? So am I. Are they Israelites? So am I. Are they Abraham's seed? So am I" (2 Cor. 11:21–22). But the punch comes as Paul takes his next turn, asserting that he is more of a servant of Christ than they. How does he prove that his mission is some sort of greater servanthood than theirs? By chronicling how his life better reflects the suffering, shame, and apparent failure of the gospel: "More labors, more imprisonments, countless beatings, often in mortal peril; I received 'forty lashes minus one' from the Jews on five occasions; three times I was beaten with rods, once I was stoned" (2 Cor. 11:23–25). And so he continues, outlining the dangers of his travels and the internal burden of caring for the churches.

What does it mean to establish a résumé as someone devoting his life to service of Christ? For Paul it means to point to himself as a living narration of the gospel of Christ crucified. To be in danger of death is to find oneself confronted with the fundamental question of Christian faith: do I trust in the God who gives life to the dead (2 Cor. 1:9)?

As a seminary professor, I teach through Paul's letters once or twice a year. But however many times I teach through the Corinthian correspondence, these letters never cease to haunt me. The letters signal the radical implications of saying that the story of the crucified Christ is the story of God's redeeming power. To hear Paul tell it, such a story subverts the competing drama that has always beckoned us to find significance, security, fulfillment, and success by reaching higher, by performing better, by overpowering and supplanting our competitors.

Why do I say that Corinthians haunts me? Because everywhere I turn I am confronted by how Western Christianity stands in the place of the Corinthians: we have written Christ's name in the byline of our culture's story and think that we have thereby made known the gospel of Jesus. "We can do what you do with equal excellence"—that seems to be our self-indulgent claim to the society in whose wake we struggle to swim.

Which Christian voices are widely heeded in our day? When I list the five or six that readily come to mind as the regular headline-makers,

I am struck by the fact that they have prominent voices because they have attained greatness by the measures of growth that fuel our capitalistic society. They have built prosperous enterprises, amassed large followings, written best-selling books. In a Walmart society, we flock to the large church that has managed to squeeze the life out of its local competition.

For those who claim to follow Jesus, our role is not to show how Christ can play the lead in society's story better than any other person. Our calling is to make manifest the Christ who plays the lead in a different story altogether, and to show that this other story is the paradoxical way to life, peace, significance, security and—I say with both trepidation and full conviction—power and glory, but all by way of the cross.

At the beginning of the biblical story, things go awry when the serpent tempts the first couple with this promise: "Your eyes will be opened, and you will be like God" (Gen. 3:5). In a story whose dramatic tension is set in motion by this grasping after God-likeness, the answer comes in one who refuses to do so. As Paul puts it in Philippians 2, "Although he existed in the form of God, he did not regard equality with God as something to be grasped, but emptied himself, taking the form of a servant." The irony of the story, of course, is that this very refusal to cling to or exploit God-likeness for selfish gain, the willingness even to set it aside, leads to the very God-likeness that Adam and Eve reached for and failed to attain. Because Jesus became obedient unto death, God highly exalted him and bestowed on him the highest name (Phil. 2:9).

When we talk about the sort of life we are called to as followers of Jesus, Paul would lead us to believe that the question before us is what courses of action enable us as Christians, and as churches, to become living narrations of our foundational story. It is an ethic that derives from the conviction that the old self was crucified with Christ so that we can now embody his self-giving love.

What Paul says about how to assess would-be Christian leaders is of vital importance because how we are led determines what it looks like for us to follow. To be a Christian leader is to say to others, "Follow me as I follow Jesus." The question is whether the leader we're following is following Jesus along the way to the cross.

A True Church

Paul writes 1 Thessalonians in large part to encourage this fledgling congregation. At the heart of his affirmation is their faithful following of cruciform leaders. Much of the first two chapters is spent reflecting back to the congregation what Paul sees as their faithfulness to the gospel of Christ.

He begins by saying that he thanks God for their faith, love, and hope—the same cluster listed in 1 Corinthians 13, here in slightly different order. Perhaps one of the surprising things for many of us, whose bread-and-butter understanding of the gospel pits faith and works against each other, is that Paul singles out the Thessalonians for their "work of faith"—the things they do because they believe (1 Thess. 1:3). Similarly, he praises the labor that is spurred by their love and the endurance that is empowered by their hope. In all of this, Paul is signaling that a true and viable Christian community is known for what it does, not just for what it thinks or believes.

A Christian community is summoned, preeminently, to embody that story of the Suffering Savior. And thus Paul goes on: he knows that God has chosen them because the Spirit worked powerfully among them (1 Thess. 1:5). What is the evidence for this? The Thessalonians saw the kind of people who were proclaiming the gospel to them and, in imitation of them, joyfully received the message in the midst of great affliction (1:6). It is not simply that they believed but, like Jesus and the apostles after him, that they entrusted themselves to God in the midst of suffering.

The connection between Jesus's suffering, the suffering of Paul and his companions, and the suffering of the church is drawn out even more explicitly in chapter 2 of that same letter. Paul first declares that he knows God's power is at work in the Thessalonians, and then tells them why he has such confidence: "You became imitators of the churches of God in Christ Jesus that are in Judaea, because you suffered the same things from your own countrymen as they did from the Jews who killed the Lord Jesus and the prophets and drove us out" (1 Thess. 2:14–15). To be "in Christ Jesus" is to be rejected and suffer—even as Jesus was and did. Paul has confidence about the faith of the Thessalonians because this church has become a living picture of the story of the crucified Christ.

Freed to Obey

Thus far, our discussion of Paul has been rather sober, if not downright gloomy. All this talk of death and crucifixion is couched so as to curtail other ways of thinking through what it means to act Christianly. It is not about obeying some sort of ever-existent "moral law"; it is not about finding what is good and valuable in our society and excelling there; it is not about successful church growth and marketing. No, Christian ethics or spirituality is about living out our foundational narratives in the communities we have been joined to as followers of Jesus. We are to be living stories of the crucified Christ.

But the good news is that the same Jesus who was crucified was also raised from the dead. While the resurrection life of Jesus does not provide as many pointers for how we are to act as the crucifixion does, it nonetheless provides a vital component to Paul's vision of the faithful Christian life.

The key place to look for the intrusion of Christ's resurrection into our current lives is Romans 6–8. There, Paul is wrestling with several things at once: What does it mean that the death of Jesus brings life? What does it mean for the status of the law that God chose to give life not on the basis of law keeping but rather on the basis of crucifixion?

Indeed, that issue of the law is so important because Paul makes a surprising claim about the story of Israel, namely, that when law entered the story of the world gone wrong, it did not have the power to fulfill its purpose. It was supposed to bring life, but instead it was commandeered by sin and death and worked against God's design.

For Paul, the death and resurrection of Jesus show beyond a doubt that the defining narrative of the Christian story can no longer be the law that God gave to Moses on Mount Sinai. But without such a law, what becomes of ethics? Does the story of a holy and righteous people then crumble? These are the questions Paul sets out to answer in Romans 6–8. His answer is that a righteous life is now possible for the first time in human history because the power of sin is defeated through "resurrection via crucifixion."[5]

Throughout Romans 6, there is a movement from dying with Christ (union with him in death by means of baptism) to living, now, in his resurrection life (and therefore in anticipation of our own future): "We have been buried with him in death . . . in order that as Christ was raised from the dead . . . so we might walk in newness of life" (Rom. 6:4). The purpose of all this co-crucifixion talk is to open new possibilities for lives that are pleasing to God.

Here Paul is wrestling not only with the all-pervading reality of death but also with the power of sin. Paul treats these as two powers that come, and go, together. To die is to succumb to both the power of sin and the power of death. Therefore, to be raised from the dead is to overcome both the power of sin and the power of death. Such resurrection from the dead is what God, by the power of the Spirit, enables us to experience now in Christ.

Christian life is resurrection life, new life that is capable of obeying God as our old self never was. New creation impinges on the present: "Consider yourselves to be dead to sin but alive to God in Christ Jesus" (Rom. 6:11). The story of Jesus draws us into itself. It not only converts our imaginations, giving us a new story line by which to identify ourselves, it also genuinely frees us to become in Christ what we were not before. Now we can become people who freely obey God.

It is precisely this movement from death to resurrection life that Paul has in view six chapters later when he begins the instructional section of the letter with these images: "Offer your bodies as a living sacrifice, holy and acceptable to God—this is your reasonable service of worship. And do not be conformed to this world, but be transformed by the renewing of your mind so that you may approve what the will of God is—that which is good, and acceptable, and perfect" (Rom. 12:1–2).

To offer our bodies as a living sacrifice is to enact the narrative of Christ crucified, the defining narrative of our Christian communities. To be transformed by the renewing of our minds is to live into the new life that is ours in Christ, a life in which we consider ourselves dead to sin but alive to God, a resurrection people who must use the power given to us to live lives pleasing to God.

Notice that Paul here advocates an ethic that comes hand in hand with, and flows from, transformation. Although he will go on to give some particular instructions, the point of Pauline ethics is not that we accept Jesus and then follow a list of rules. The point of Pauline ethics is, instead, that we become the kind of people who can faithfully express our corporate narrative of a crucified and risen King. Such transformation is what ethicists speak of as virtue.[6]

Authentic Witness, Well-Played Roles

Rightly read, Paul shows us that as followers of Jesus we are called to get our story straight, not just for the purpose of telling our story with words but even more importantly for the purpose of telling our story with our lives. As Samuel Wells puts it: "Narrative and practices form *witnesses*—disciples who embody the church's life in prayer and service. These witnesses are the church's truth claim—it has no purchase on truth that is detached from the transformation of lives and communities brought about by its narrative and practices. . . . Changed lives embody the hope of the community."[7] If the Paul you have met is one who seems to have too little to say about how to follow Jesus, then the heralds who have introduced you to him have likely been living out a truncated gospel story at best.

As for the apostle, he would beg his churches to hold fast to the gospel message with one hand while holding his ministry up for examination in the other. His invitation was clear: Measure what you see. If my life does not tell the story of the gospel I proclaimed, then my apostleship is worthless. However, if his life has shown forth the power of the resurrection in a life that bears all the marks of cruciform self-giving, then he is a true messenger of this gospel story. This is how we should assess him as well.

The Christian story and the stories of our lives are inseparable. I would argue that this is not only an imperative we are called to implement, but an indicative statement of what is true whether we are aware of it or not. How we understand and articulate the Christian story will always determine how we act.

If we tell a story of a principle of grace, we will inevitably create communities of "cheap grace" demanding no transformation, no lives of self-giving love, because grace as some kind of universal principle is a story of grace without the cross.

If we tell a story whose lead is played by a human disposition of faith, we will inevitably create introspective communities, devoid of costly reconciliation and lacking in acts of mercy, because faith as a human disposition is a story of faith without the faithfulness of Christ unto death on a cross.

If we tell a story of an unassailable theology, we will inevitably create contentious communities that consume the saints as they defend their borders, because unassailable human theology is a story that raises itself up against the story of the self-giving Messiah who gave himself to assail, overturn, and conquer every human system of control and power.

As humans, we cannot curtail the power of story to determine the lives of those who participate in a particular, defining narrative. What we can do, however, is tell new stories and, as followers of Jesus, return repeatedly to our gospel story. We can rehearse it in the words spoken in our communities. We can illustrate it in the giving of the bread, which is Christ's self-given body, and the wine, which is his self-given blood. We can symbolize it in the cross. And we can beckon one another into it by creating communities defined by self-giving acts of love.

If this storied ethic is true to the Paul of the New Testament, why have so many of us encountered a Paul who seems to ask so very little of us? Doesn't Paul tell a story of justification by faith alone, a narrative that would seem to bear its inevitable fruit in lives where faith remains alone, devoid of contaminating works? Not quite.

Responding to the Message: The Obedience of Faith

The rallying cry of the Reformation, that we are "justified by faith alone," has produced an understanding of Paul that severs the connection between assent to the gospel message and the transformed life that Jesus calls forth.

I can say from my own experience that a commitment to "justification by faith alone" has the power to produce an underdeveloped sense of Christian responsibility. This is not merely a stereotype, even if it does not represent the best of what the Reformed tradition has to offer. I have heard expositions of the Christian life that quote Paul's saying to "keep in step with the Spirit" (Gal. 5:25) as proof positive that we shouldn't try to outrun God, or even take any initiative, in our pursuit of holiness—we should wait for the Spirit to move. I have heard faith and "law" set in such antithesis that the audience was invited to "blow off" anything in "the law" that caused them to stumble. I have heard Reformation justification theology paired with Luther's claim that Jesus's call to repent means that all life is to be a life of repentance—such that our only "work" is to repent of any work we might have tried to do.

In light of the widespread popular idea that Paul sees faith and works as antithetical, and that saving faith has nothing to do with our obedience, I want to spend some time here looking at a few key texts that paint a very different picture. We will then see how Paul's articulations of faith and works fit within the biblical narrative of the ongoing work of Israel's God. Like Jesus, Paul calls believers to participate in the narrative of God's restoring of a scattered people to himself and in the larger project of God's renewing all things.

One of the first things that must be said is that we should not pin the phrase "justification by faith alone" on Paul. Indeed, there is only one verse in the Bible where the words "justification," "faith," and "alone" appear, and it is in James 2:24: "See, then, that a person is justified by works, and *not* by faith alone."[8]

When Paul speaks of faith, works are often not far behind. As often as not, works are written into Paul's descriptions of faith. We have already seen how in 1 Thessalonians Paul is thankful for the deeds the church does that make known its faith, hope, and love (1 Thess. 1:3). Faith does not simply assent. Faith does not simply receive. Faith works.

Later in this same chapter, Paul continues to praise the Thessalonians for their faith, the report of which has gone out far and wide. What is the report? First, that the Thessalonians received Paul and his traveling companions (1 Thess. 1:9). Also, their service of worship has changed: they no longer serve idols but the true and living God (1 Thess. 1:9). Finally, their whole life is reoriented to the eschatology of God's story: God is bringing history to its culmination with the return of Jesus, and the Thessalonians are looking forward to this coming (v. 10). Each of these is part of the report of their "faith" that has gone out far and wide.

Faith is at work not only in a disposition toward God, but also in dispositions and actions directed toward other people. It is made known in worship and in a whole life orientation that is transformed in light of the proclamation of Jesus.

Lest we should think that such descriptions of faith were articulated in a context that had not yet drawn to the apostle's attention the need to keep faith and works categorically distinct, we should take stock of the way that this very same idea is repeated in both Galatians and Romans.

In his fiery letter to the Galatians, Paul is at his most adamant about justification by faith: "We know that a person is justified by faith and not by the works of the law," he says in chapter 2. And yet in this same letter Paul enunciates the one thing needful for Christians: "Neither is circumcision anything or uncircumcision, but *faith working* through love" (Gal. 5:6). Yes, Paul does take certain kinds of actions (or markers of Jewish identity and covenant faithfulness) off the table, and yet he still insists that the kind of faith that matters is not faith that stands alone. The faith that is of utmost value is faith that works through love.

Similarly in Romans, another book that gives no little attention to the question of justification by faith, Paul states at the outset that his missionary goal moves well beyond assent and internal embrace of a set of teachings. He says that the reason he has been given the charge to be an apostle is "to bring about the *obedience of faith* among all the gentiles" (Rom. 1:6). Like Jesus, Paul, when he issues his summons to follow, anticipates a transformation of life and action that correlates with a new, life-ordering reality: the crucified Christ is the resurrected Lord over all. To exercise faith in such a Messiah is, at least in part, to obey him.

To be justified by faith is never to be justified by faith that stands alone. In this, it's time for many of us to revisit the letters of Paul and have our story straightened out.

Reconfiguring Western Christian Mores

Somehow, Christians in the Western world have backed themselves into a peculiar corner. Some of us have inherited the Reformation by insisting that anyone who demands a life of costly obedience is denying the gospel. Some of us are living into the secularized ideal of a "Judeo-Christian ethic" that in actuality divorces morality from both the Jewish and the Christian stories. Some Christians have partially corrected this, insisting on adherence to the Ten Commandments themselves, with clear commitment to their origin as given by the God of the Bible. But to insist on such a standard is to ignore a cluster of problems such as the fact that almost no Christian communities keep the Sabbath (what *did* you do last Saturday?), that God's revelation of himself has occurred in visible form, that the name by which God is known is not (in the Christian story) summed up as Yahweh, and that the great act of salvation by which God's name is made known and from which our commandments flow is no longer bringing a people up out of the land of Egypt.

Instead of a Ten Commandments whose grounding is the saving event of the exodus, Christian faith demands actions that correspond to its foundational story of the self-giving Christ. Its ethics derive from our particular story, not a universal ideal or moral law. And its spirituality is defined by Jesus's story, with the exodus and its Decalogue spirituality standing as fitting forerunners to God's ultimate act of redemption, but insufficient for Christian identity and, therefore, for Christian practice.

Paul's voice has been co-opted to advocate for such misarticulations of Christian performance as I have outlined here. Such misemployment of the apostle is both the fruit and the cause of a misread story. Reclaiming Paul will entail reclaiming the gospel story in the process of rearticulating a viable Christian ethic. Wayne Meeks puts it like this: "Paul's most profound bequest to subsequent Christian discourse was his transformation of the reported crucifixion and resurrection of Jesus Christ into a multipurpose metaphor with vast generative and transformative power—not least for moral perceptions. In that gospel story Paul sees revolutionary import for the relationships of power that control human transactions."[9] Too few of us, I fear, have met this Paul.

Too often the Paul I have encountered in my ecclesiastical wanderings has been a caged Paul, restrained from revolutionizing human relationships of power. Those in power have, instead, used his words to reify the status quo. When proclaiming that Paul forbids "doing," they call people away from activities that, conveniently enough, fall outside the control of those who hold positions of power in the church.

Thus Paul is used to forbid what the powers cannot control. Paul's own vision of the obedience of faith redefines faithfulness in such a way that it is less predictable, and perhaps even uncontrollable—something that cannot be said for the static system of moral law that demands one and the same set of actions for all people at all times. Even keeping the Ten Commandments can be a convenient shield against the calls to self-giving love that both Jesus and Paul summon us with.

I daresay that most of us need to have our entire understanding of what it means to live faithfully before God restoried. We need to come back to the narrative that is given its definitive shape by the life, death, and resurrection of Jesus. Such is the call of discipleship we find coming from both Jesus and Paul.

When we turn to wrestle with particular issues, we cannot simply scour the Bible for what it says about x, y, or z. We are called to so embody the story we inhabit that our transformed mind will test and approve the will of God. Having laid out the importance of story, the all-embracing new creation that provides both the stage and the content for God's work of redemption, the church community that becomes the living narration of that story, and the implications for individual ethics, we turn now to explore the implications for various pressing issues.

It seems that a fitting place to start is to answer the question that many readers will feel went unanswered in this chapter. If "justification by faith" is not about establishing faith as something that stands by itself, then what was Paul going on about in Galatians and Romans? The answer to that question, perhaps surprisingly, is to be found in our next discussion, on the topic of unity, inclusion, and universalism in the church.

5

Judgment and Inclusion

> As God does not abandon the godless to their evil but gives the divine self for them in order to receive them into divine communion through atonement, so also should we—whoever our enemies and whoever we may be.
>
> —Miroslav Volf, *Exclusion and Embrace*[1]

Up to this point I have been developing a narrative interpretation of Jesus and Paul, arguing that their theologies are storied engagements with God. These stories expand as wide as the cosmos, enfold the people of God, and come to a point in the lives of individual followers of Jesus. Now we need to probe a bit deeper into the universal scope of this message. To paraphrase a common concern, does Paul adulterate Jesus's message of inclusion and embrace by creating judgmental and exclusive communities?

When we ask this question, we find ourselves having to wrestle quite quickly with the history of the Western church. The Paul that so many are uncomfortable with had a major boost in his career when his writings provided the theological backbone for the Reformation. In the years that followed, correctly articulated theology became the hallmark of Protestant Christianity's claims to spiritual authority.

The upside of this return to the Bible, and of the challenges fostered by fresh readings of Scripture, was that a genuine reformation was had. Not only did the likes of Luther create new forms of worship and theology better fitting to the early years of the late and post-Middle Ages, but the Roman Catholic Church was also pressed to curtail a number of abuses.

But if there is a dark underbelly to the Reformation, it is to be found in its opening of a Pandora's box of division in the church. And if the tens of thousands of denominations we have now illustrate the dicing up that will inevitably occur when we give free reign to our divisive spirits, the first instrument of our division was the doctrine of justification by faith alone. So for many who are passionate about unity, reconciliation, and inclusion in the church, Paul stands out as a biblical hurdle to overcome rather than an ally to be mustered.

In the previous chapter, we started a process of deconstructing the Paul who advocates justification by faith that stands alone. We were introduced to a Paul who calls for the "obedience of faith," a Paul who summons us to live into the Christian narrative of a crucified Messiah as proof of our "faith" in him. The faith Paul commends is a faith that works, a faith that is never alone.

But if being introduced to a Paul who advocates working takes us aback, an even greater surprise awaits us when we settle into the original context for his fighting words about justification. What for the past five hundred years has been a linchpin doctrine for the division of the Western church was, at its inception, a radical plea for unity, reconciliation, and embrace.

But before coming to Paul, we need, as always, to see what sort of groundwork Jesus lays in his ministry. For if Paul stands out in many minds as the perpetrator of division, rancor, and judgment, it is often as a foil to the Jesus who welcomes all.

Do Not Judge: The Embrace of Jesus

"That book you're writing is for me," my friend confessed over lunch. "I can't square the Jesus who says, 'Do not judge lest you be judged,' with the Paul who condemns homosexuals." And in numerous parallel conversations I have seen Jesus's admonition, "Do not judge," raised as a banner of refuge that people flock to as they flee from the apostle. We will deal with homosexuality in another chapter. But what about the issue of judgment itself?

We are dealing here with a question that is an outgrowth of the community discussion in chapter 3. If Jesus came to form communities, what kind of communities are these? When we are united to Christ, with whom are we (and can we be) living in unity? And as one people, united to Christ, how universal is the embrace we are called to extend?

Do Not Judge Those Pigs and Dogs

We find Jesus's warning against judgment in the Sermon on the Mount (Matt. 7:1). It is a warning that seems appropriate given what we saw above (chap. 3) about Jesus's expectations for his followers. Because Jesus's family consists of those who have been enfolded by God's forgiving embrace, he summons us to extend the arms of that embrace to one another. The admonitions to be reconciled and to extend forgiveness also come from the Sermon on the Mount (Matt. 5–6). And so "Do not judge" finds a natural home in a sermon that compels us to a life of mutual forbearance, patience, forgiveness, and love.

But Matthew 5–7 also raises some caution flags for us when we are tempted to hold on to one isolated saying as giving definitive shape to Christian community. After Jesus states emphatically that we are not to judge, he elaborates the dangers entailed in judgment: we will be judged by the same standard we measure others by (7:1–2). He illustrates the hypocrisy that so often embeds itself in the task of judgment: we are warned against trying to clean the speck out of our brother's or sister's eye while carrying about a log in our own (Matt. 7:3–5). Such a warning also helps to establish the world that these actions are envisioned in: this talk of judgment is family business. It has to do with how the brothers and sisters within God's family treat one another.

But the surprising conclusion to this paragraph of teaching in Matthew 7 is that Jesus does *not* say, "Therefore, do not worry about your brother or sister; rather, attend to yourself." Instead, he says, "Therefore, first take the log from your own eye and then you will see well enough to take the speck from the eye of your brother or sister" (Matt. 7:5).

My conversation partners are right to trumpet Jesus's warning against judgment: judgment is a serious business that is as likely, or more likely, to lead to the judge's own condemnation as it is to lead to the condemnation of the person judged. Those who cling to this verse utter a needful prophetic warning to the church—an institution that is too often guilty of clubbing the world with its own eye-log in its attempts to remove other people's splinters.

But when "do not judge" becomes a cipher for "mind your own business and leave your siblings alone," we have lost a crucial component of our life in Christian community. Yes, Jesus does summon us to mind our own business. But that command is not to mind our own business, full stop. Instead, it calls us to mind our own business so that we can, in turn, more faithfully attend to that of our siblings. If we follow his teaching about judgment to the end, Jesus's speech leaves us not forsaking all judging of one another, but monitoring ourselves lest we become arrogant and judgmental.

Let us explore a bit further the suggestion that judgment is a part of the Christian community's family business. Throughout, Jesus tells us how we are to interact with our brothers and sisters. This is not a command to the church about assessing outsiders; it is intramural talk about how we live as God's family.

Too often, the volume of our disagreements is turned up so loudly that we quickly begin assessing our opponents as those who are not really Christians. We label people "false teachers," or "deniers of the gospel." But when we find ourselves compelled toward judgment, Jesus's humbling requirements for us have not been met until we can address our interlocutor as "brother" or "sister." Only then can we engage in the kind of dialogue that befits a family whose rule is the Sermon on the Mount.

In light of these strong words of warning about judgment and the urgency of Jesus's admonition to self-examination, the command that follows is jarring: "Do not give what is holy to dogs nor cast your pearls before pigs, lest they trample them with their feet and turn and tear you to pieces" (Matt. 7:6). Whatever else we might learn from this difficult passage, its juxtaposition with the famous "do not judge" teaching warns us against too facile an adoption of the notion that we are not to assess the people around us.

The statement about dogs and pigs contrasts with the sayings about judgment on two points. First, the warning applies to how Christians posture themselves before outsiders in stark contrast to how we conduct ourselves toward one another. Second, in this context of dealing with people outside the family we are not called to the same dangerous business of loving, self-critical judgment as we are with one another. One way to view the "holy things" and "pearls" is to see them as acts of judgment themselves.

When a brother or sister confronts us with our failure to live up to the family name, this is a holy act, a valuable gift, a pearl of love and affection. Engaging in "judgment" places both the "judge" and the "judged" in a vulnerable position. We find in Matthew 7 that this type of intimate vulnerability is appropriate within the family, but that Jesus dissuades us from approaching "outsiders" with such judgment. Of course, this does not present anything close to a holistic picture of how Jesus perceives our posture toward outsiders. They are not to be judged, and they are not seen as part of the family, but this is not the end of their story (as we will see momentarily).

Later in the same chapter, Jesus once again demands that we judge. Specifically, we are to assess prophets. Who are the teachers who would command our attention? We must beware (7:15), and we must assess would-be teachers by the "fruit" they produce (7:16, 20). At its best, judgment is an act of loving protection for the family of God.

Without beckoning us toward a naive ignorance about the realities of people's ultimate allegiance (either part of the family of God or not) or of our sisters' and brothers' shortcomings, Jesus demands a cautious self-awareness that should make us slow to judge insiders, keenly attuned to the lives of would-be teachers, and not at all willing to exercise judgment toward those outside the community.

The End in the Sermon

But even the basic distinction between "follower of Jesus" and "one who does not follow Jesus" is one that many are increasingly uncomfortable with. However hesitant we might be about including such a division within our own theology, we cannot ignore that Jesus consistently makes this distinction: the decision to follow him or not to follow him is of ultimate consequence.

As with the various actions of Jesus, so also in his teaching we hear not only a broad summons to participate in the family of God, but also a warning that not all are so included. And Jesus is in the middle of this division.

The Sermon on the Mount ends with two sayings that underscore the pivotal place that Jesus occupies as the means of entry into God's eternal kingdom. In the first, Jesus warns that not all who say to him "Lord, Lord" will enter the kingdom; rather, those who do the will of Jesus's Father are invited in (Matt. 7:21). But as the saying concludes, Jesus tells us that we cannot detach "doing the will of the Father" from knowing Jesus, who is the Judge. The words of rejection that he speaks to many who address him as Lord are these: "I have never known you" (Matt. 7:23). Knowing Jesus and doing the will of God are inseparable.

As if to underscore the point, the final unit of the sermon is the story about the wise man who built his house on the rock and the foolish man who built his house on the sand. How does one attain to the status of "wise man"? By hearing the words of Jesus ("these words of mine" [Matt. 7:24]) and doing them. And what does it mean to be a fool? It is to hear the words of Jesus and disobey ("Everyone who hears these words of mine and does not do them" [Matt. 7:26]).

The point here is simply that Jesus was not a universalist. As we discussed in chapter 3, Jesus formed a community around himself. He was the determining factor for participating in the family of God. The upshot of this is that those who reject Jesus's teaching as the way to faithfully follow God do not belong to God's family as God's children. Jesus came not to proclaim that everyone is part of the family of God (the mistake of nineteenth-century classical liberal theology) but to form that family around himself.

Go to All—Jesus's Universalism

And yet Jesus's ministry is rightly seen as a work of embracing the outsiders, of celebrating the arrival of the kingdom "with all the wrong people," as N. T. Wright puts it.[2] Watching Jesus's ministry unfold, one might even perceive a type of "universalism"—an embrace that goes far and wide, transcending the old boundaries between insider and outsider. Or perhaps we might even perceive an inversion of the old system.

If we follow Jesus down from the mountain of his famous sermon, we can observe his engagement with two quintessential outsiders. First, a leper runs up to Jesus and asks to be cleansed from his disease (Matt. 8:1–4). Notice the language. The leper asks not to be "healed" but rather to be "made clean" or "purified."

One of the greatest burdens to bear for those afflicted with skin maladies in ancient Jewish contexts was that such diseases disqualified people from entering public spaces. Their presence would defile not only the holy places of worship in the temple but also the less holy place where the Israelites lived. They were therefore prohibited from entering not only the temple but also the towns. In keeping with the laws of Leviticus 13–14, lepers were excluded from the life of the people, living in colonies beyond the pale of Israel's holy community.

By cleansing the man, Jesus enables him to be reembraced by the people. Social exclusion is undone and the outsider is brought within.

If lepers lived, at best, on the fringes of Jewish society, gentiles occupied the place of the proverbial "other"; they were the quintessential outsiders. Gentiles were uncircumcised, unclean by Jewish purity standards, and living in constant violation of the Torah (at least stereotypically) through their manner of eating, treatment of other people, sexual activity, and especially worship.

But from Israel's point of view, things could be still worse for a gentile. The Jewish people longed for God to fulfill his promise to make them a free people on their own land under their own king and governed solely by their own laws. Under Roman imperial rule, the Jewish people were perpetually confronted by the as-yet-unfulfilled promises of God in the persons of Roman officials, military officers, and soldiers. If there was anything worse than a gentile, surely it was a gentile Roman "peacekeeper."

Enter the Roman centurion whose son is experiencing a tormenting paralysis. This second supplicant tells Jesus that there is no need for Jesus to come to the house: "But only speak a word, and my child will be healed" (Matt. 8:8). The centurion has eyes to recognize Jesus's authority, much to Jesus's amazement (Matt. 8:10). And Jesus proceeds to spell out the implications of this foreigner's faith: he is emblematic of a stream of outsiders who will recline at the great, eschatological banquet with Israel's honored forefathers in the coming kingdom of heaven (Matt. 8:11).

Approaching Jesus with faith is not merely about receiving a one-off blessing of healing. It is an expression of rightly apprehending, and submitting oneself to, the reign of God as it is present in God's Messiah. Jesus embraces the despised outsider on this basis.

So on the one hand, Jesus appears to be extending the boundaries of God's people—by his transforming power Jesus is simultaneously extending healing and embracing people into God's family. But on the other hand, even as he does so, he issues a stern warning. Not only will Abraham, Isaac, and Jacob be joined by gentiles from east and west, Jesus also warns that "the children of the kingdom will be cast out" (Matt. 8:12). In their responses to Jesus, outsiders may become insiders, but the equal, opposite danger is that the insiders might be made outsiders.

Two subsequent stories in Matthew drive this point home. In stark contrast to the gentile centurion, the Jewish scribe stands as Judaism's quintessential insider, an expert in the very law that gave Israel its self-understanding. When one scribe professes a willingness to follow Jesus wherever he may go, Jesus appears to rebuff his advance, warning him that the Son of Man has no place to lay his head (Matt. 8:19–20).

A second pious Jew wishes to fulfill his filial duty to bury his father before following after Jesus—a widely recognized obligation that would have been seen as essential to keeping the commandment to honor one's father and mother. But Jesus says to leave such tasks to others and to follow him (Matt. 8:22). If the man followed, he did so by leaving aside the very sort of practice that would have marked him as a faithful member of God's family according to Jewish standards.

Stepping back, we see that Matthew paints a complex picture of inclusion and judgment. First, as we see throughout the Gospels, Jesus's teachings in the Sermon on the Mount and his subsequent actions set up Jesus as *the* defining characteristic of the dominion of God. We must not mistake the surprising scope of his embrace for a universalism that has no need of it or for a universalism that minimizes the consequences of rejecting it. Second, for those who have been embraced by Jesus, we discover a "family life" that includes the sacred duty of cautious judgment—perhaps with a warning against turning to the "outside world" with such a posture. Third, however, we see an expectation that the reign of God will bring with it surprising reversals—that outsiders confronted with Jesus will express hope and faith and thereby find Jesus's embrace, while insiders confronted with Jesus will retreat from his call and thereby discover themselves excluded.

Thus, while the way of Jesus is open to all, and while it tears down traditional Jewish means of delimiting the people of God, it also manufactures a new badge of membership from the divine family. A person must recognize Jesus and follow him.

The Gospel of Matthew famously ends with Jesus sending out his disciples to go and make other disciples. They are to go out into all the earth—a universalism that indicates the absence of geopolitical boundaries on the people of God. But this disciple-making is inseparable from being marked by the name of Father, Son, and Holy Spirit; and it strives to bring people into obedience to the teachings of Jesus. The potential for being the wise man depicted at the end of the Sermon on the Mount is now open to all: anyone may hear Jesus's words and do what they say. But the possibility of playing the fool is also carried along with it.

One People, One Lord

Is Paul a promoter of division and exclusion, an adulterator of Jesus's inclusive mission of universal love? The first part of this chapter, and indeed this book as a whole, has tried to work on such a stereotype from both ends. On the one hand, such a reading of Jesus's ministry is naive at best. And on the other hand, Paul is most passionate and fiery when fighting for the unity of the church and the inclusion of those who formerly were outsiders.

We should not lose sight of the reality that for me, and most of you reading this book, the primary historical reason that, as non-Jews, we worship the God of Israel is the missionary work of Paul. Paul's vision of the universal lordship of the resurrected Jesus propelled him out to the nations, extending the embrace of God around the Roman

Empire. And it led him to wage the battle against a conservative form of early Christianity that wanted to require all of us to become Jewish through observance of key rituals such as circumcision, Sabbath keeping, and food laws.

This brings us back once again to the question of justification. I'm going to be offering what, to many of you, will be a shocking rereading of this concept. An issue that, for the Western church, has been a source of unparalleled division was, for Paul, the rallying cry for the oneness of the people of God. As N. T. Wright puts it, justification is Paul's "ecumenical doctrine, the doctrine that rebukes all our petty and often culture-bound church groupings, and which declares that all who believe in Jesus belong together in the one family."[3] How can this possibly be correct? I want us to wrestle with the very real possibility that the points at which Paul looks most prone to division and exclusion appear this way to us because of how we have been taught to read them. In their first-century context, they read quite differently.

One People: Justification by Faith

To come to grips with Paul on the question of judgmentalism and division, we should start with what we have seen already in this book: Paul expects the churches to know the story of the crucified Christ and to walk in step with this defining narrative. Given this narrative, Paul pulls justification by faith out of his theological toolbox for one primary purpose: to hammer home his conviction that Jews and gentiles are coequal members of the people of God. United in the story of the crucified Christ, the conservative Jewish Christians cannot require non-Jews to keep the law in order to be received into the church on equal footing. God has already received them on equal footing, on the basis of Jesus's death and resurrection. All are justified through faith.

Paul and Jesus ministered in two very different contexts. Jesus almost never left the confines of Israel, did not engage in a substantial mission beyond the Jewish people, and did not attempt to integrate gentiles into the community of his followers. But Paul recognized that the message of the crucified and risen Messiah was not simply about the restoration of Israel but also about the rescue of the nations. Paul shows us that "Jesus is Lord" is a universal claim about the significance of Jesus's kingship, a component of the story that subverts our tribal or colonial claims to superiority.

We must remember as we get into Paul's letters that we are dealing with the pastoral correspondence of someone deeply involved in the mission of God, extending God's embrace in Christ around the northern Mediterranean Sea. His work enveloping the gentiles into the narrative of Israel raised crucial questions that plagued the first half-century of the church's mission work.

In Galatians 2 we read of how Paul came to Jerusalem with an uncircumcised Greek man named Titus. The questions before them are these: How do gentiles (non-Jews) get written into the story of Israel? Do they have to enter by way of the covenant with Abraham, complete with circumcision (as Gen. 17 indicates)? No. The conservative, law-keeping group of Jewish Christians who wanted all to be circumcised did not win the day. Paul's gentile converts could come into the people of God without adopting the ethnic and religious identity of the Jewish people.

Paul is demanding that the story of Jesus as the crucified and risen Lord be the determining narrative for the people of God, not the story of Abraham's circumcision.

Galatians 2 goes on to tell a second story about the conflict between Jewish identity markers and gentile Christians, this time over food laws. Initially in Antioch Peter has been treating the gentiles as family members, expressing their mutuality by eating together. But when some representatives of a conservative, law-keeping Christian group come to town (the circumcision party—note the ties with the earlier story), Peter stops eating with the gentiles. The implicit demand seems to be that the gentiles would have to keep Jewish laws, adopting Jewish practices that set Jews apart not only religiously but also ethnically within the first-century world. But to Paul, such an implication amounts to "compelling the gentiles to become Jewish," something that undermines "the truth of the gospel" (Gal. 2:14).

So here we have another story where, to hear Paul tell it, the unity of the church is being disrupted by the imposition of Jewish law. A narrative of God's people is being told that places the law at the center, as the marker of God's people. But for Paul, requiring everyone to, in essence, become Jewish denies the gospel narrative that defines the identity of the church. The gospel story is that "Christ loved me and gave himself up for me" (Gal. 2:20). Paul's vehement opposition is leveled against those who hold on to alternative narratives and require other would-be members of the church to live out these substitutes. The conservative Jewish Christians are introducing division into the church by demanding that gentile Christians become like them.

And here is where justification comes into the picture. Unity is Paul's chief concern. He refuses to allow his gentile converts to be judged as having an inferior or outsider status due to the standards of traditional, even biblical, Jewish piety. Simply put, judging by the standards of law keeping gets the story wrong. Why? Because justification has to do with judgment. Justification is God's own judgment that a person is rightly related to God, a member of God's covenant people, God's family. Therefore, the basis on which God justifies someone is the same measure that God's people should apply in judging others to be part of our Christian family.

And so Paul confronts Peter and begins by relegating their own Jewish status to something of secondary value: "But knowing that a person is justified not by the works of the law but rather by the faith of Jesus Christ, *even we* [Jews by nature! (v. 15)] have believed in Christ Jesus in order that that we might be justified by the faith of Christ" (Gal. 2:16). At stake here are two renditions of the story of God's people, one whose central character is law and one whose central character is the crucified Christ. These two Jewish followers of Jesus know that God's story of salvation is defined by Christ's faithful death on the cross and not by the law of Moses. And so the final sentence of Paul's rebuke to Peter for disassociating from gentiles is this: "I do not set aside the grace of God, for if righteousness is through the law, then Christ died needlessly" (Gal. 2:21).

Throughout Galatians Paul is arguing that the law and Jesus's crucifixion had opposite purposes. Whereas the law's purpose was to set Israel apart from the world as God's people, thus erecting a dividing wall among people as to who was in and who was out, the crucifixion's purpose was to enable Israel's blessings to break beyond its borders to the gentiles. "Christ redeemed us [Jews] from the law's curse . . . so that the blessing of Abraham might go forth to the gentiles" (Gal. 3:13–14).

This is the story that enables us to see that justification is, as Wright claims, Paul's ecumenical doctrine. When Paul gets worked into a frenzy over justification by faith, it is not to divide the church into those who have the doctrine right and those who do not. It is to call the would-be dividers to be reunited in the narrative that all confess together: the death and resurrection of Jesus are God's way of rescuing us from the present evil age. We are justified as we participate in the story of the self-giving Christ.

In our section on community (chap. 3 above), we discussed how Paul's most basic model of salvation is one of "union with Christ." Justification fits within this larger framework such that Paul can say that we are justified in Christ (Gal. 2:17). Because Christ is God's Son, and because we have been baptized into him, we share in his work and all its benefits—including becoming children of God (Gal. 3:26–27). On this basis of unity, Paul inveighs against the world's divisions being sustained within the church: "There is no longer Jew nor Greek, no longer slave nor free, no longer male and female, for you are all one in Christ Jesus" (Gal. 3:28). To deny this unity, to exclude gentiles from coequal standing in the people of God, is to deny "the truth of the gospel."

Only oneness in the church, a mutual embrace of all those who affirm the saving narrative of Jesus's death and resurrection, gets our story straight. Justification is Paul's doctrine of unity. It is a doctrine hammered out as he put into practice his vision of the universal lordship of Jesus being fulfilled in a worldwide and diverse community of Jesus's followers.

Do We Not Judge?

If Jesus is famous for saying, "Do not judge," it seems that Paul is equally infamous for asserting, "Are we not supposed to judge those who are inside the church?" (1 Cor. 5:12). Is Paul more judgmental than Jesus? Having reexamined the Sermon on the Mount, hopefully our understanding of Jesus on this point has already taken a step closer to Paul, and as we work through Paul's advocacy of judgment, we find him stepping closer to Jesus as well. The summons issued by both is that we live in keeping with the story of Jesus the Messiah.

In 1 Corinthians 5, the issue at hand is that someone in the community is having sex with his stepmother. We will deal more extensively with questions of sexuality in chapter 8. Here I want us to look at why Paul mounts an argument for judging the offender and excluding him from the community.

First, as Richard Hays points out, Paul rebukes the entire community.[4] There is a corporate responsibility for appropriate behavior. This grows from the conviction we examined in chapter 3 above that Christian life is inherently communal. Moreover, the identity of this community is not simply that it is an amalgam of people from Corinth. They are a transformed people—despite their not being "Jewish," Paul seems to distinguish them from "gentiles" when he says that such sexual immorality as they countenance is not even tolerated "among the gentiles" (1 Cor. 5:1). They have a new identity, a new story to live out in their life together.

This new story is a second exodus, a delivery from the power of Satan, sin, and death by the death of Jesus. Paul likens Jesus to a Passover lamb, one whose blood marks out a people as belonging to Israel's God so that they might live free as God's own people (1 Cor. 5:7). The Passover custom of eating unleavened bread is a metaphor for the purity that God demands of his people. "Clean out the old leaven so that you can be a new lump of dough—just as you are, in fact, unleavened" (1 Cor. 5:7). Freed from the power of sin and death, they must not once again return to the sin from which they have been delivered. Their calling is to live out the identity that God has given them as a result of Jesus's death. The danger is that the sin will spread to others in the community (1 Cor. 5:6–8). We note, once again, that the entire context is intramural: it's about the family of God getting its story straight. The story of Jesus's death is a story of purity and holiness.

Expelling the offender from the community is described as an exercise of the Spirit's power—a power present when the community as a whole is assembled (1 Cor. 5:3–5).[5] As these verses have the potential to make us increasingly uncomfortable, we do well to remember that the Jesus we meet on the pages of Matthew makes similar provision for the community, outlining for it how an unrepentant brother or sister is to be confronted, challenged, and eventually turned out (Matt.

18:15–19). And in both cases, the promise of Jesus's presence among the community is central to the authority it has for such binding and loosing. Whatever else we might think of Paul's relationship to Jesus, the apostle's call for judging within the community is not a point at which he distinguishes himself from his Master.

Paul makes a startling, puzzling statement about the excommunication he advocates. Its purpose is "to deliver the person to Satan for the destruction of his flesh so that his spirit may be saved in the day of the Lord" (1 Cor. 5:5). Whatever this "handing over to Satan" might mean, the outcome is the crucial point: Paul envisions this earthly judgment to have saving force when it comes to the final, heavenly judgment.

This is parallel to what Paul says later in the letter, when he maintains that some people in the Corinthian church are growing sick and dying due to the Lord's discipline—but that this happens so that they may not be condemned along with the world (1 Cor. 11:32). Judging a person in the present condemns his or her actions as out of sync with the story of Christ; however, it is not a statement of eternal condemnation. In a paradoxical fashion, judgment within the church is a means of pronouncing, and producing, ultimate deliverance. Judgment in the present works salvation in the future.

In this context, Paul contrasts the church's posture toward insiders and outsiders. Like Jesus, he anticipates that judging among insiders is necessary (1 Cor. 5:11–13). Also like Jesus, Paul maintains that there will be a judgment where outsiders will have to answer for themselves—but that this is in God's hands.

In addition, though, Paul's missionary endeavors provide him a perspective that we don't find in the Gospels. Paul insists that there is no point trying to remove ourselves from engagement with those who are not part of the church. This would entail removing ourselves entirely from the world. Too often modern church concerns for purity entail a withdrawal from the world around us, creating an isolated community that stands in perpetual judgment of the world. This is not the picture that Paul advocates. In fact, it gets Paul exactly backward. Moreover, Paul as much as Jesus condemns our propensity to use judgment as a means to pronounce fellow Christians to be, in truth, outsiders. When we take such a route, we distance ourselves from Paul, who sees discipline as a guarantee of final deliverance.

Judgment is part of the story of salvation. Both Jesus and Paul recognize that the community called to narrate the saving work of Jesus in its life together will, at times, need to summon its members to more faithful performance. Judgment is part of the work of the body, an inherent component of the communal nature of Christian identity and calling. In his book *Manifold Witness*, John Franke strives to hold together the always-contextualized nature of the gospel that enables it to burst beyond the bounds established by social mores (what he calls "the indigenization principle") with the gospel as a transforming power (what he calls "the transformation principle"). He puts it like this:

> While the indigenization principle affirms that Christians remain appropriately related to the relationships and thought-forms in which they are raised and seeks their renewal in Christ, the transformation principle points to an entirely new set of relations with others who are part of the community of Christ's disciples. These relations call on us to be accepting of others and all of their group relations just as God has so accepted them, while at the same time seeking the transformation of all things in Christ in accordance with the will and mission of God.[6]

As Paul contends when speaking of justification, the gospel forbids that we erect standards that draw all people into cultural conformity with ourselves. And as he also asserts when he calls for judgment, we are called together in order to experience transformation by the power of the Spirit of God. The unity that is ours is a oneness we share "in Christ"; therefore, our life together must show forth the Christ story of salvation. It must follow his teaching, walk the way of his cross, live by the power of the resurrection, and honor the purity to which his sacrifice summons us.

Breaking Down Our Dividing Walls

Paul and Jesus share a frame of reference when it comes to questions of judgment and inclusion of outsiders: Jesus is the Messiah who is therefore Lord over all things and the One to whom we must be faithful if we would enter into the eternal salvation that Jesus's death and resurrection bring about. Those who submit to Jesus's reign are themselves the family of God. And because following Jesus determines the family identity, anomalous behavior that strays from the way of Jesus is a matter of mutual concern and correction. The flip side of this familial identity, however, is that judgment of outsiders is left in the hands of God while we are simultaneously called to see Jesus's reign more fully realized on earth through our own being sent into the world to make disciples.

Thinking about our postmodern cultural context, this complex set of interrelated themes creates both opportunities and challenges. First, the opportunities.

The Jesus who is Lord over all things will not demand that the church become culturally homogenous. The gospel is always contextualized. This, Franke's "indigenization principle," is what we have seen throughout this book as Jesus and Paul have told the same story for different contexts. The whole New Testament is a testimony to how people in different contexts think about, articulate, and perform the gospel differently. Even with an all-encompassing, cosmic narrative to tell, Christianity admits of a rich diversity. More than this, it demands that we continually reassess how to tell the story so that it makes sense in the worlds that we live in.

In a society marked by its plurality of cultures, we discover that many of our judgments about the world seem normal to us simply because of the context we are immersed in. Encountering people from countries that do not share the industrialized world's perspectives on historical "development," people from other parts of our own countries, or even simply people from our same towns who do not traverse the same Christian terrain where we so freely move—each of these can have the effect of making us more self-aware and self-critical about how we articulate the Christian message.

And here is where Paul becomes an invaluable resource for the church. As the first person to take the gospel across cultural boundaries, he simultaneously insisted that his gentile converts had become part of a story that had not previously defined their identities (they are transformed) and that they did not have to adopt the peculiar ethnic identity that marked out Jewish Christians (the gospel became indigenous to their culture). A transformation had taken place, but it was a metamorphosis into the story of the crucified Christ and the God of Israel, not a metamorphosis into the likeness of the dominant Christian subculture.

And so as we grow in our awareness that our ways of articulating Christian theology are deeply contextualized, we open ourselves to the possibility that postmodern or non-Western cultures might choose not to adopt our way of speaking and living Christianly—and that such difference within the body need not be a source of division. The universality of Jesus's reign means that he can accommodate a world's worth of diverse expression of the Christian story. White, Western, and—in our day and age perhaps we should say, especially—American ways of performing the Christian story and judging its fidelity to its founding narratives need not, indeed must not, become Procrustean beds to which all other enactments are made to conform.

We are right at the point where Paul has sometimes been given a bad name entirely against his will. A friend of mine recently complained that Presbyterians would do better with Paul if they remembered that he was a missionary. My friend went on to clarify that the mistake we so often make when reading Paul is to think that his thought is designed to be tightly organized into a system. While there are varying degrees of value to be had in systematizing our theology, the snare we must avoid is in thinking that we have a singular hold on the truth, such that anyone who wants to follow God in the way of Jesus must think exactly as we think and do so exactly as we do. Paul has been unjustly saddled with just this reputation.

As Paul tells the story, at least, it is just such a homogenization of the early church that his own letter to Galatia was written to ward off. Such a resource in our biblical canon helps clear the way for the plurality of expression that many in today's church long for. When Paul insisted that all are justified by faith in the faithful Son of God, he simultaneously closed the door on any competing narrative as the litmus test for faithfulness to God's story. Yes, we do have to follow Jesus. But no, we don't have to become Presbyterian, Baptist, Methodist, or Anabaptist. No, we don't have to embrace modernity or premodernity or postmodernity. Our mode of Christian expression does not have to be traditional or contemporary or emergent. When Paul said that gentiles did not have to keep the God-given laws of the Old Testament in order to fully participate in God's family, he blew the door of cultural conformity off its hinges, forever invalidating any church's would-be baptism of social patterns of exclusion or alienation.

This movement toward a more faithful embodiment of the multicultural Christian story is just what I saw being attempted at a conference website recently. Promoting themselves as representatives of "Big Tent Christianity," the conference organizers were striving to articulate what "unites us as followers of Jesus Christ" in an explicit effort to transcend "old battle lines" that many today find irrelevant.[7] Such a movement finds warrant in the story of the Jesus who is Lord over all and is one way we see that Paul in particular has created space for a type of Christian performance that might well resonate with several currents of our postmodern culture. We need new, more unified ways to follow Jesus so that we will more faithfully perform the story of the crucified and risen Christ. The conclusion of our study of Paul is that he should be enlisted as an ally in the defense of this type of work. He, no less than Jesus, insisted on including within the family of God everyone who acknowledged Christ as God's means of gathering a people for himself.

This is where, I believe, the contemporary aversion to judgment might have a healthy outlet. When union with the universal Lord is the standard we judge our Christian storytelling by, we find significant validation for the modern-day impulse for transcending old theological and denominational dividing lines.

But those who would be faithful to Jesus can go little further. While indigenizing within various cultures, we must not lose sight of the gospel as a word of judgment itself. One possibility of living an insufficiently Christian story comes through our complicity with culture—a mistake we make when we fail to see the difference between what God is doing in the world and what just so happens to be occurring in the world. Miroslav Volf issues this warning: "Our coziness with the surrounding culture has made us so blind to many of its evils that, instead of calling them into question, we offer our own versions of them—in God's name and with a good conscience."[8] Recognition of the inherently contextualized nature of all human activity must not blind us to the fact that each context will approximate holiness and mask evil in varying degrees.

While the dividing lines within the church must continue to crumble, and while we must endeavor to appreciate and celebrate the diversity of the family of God more and more, we are not free to say that there is no dividing line between the family of God and those without, or that the Jesus narrative does not demand behavioral standards befitting a particular story.

Once we have done everything in our power to remove the aberrations that have made the story more offensive than it should be, we are still left with a story that will always be offensive in its very claim to exclusivity. God was in Christ reconciling the world to himself (2 Cor. 5:19). This means that the world outside of Christ is a world in some sense hostile to God. The world that lives in faithful submission to God is only that world that is the new creation begun in Christ, and the only way for us to participate in reconciled relationship with God is to be in Christ by faith, Spirit, and baptism.

Simply being human is not enough to claim membership in the family of God. There is a new humanity in Christ, the Second Adam, and membership in God's family is inseparable from this Person. The deeply offensive message that we are not good enough on our own, that we require freedom from slavery, that we require freedom from guilt, that we require, in short, the cross of Christ, must always be our message if our story is to be truly Christian.

Like so many other elements of Christian theology, however, this conviction becomes problematic if not held with a degree of humility. Christian talk about hell is often triumphalist and rarely tinged with the reverent caution and even sadness that should attend a conviction that some might be permanently excluded from the life with God they were intended for. But as we ponder the gravity of ideas such as hell, there is an element of the Christian story that we must make sure not to neglect: the element of surprise.

The Jewish people who best knew the Scriptures were so unprepared for the kind of ministry Jesus enacted that they could not recognize him as Messiah. Jesus's message was a genuine surprise. Further, when we come to Revelation and its story of the end, people who seemingly should have been excluded, the kings of the earth, come bringing the glory of the nations into the New Jerusalem (Rev. 21:24). Without embracing universalism, I do think our story demands that we anticipate surprise: many who were thought to be children of the kingdom will be excluded, while those whom we would have thought to be outsiders will be recognized as family and ushered in by Jesus.

The basic movement of people into the story, from the realm alienated and hostile to God to the realm in which God's faithful King Jesus reigns, must continue to define our life together. Not only does this mean embracing people across multiple cultures and expressions of faith—not only does this mean that we must, in fact, *enter*—it also means that we must vigilantly guard ourselves and our communities against actions that express hostility and alienation toward God rather than reconciliation and peace. We must judge.

We have a story to live. The community that hears, learns, and performs the drama will always inevitably be assessing various performances as more or less in keeping with the narrative we have been given. Judgment is a dangerous business, to be sure, but its place in our communities becomes intelligible when we recognize that we are the story. The community of believers is the continuing narrative of Jesus Christ on earth. As such, we who comprise the family must enact a drama that truly displays what makes us who we are. We are to be one people, diverse in our manifestations of the gospel, living in faithful harmony with God our Father.

6

Women in the Story of God

> How great is the wisdom of this woman [Junia (Romans 16:7)], that she should even be counted worthy of the name of apostle!
>
> —John Chrysostom[1]

One reason that Paul gets a bad rap is that letters bearing his name provide biblical ammunition for almost every injustice that Christians have perpetrated in the name of Jesus. Slavery? Check (Col. 3; Eph. 6; 1 Tim. 6). Subjugation of women? Check (Col. 3; Eph. 5; 1 Tim. 2). Anti-Semitism? Check (1 Thess. 2). Tyrannical governments? Check (Rom. 13).

With such a history, what hope can we possibly have of finding in Paul the voice of a liberator, of one who, like Jesus, sees the gospel as a message of freedom to the oppressed, of liberty to the captive? The task is daunting, but there is hope.

In Paul's letter to Galatia we read a statement about unity in Christ that overcomes the polarities that define (ancient) society: "You have been clothed with Christ. There is no longer Jew nor Greek, no longer slave nor free, no longer male and female, for you are all one in Christ Jesus." New Testament scholar Paul Jewett called this statement, found in Galatians 3:28, the "Magna Carta of Humanity."[2] If such a charter of freedom and equality is, in fact, in the Bible—and in one of Paul's letters of all places—then why has the church so often failed to live up to its potential? Is the problem to be found in Scripture, in the church's uses of Scripture, or both?

I am going to sketch in this chapter and the next why I think that the answer is both/and. As for Scripture, it not only sows seeds of equality whose flowers never fully bloom on its pages; it also continues to reflect and, at times, affirm the inequalities endemic to its ancient cultural context. With such ambiguity on the table, the question that squarely confronts the church becomes what it means for us to faithfully embody the biblical narrative in our own time and place.

This chapter focuses on the issue of women's roles in the communities formed under the leadership of Jesus and Paul. Having explored the question of gender equality in some detail, we will turn in the next chapter to apply the same line of interpretation to issues of social justice. In what may come as a surprise to many, I am going to argue that Paul's letters, to a greater extent even than the ministry of Jesus itself, establish a narrative trajectory of unity through equality. We will begin with a look at female coworkers in the stories of Jesus and Paul.

Jesus's Female Followers

Each Gospel writer tells his own story about Jesus, some of which depict more prominent places for women than do others. However, they each contain indications that Jesus follows the cultural norm of appointing men to leadership positions while at the same time affirming and commissioning women in some unexpected ways.

Mark's Nameless Women

Let us look first at some of the ways that Jesus does less than some of us might wish when it comes to including women in his ministry. When Jesus chooses his inner circle of followers, he chooses twelve men. These are the ones to whom he gives special authority to extend his ministry. Jesus preaches, heals, and exorcises, and he selects these twelve men so that he might spend time with them and then send them to preach and have authority to exorcise demons (Mark 3:13–15). When, a few chapters later, Jesus does send them out, their ministry is one that extends Jesus's own in its preaching, healing, and exorcism (Mark 6:12–13). In addition, when the resurrected Jesus appears to his disciples and commissions them to continue extending his ministry to the world, he gives this charge to the men. Matthew 28:16 tells us that the great commission is given to "the eleven" who remained (since Judas has hanged himself).

But we must not allow the pride of place given to this special inner circle of men to obscure the story that the Gospels tell about them. The Gospel of Mark in particular depicts these closest companions of Jesus as much less than ideal followers and leaders. The turning point for them is when Peter confesses Jesus to be the Messiah but subsequently refuses to allow Jesus to redefine messiahship in terms of suffering (8:27–33). The latter half of Mark's Gospel shows us the effects of failing to apprehend the cruciform character of Jesus's ministry. Those previously sent to cast out demons now fail in their exorcism (9:14–29). Those previously sent to help enlarge the family of God by preaching in Jesus's name are now forbidding others from extending his reign (9:38–40) and preventing children from being brought to him (10:13–16). The last we see of the disciples in Mark's Gospel is when Jesus's prediction that they will all fall away reaches its climactic fulfillment with Peter's swearing and cursing in denial of the accusation that he is one of Jesus's followers (14:71–72). And thus, it seems that Peter (whose name means "the rock") embodies in himself the destiny of the disciples to be rocky soil whose young plant withers, people who fall away when persecution arises on account of the word (4:16–17).[3]

One of the most important dynamics of the Christian narrative is its turning of the economy of the world on its head. Where the world sees power and glory, the gospel proclaims that there is only weakness and shame. Conversely, where the world sees only weakness and shame, there the gospel proclaims power and glory. This is exactly what the twelve men closest to Jesus could never accept. And in refusing to accept the upside-down nature of the dominion of God, they who were the consummate insiders found themselves, at the end, far from the crucifixion by which Jesus came into his kingdom. They are absent from his paradoxical coronation. Outsiders.

So when we make a return trip through the Gospel of Mark and find that the commendable women are nameless and ill-suited to our ideas of greatness, we must not make the mistake of thinking that such lack of glory is a judgment on them or a relegation of them to a position of secondary importance in the kingdom of God. Indeed, if this is how we read such stories, then we show ourselves to be, like the disciples themselves, culpably ignorant of the upside-down economy of the dominion of the crucified Christ.

A first such faithful female character in Mark's Gospel is the woman with a seemingly incurable flow of blood (5:25–34). Though she has suffered under the care of doctors for a dozen years, she approaches Jesus with confidence that even touching the hem of his robe will deliver her from her affliction. Her faith in the flow of Jesus's power is so great that she is willing to initiate physical contact even though her illness renders unclean both her and everyone she touches. Jesus responds to her faith by tenderly addressing her as part of his family ("daughter") and sending her away with peace and healing. The power of this story is found, in large part, from its being intertwined with the story of a consummate Jewish insider, a synagogue official, whose daughter Jesus heals. Moreover, Mark positions the story of the healed woman immediately before Jesus's trip to his homeland, where those closest to him demonstrate the least amount of faith. With faith that measures up to, or even exceeds, that of the Jewish leader, and faith that puts to shame the faithlessness of Jesus's own community, the woman with the flow of blood surprises us by playing the role of a consummate outsider who ends up enfolded within the family of God as an exemplar of saving faith.

Other nameless, remarkable women in Mark's Gospel include a gentile woman who persists in requesting an exorcism for her daughter despite Jesus's calling her a dog (7:24–30) and a poor woman who puts her two coins in the temple treasury (12:41–44). But I want us to look at the fourth nameless woman in Mark, the one who received the highest commendation because her actions held together the very idea that the disciples could never accept: Jesus is a Messiah who must die.

Mark introduces us to the final scenes of Jesus's life by framing a story of a dinner party (14:3–9) with the plans of the Jewish leaders to have him killed (14:1–2, 10–11). At this gathering, a woman comes in and pours costly, fragrant oil on Jesus's head. For those familiar with the biblical imagery, and privy to the narrative indications of Jesus's identity as Christ, the pouring of oil on Jesus's head would seem to point to his own role as God's "anointed one"—Israel's Messiah. But when those sitting at the party complain of this wasteful act, disposing of nearly a year's wages on Jesus's head, Jesus rebukes them by saying that this good work is a preparation of his body for burial (14:8). The mystery that the disciples refused to accept, that as Messiah Jesus has to die, is proclaimed in this woman's action—an anointing, as of a king, but for burial. And this is why Jesus promises that wherever the gospel is proclaimed in the whole world, this woman's deed will also be told in memory of her (14:9). Her deed is the one deed of any person in the story that captures both Jesus's authority to reign as Messiah and his death as the means of his enthronement.

And so, in what is likely the earliest of the biblical accounts of Jesus's life (Mark's Gospel), we are presented with a bit of a paradox. On the one hand, traditional ancient gender roles are upheld as the men are given positions of greater prominence and become the main supporting actors in the story. But on the other hand, the power and purpose of the narrative is found in its insistence that the kingdom of God inverts such judgments. Greatness is not found in worldly prominence or through insider status. To be great is to be least and servant of all (Mark 10:44). Thus, as Mark narrates the account, the woman who acts as servant to Jesus is the servant who receives the highest word of commendation. Other than Jesus, she is the greatest character in the story. We will work out the implications of such a world-subverting paradigm below. For now, let's see what other Gospel writers might add to our picture of women in the life of Jesus.

Women as Disciples in Luke

Luke presents numerous unique scenes in which Jesus has significant engagement with women. In one such engagement, an expansion of Mark's story discussed above, Luke seems particularly keen on undermining the notion that Jesus's selection of twelve male apostles marginalizes the role of women among his followers. A summary statement about Jesus's ministry tells us that Jesus was going around with the twelve, but also with women he had healed from evil spirits and sicknesses, Mary Magdalene in particular, as well as Joanna and Susanna "and many other women who were ministering to them from their resources" (Luke 8:2–3). Joel Green comments that even without any explicit indication that these women participated in preaching and healing, their mere presence among a group of Jesus's itinerant friends would have been extraordinary in the Greco-Roman world.[4] In the narrative itself, depicting these women as those who serve and who use their wealth in service of the kingdom of God singles them out "as persons who both hear *and act* on the word of God."[5]

Other stories in Luke's Gospel provide hints that the kingdom of God might come with the latent power to burst socially established gender roles. One such episode tells us of Jesus coming to the house of Martha and her sister Mary (10:28–42). Martha assumes the role of hostess, extending hospitality and ministering to her guest. Mary, however, sits at Jesus's feet in the posture of a disciple, a student learning from the master. In that cultural context, when Martha implores Jesus to send Mary to help her, she is looking to him to prod Mary away from the typically male role of disciple and toward the woman's work around the house. But Jesus, as "the Lord" (which is how he is designated throughout the passage), has the authority to upset the applecart of social conventions. As Green summarizes: "Mary (and, with her, those of low status accustomed to living on the margins of society) *need* no longer be defined by socially determined roles."[6] Propriety within the kingdom of God is not determined by the gender roles established by the dominant patriarchal society.

Women at the Resurrection

Additional Lukan stories point in a similar direction. But perhaps most important for our purposes is the trust given to the women Jesus appears to after the resurrection. In the New Testament, the resurrected Jesus propels the mission of the church by sending people out into the world to speak for him. In Acts, the apostles become witnesses of the resurrection (Acts 1:22; 2:32). Paul defends his apostleship by saying, "Have I not seen Jesus our Lord?" (1 Corinthians 9:1). It is therefore all the more significant that the resurrected Jesus entrusts the message of his resurrection, first of all, to the women who come to the tomb to attend to his body.

In Matthew's Gospel, Mary Magdalene and another Mary come to the tomb. First, an angel appears, tells them that Jesus is raised, and sends them to tell the disciples that Jesus is going ahead of them to Galilee. Then, as they run off, Jesus appears. After the women bow before him, Jesus sends them with the same message: they are to go and tell Jesus's brothers (the eleven remaining disciples) that he will appear to them in Galilee. Women are not only the first ones to whom the message about Jesus's resurrection is proclaimed, and they are not merely charged by angels to make the message known; they also witness the resurrected Christ and are the first ones Jesus sends to announce and bear witness to his resurrection. The job later performed by the "apostles" is first performed by the faithful women who came to anoint Jesus's body at the tomb.

The full potential latent in these early inclusions of women in the Jesus story is not fully realized in the ministry of Jesus. And yet they function as cracks in the glass ceiling of social hierarchies that would apportion women a role of subservience to and dependence on men as the mediators of the new covenant. How, then, do these trajectories play out in the ministry of Paul?

Paul's Coworkers

Paul's letters give significant indications about the roles women played in the early church. In this section we are going to look at the "positive" evidence before tackling the counterevidence in the next part of our discussion. This section will consist largely in examining some texts that show quite clearly that women were engaged in teaching, working, leading, and otherwise exercising authority in the early church—precisely the sorts of activities they should have been excluded from had the instructions of 1 Timothy 2:8–15 been the consistent practice of the apostles.

Deacon and Apostle

Romans 16 is a treasure trove of just this sort of evidence. The chapter begins with Paul's commendation of Phoebe, a servant or deacon (it's the same word in Greek) of the church in Cenchreae. Few translations opt for "deacon" here, though some provide a footnote suggesting that "deaconess" might be appropriate. In my view, "deaconess" is perhaps the least appropriate, because it gives the impression that the Greek word refers to a specific function performed or office held by women. It does not. The Greek is not a feminine form, and rendering it "deaconess" can create the false impression that there was a separate stream of ministry within which women could participate in Paul's churches. This is not the case.

In wrestling with how to translate the word, however, we should not lose sight of the role she plays. Paul is commending Phoebe as someone who represents the church in the city of Cenchreae. In all likelihood, it is not simply that she happens to be a servant of that church but that as someone who is a patron of the church and of Paul's own ministry, she is being sent to Rome in Paul's and the church's name to do their work and represent them before the Romans.

Next, Paul greets Prisca and Aquila, a husband-wife pair whom he describes as his "coworkers in Christ." These coworkers seem to have been host to a house church in Ephesus (Rom. 16:3–5; 1 Cor. 16:19). Both husband and wife are acknowledged as sharing in the work that Paul does. Moreover, being a "fellow worker" in Paul's gospel ministry is not merely something women can participate in if husbands lead the way. Other names in Romans 16 also refer to women who are ministering the gospel: Mary (v. 6), Tryphena and Tryphosa (v. 12), and Persida (v. 12, a woman's name that is often rendered "Persis" in English). The upshot of this set of data is that Paul views women as active participants in gospel ministry, people who extend his own work in a manner analogous to what we see Titus and Timothy doing elsewhere in his letters (e.g., 1 Cor. 4:17). Of the remaining men in the greetings, only Urbanus is commended as a fellow worker (v. 9).

But more important than these coworkers and more important than Phoebe the deacon (or servant) is the apostolic couple, Andronicus and Junia (Rom. 16:7): "Greet Andronicus and Junia, my kinsfolk and my fellow prisoners, who are outstanding among the apostles, who were also in Christ before me." Junia was an apostle. Any idea that Paul's standard practice was to deny women any authority or opportunity to teach is undone once we recognize that a woman was, in fact, among the number of apostles.

In his book *Junia: The First Woman Apostle*, Eldon Jay Epp chronicles the history of how the reality of a female apostle has been buried through mistranslation and editing of her name so that it was rendered as a man's name instead.[7] The most common approach today among more conservative Bible translators is to acknowledge that Junia is a woman but to deny that Andronicus and Junia are being referred to as apostles. And so several Bible versions render the verse as though Andronicus and Junia are "well known *to* the apostles" rather than "well-regarded apostles."

But there are several strong indications that this is not the best reading. One piece of evidence is the quote from the fourth-century Chrysostom that serves as the epigraph for this chapter: a native Greek speaker, he reads Romans 16:7 as an indication that Junia was honored to be numbered among the apostles. Added to this is the very history of changing the form of the name Junia that Epp outlines in his book. The only reason for a history of changing the form of her name is that it struck early scribes as incongruous for a woman to be called an apostle. If a native reader of Greek would have understood that this was referring to people who were known to the apostles, then there would be no offense to their sensibilities, and no apparent contradiction with 1 Timothy 2, and therefore there would have been no reason to hide the fact that a woman was in view. Likely, Andronicus and Junia are a husband and wife who were both witnesses to Jesus's resurrection and both sent out to bear witness and proclaim the gospel. (For an idea of "apostles" that goes beyond the twelve original disciples of Jesus, see 1 Cor. 15:5–9.)

Romans 16 depicts women as coworkers, as servants (possibly a deacon), and as apostles. The value of this list, and what we will see below from 1 Corinthians 11, is that it reflects life in the early church as it was. No special instructions are being given to regulate the work that these people are doing, no controversies are creating the need for an expedient answer, and nobody is being rebuked. Paul is reflecting the reality of the first-century church, in which women were integral in every facet of its ministry.

Teaching and Exercising Authority over Men

A couple of passages from 1 Corinthians provide other surprising glimpses at Paul's views toward women. One such view comes in chapter 7, where Paul is giving instructions on sex within marriage—essentially affirming the importance of it. He calls for a mutual self-giving: the wife giving herself (sexually) to her husband and likewise the husband to his wife (1 Cor. 7:1–3). But the truly astonishing thing is what comes next. Paul not only says that a husband has authority over his wife's body (which we might expect in the first century) but also says that the wife has authority over her husband's body (1 Cor. 7:4). The idea that a woman would possess authority over her husband's body is an astounding claim to mutuality in the marriage relationship, one we should not lose sight of when we look at possible counterevidence.

Moving to the context of church practice, the instructions that Paul gives to women in 1 Corinthians 11:5–16 are complex, to say the least. Arguing for appropriate dress in public worship, Paul moves from a discussion of head coverings to one of long hair versus short hair, and bases his admonitions on creation, natural birth order, and finally "the angels." But for now the main point I wish to emphasize is that these instructions about head coverings and the like are given in order to ensure that women who are praying and prophesying in public worship are doing so appropriately. In the worship service it is assumed that women are speaking, speaking authoritatively, and that this is not something to be hindered but rather to be done appropriately.

When looking through the evidence in favor of full inclusion of women in the life and ministry of the early church, we find several indications that they were involved in every facet of the church's life, and that they were disciples in ways that crossed the boundaries of societal expectation in the first century. We do not find, and we would be wrong to look for, a Jesus or a Paul who fit the expectations of modern-day egalitarians. But neither do we find blind affirmation of male superiority or of male leadership.

Pauline Tensions

If Paul's letters show some indications of transcending the sexism of their cultural age, they also show how the biblical narrative can be used to reinforce gendered hierarchy. There is a true ambiguity of evidence in the New Testament. We have already seen how Jesus plays into cultural expectations by selecting twelve men to follow him, and how the Gospels seem to relegate women to secondary story lines. With Paul, too, there is ample evidence of distinction based on gender.

Women in Worship

Returning to the 1 Corinthians 11 passage we just discussed, we discover that the way that women are instructed to conduct themselves while praying and prophesying seems to derive from a biblically based gender hierarchy. Women should veil themselves, Paul says, because they are under the authority of a man, were created for man's sake, and are man's glory (1 Cor. 11:5–9). Interestingly, however, Paul steps back from the hierarchy he seems conscious of having articulated. "But neither is woman without man nor man without woman *in the Lord*" (1 Cor. 11:11). Mutual dependence turns out to be more ultimate than hierarchy. This is because the argument for hierarchy is based on creation, while mutual dependence derives more directly from the gospel story in which all are one because they are united to Christ. Here we catch a glimpse of how Paul's narrative theology modulates the biblical story and hence the church's faithful performance of its defining narrative. New creation is more determinative of our life together than first creation.

What I just said runs strongly against many of our instincts when approaching the tasks of theology and ethics. We tend to treat all biblical passages the same, looking for instructions and paradigms throughout Scripture, assuming that an integrated picture will form in that process. But for both Paul and Jesus the decisive moment of Jesus's ministry has the potential to change everything. And so we find places like this, where Paul shows us how important it is to take full stock of the place we occupy in the development of the narrative. New creation is more determinative of our life together than first creation.

In light of this, Paul even revisits the question of "natural order," and when he does so he now recognizes that men come into the world through women, even if the first woman was made from man (1 Cor. 11:12). Each can claim to "come from" the body of the other. Hence, even in nature (we now know, having been pushed to reread the story in light of Christ) there is no final superiority or primacy for males.

What, then, are we to make of the hierarchies with which Paul begins his instructions about how men and women are to dress in public worship? As we dive into this complicated passage, we should note that the instructions lead off not with a command to women but with one directed to men: it is disgraceful for them to cover their heads while praying or prophesying. Throughout the passage, there is a concern that social norms be upheld. When we say "social norms," we often think of these as rather trivial. However, two dynamics are at play in Corinth that make such norms tremendously weighty.[8]

First, we are reading not simply about styles of dress but about coded ways of dressing, about how and what people communicate to others through their clothing.[9] In the ancient world how one wore one's hair and/or adorned one's head communicated sexual availability. A woman's shaved or uncovered head might well connote such availability. Thus, the problem seems to be that women, and quite possibly men as well, were leading worship while communicating sexual availability through their dress.

And this brings in the second dynamic that is perhaps foreign to our context: the basis on which this is being assessed is a system of honor and shame. In a society governed by these dynamics, the concern is to maintain your own honor by behaving in such a way as to bring honor to those "above you" in the social hierarchy, as well as by behaving in an honorable way to those beneath. In the hierarchy as Paul has drawn it, both men and women bring shame, rather than honor, to Christ and ultimately to God when they dress shamefully in public worship. By putting themselves on display, perhaps with connotations that they are sexually available, they are detracting from the worship that the community as a whole is to be rendering to God and thereby bringing shame on God and Christ.

How does this happen? How does a church like Corinth find itself in a situation where people seem to be behaving inappropriately such that it disgraces God? While constructions of the past must always remain tentative, it seems likely that some Corinthians' holistic understanding of freedom in Christ (including not only gender equality but also complete freedom from dietary restrictions) had created a level of indulgence in purportedly Christian freedom that was disrupting the community. The Corinthians themselves seem to have championed the idea "all things are lawful for me," which Paul quotes back to them twice (1 Cor. 6:12; 10:23). Each time, he responds by qualifying their freedom: not everything is beneficial, either for building up others or for oneself.

In 1 Corinthians 11, the fact of gender equality seems to have led to a wrong conclusion about how people could act in worship. Had Paul's gospel not proclaimed a fundamental equality between men and women in Christ, the Corinthian church would not likely have had the problems he addresses in this chapter. The specific issue of equality between the sexes had led some to the mistaken conclusion that there is no difference between them to be maintained.[10] Because Paul proclaimed "no longer male and female" in Christ, we find these instructions issued for appropriate dress and action in public worship.

What then does all this tell us about Paul's views on women? First, women are different from men. Also, for the sake of honoring God in public worship, he urges that the social embodiments of some of these differences be maintained by both men and women. The passage also shows us that Paul assumes that, though different, men and women are equal participants in the leadership of public worship. Moreover, the very fact of their wrong conclusion about gender equality likely indicates that Paul's gospel includes a fundamental affirmation that such equality exists. In Christ, the inequalities of Jew and gentile, slave and free, male and female are done away with.

Hierarchy Affirmed?

The most challenging passages for my project of painting Paul with a more sympathetic and egalitarian view toward women are those letters bearing his name that tell wives to submit to their husbands (Col. 3:18; Eph. 5:22–24) and tell women to remain silent and forbid them to either teach or exercise authority over a man (1 Tim. 2:9–15). Many New Testament scholars question whether Paul wrote these particular letters, and for good reason. However, distancing the historical Paul from these difficult books does not answer the question of what we are supposed to do with them as part of the Christian canon. So we will set aside the question of authorship and delve into them here.

Subject Wives

The commands that wives submit to their husbands, and that husbands love their wives, are found in household codes. Household codes are ways that ancients both gave instructions and expressed the order of the world as they understood it. The instructions are given in pairs, and in each pair one member is considered superior, and one is considered inferior. The codes exhort people to act in a manner befitting one's standing in the relationship. Thus, household codes reflect the idea that husbands are superior to their wives, parents superior to their children, and masters superior to their slaves. In the Greco-Roman world, maintaining such order was crucial because the house was considered a microcosm of society as a whole and its foundational building block. Just as some are superior in household relationships, so too in the state some are superior at ruling while others are "superior" at being ruled; some are superior at governance while others are "superior" at manual labor and service. Such presuppositions of the natural order of the world stand behind the household codes articulated in the New Testament.[11]

If the household codes are carryovers from the surrounding culture, how did the gospel story impact Paul's articulation of them? Are they simply brought in and affirmed of a piece? Or has the story of God's work in Christ transformed the cultural expectation?

As we explore the ways that the household codes have been integrated into the story of Christian family life, we must acknowledge that a Christian adaptation of such codes has the power either to strengthen the social disparities and power relations or to subvert those inequalities. Thus, when Colossians says that wives should submit to their husbands "in the Lord," without further commentary, this can be and often is read as placing God's seal of approval on a hierarchical view of society in which men are to take the superior position of leadership and women the inferior position of subservience.

The household code in Ephesians 5:21–6:9 provides a fascinating both/and of reifying the existing social structure and transforming it by writing it into the gospel story. On the one hand, this code heightens the importance of wives' subservience to their husbands by drawing an analogy with the church's relationship to Christ: as the church submits to Christ, so wives are to submit to their husbands in everything. The basis of this submission is the superiority of the husband in the relationship: he is the head, as Christ is the head of the church. Not exactly what we might hope for from a gospel narrative that otherwise reaches out to the outcast and subverts society's gender-based value judgments.

On the other hand, when the instructions turn to focus on the husband, the narrative dynamics of the crucified Christ come more to the fore. The idea that the Christian community, in general, is to be a living depiction of the story of cruciform love finds expression in the mandate that the husband is to love his wife as Christ loved the church and gave himself up for her. The husband to whom the wife is supposed to submit is a husband who is living out the surprising surrender of power that defines the life, and love, of Jesus. This is a husband who, like Jesus, does not lord his authority over his subject but stands with her as the slave of all (Mark 10:41–45). Husbands are placed in the role of Christ, but this is the Christ who does not regard equality with God as something to be grasped after, instead emptying himself, taking the form of a servant (Phil. 2:6–11).

What are we to make of this? While these letters are working within the givens of Paul's hierarchical culture, the gospel is transforming what it looks like to fill the role of the "superior" in the relationship. Although these household codes give clear evidence that the gospel story did not blow up the social categories of the ancient world, they do radically transform what it looks like to be "first" in the new creation community: it means to be least, to be servant of all.

Recently, N. T. Wright has argued that a driving theme in Ephesians is the oneness brought about by the reconciling work of Christ: God and humanity are reconciled and made one; Jews and gentiles are reconciled with one another in Christ's body and thereby made one; and here male and female are reconciled in Christ's body and made one.[12] In the last section of the chapter we will explore what all this might mean for those of us who want to faithfully embody the Christian story today. But first, we need to allow one final biblical witness against gender equality to speak.

The Voice for Subordination

First Timothy 2:9–15 is the linchpin passage for the position that leadership and teaching in the church are charges entrusted to men alone. At the seminary where I received my master's degree, the lecture on women in the church began with a serial elimination of the relevance of all other passages in the New Testament, imploring us to recognize that 1 Timothy 2 is the decisive statement of the issue. The passage in question reads as follows (backing up to include verse 8):

> I desire, then, that in every place the men should pray, lifting up holy hands without anger or argument; also that the women should dress themselves modestly and decently in suitable clothing, not with their

> hair braided, or with gold, pearls, or expensive clothes, but with good works, as is proper for women who profess reverence for God. Let a woman learn in silence with full submission. I permit no woman to teach or to have authority over a man; she is to keep silent. For Adam was formed first, then Eve; and Adam was not deceived, but the woman was deceived and became a transgressor. Yet she will be saved through childbearing, provided they continue in faith and love and holiness, with modesty. (NRSV)

The heart of our concern is verse 12: "I permit no woman to teach or to have authority over a man; she is to keep silent."

We should be clear as to how absolute this prohibition is. Some, feeling the tensions between this passage and others, have suggested that women may teach in public worship (for example), so long as they are not teaching under their own authority but rather under the authority of the men who comprise the church's leadership. These interpreters combine "teach" and "exercise authority" such that together they now mean "teach authoritatively" or "teach on her own authority." But this is not what the passage states. The contrast the passage establishes is between teaching and remaining silent, not between teaching authoritatively and teaching nonauthoritatively.

The next important element to explore is the way that this restriction is tied to the narrative of creation and fall from Genesis 2–3. It seems to imply that what went wrong in humanity's rebellion against God was an upending of the order of creation. Adam was created first, but he chose to listen to the woman. The priority of Adam in creation seems also to imply that his superiority to Eve includes being less prone to deception: "the woman was deceived and became a transgressor." The implication is clear: women should not teach now in the church because, being more prone to deception, their teaching would lead not only themselves but also the entire church into transgression. This reinforces the point that the mandate of this passage is to keep women not simply from "authoritative teaching" but from all teaching.

It is important to paint this passage with such stark colors because only then can we see that it stands in direct tension with the actual practice of the early church as evidenced in numerous places, including Paul's own letters. Once we allow for the softening of its force such that teaching is okay, so long as it is under the authority of the male leadership, we blind ourselves to the contradiction it presents to the presumption, visible in passages such as 1 Corinthians 11 and Romans 16, that women will participate fully in worship and the life of the church. This passage is counterevidence to those texts. It provides testimony that, if vindicated, would call into question not only modern ordination of women but also the ancient practice of the apostles' churches and fellow workers.

We need to say more about this passage as well, because not only does the ancient church serve as a living counterpoint to this passage of Scripture but almost every modern-day church does as well—even those that cling to the prohibition of women teaching on the basis of a commitment to the Bible as the inerrant Word of God. To see how this is so, let's broaden our vision to the other commands contained in this paragraph.

The first command mandates that women dress simply, adorning themselves with good works rather than external adornment: "Women should dress themselves modestly and decently in suitable clothing, not with their hair braided, or with gold, pearls, or expensive clothes, but with good works, as is proper for women who profess reverence for God" (vv. 9–10 NRSV). One question for those who base their views of women in church leadership on verses 11–14 is whether they also enforce verses 9–10: Do they forbid people from dressing up to come to church on Sunday? Do they forbid women from braiding or otherwise styling their hair? Do they forbid women from wearing a gold necklace or a diamond ring? With rare exception (such as Amish communities), the answers are no.

We recognize that these are culturally or temporally bound restrictions and that there may be other considerations that would pull a community in a very different direction. But once we have made such concessions to our own cultural context, we begin to strip away the veneer of simply "obeying the Bible" as the reason for enforcing the subsequent verses. All application of the Bible is mediated by a host of considerations about how our own time and place, and our own location in the unfolding narrative of God's redemptive work, is similar to or different from the cultural contexts the biblical texts are situated in. Are not the mandates about dress in the very same paragraph as those about women teaching? Are they not set down to regulate the very same ecclesiastical context of worship? Why then are we happy to enforce literal restrictions on teaching but not on dress?

Another set of related questions arises when we keep reading beyond the Adam and Eve allusion. The final verse of the paragraph states that the woman (Eve? all women?) will be saved through childbearing if they (all women?) continue in faith and love and holiness. The typical meaning of "through" in the Greek is "by means of." Again we are face-to-face with a verse that not even the most biblically adherent incorporate directly into their theology. Nobody, in short, thinks that women will be saved only if they add "having babies" to the standard markers of faith, love, and holiness. Some have attempted to find in this verse a continuing allusion to the fall narrative, in which Eve is told that her seed will bruise the head of the serpent. This is unlikely, however. The verse in 1 Timothy looks at the action of women in the present-day church ("they continue in faith . . ."), and "childbearing" is not well suited to evoke an allusion to "seed" from Genesis 3. Another possibility is that the verse evokes the curse of pain in childbirth (Gen. 3:16). It is conceivable that "saved through childbearing" means something akin to "preserved through the act of bearing of children." But again, this is an unlikely meaning for the Greek phrase and is ill-suited to the context of 1 Timothy 2.

Reading through various commentators' attempts to make sense of this admittedly difficult verse, I am struck by the irony that some scholars reject the idea that the verse about being saved through childbearing refers to how women obtain salvation simply because this would contradict other passages of Scripture. And yet many of these same scholars are unwilling to apply the same criterion for making sense of the verse on women's silence that, as it is commonly applied, contradicts the apostolic practice we see in other passages of the New Testament.

First Timothy 2:9–15 contains three statements about the activities of women in the church: (1) they are to dress plainly; (2) they are to remain silent; and (3) they will be saved by having children. The vast preponderance of the church has rightly concluded that cultural and other hermeneutical considerations call for a mitigation of the force of (1). It should not be enforced literally. The near entirety of the church has, for various theological and hermeneutical reasons, subordinated (3) to other texts that speak differently. This being done, however, any appeal to "submitting to Scripture" as the reason for continuing to enforce (2) is rendered impotent. This passage shows us that all application of Scripture is subject to reinterpretation in light of both other teachings in Scripture and the complexities of bringing the text into our own cultural contexts. This brings us to the question, then, of how we are to plot gender roles within the gospel story.

Storied Redemption and Gender in the Church

First Timothy 2:9–15 is a difficult passage. At some point in these seven short verses, nearly every one of us will read something that we are all but unwilling to hear, something we are either unable or unwilling to integrate into our theology or practice. As troubling as this is for those of us who receive the New Testament canon as our rule of faith and practice, the benefit is that it provides us with a striking case study for how we read and apply the Bible. All our readings of the Bible are deeply wedded to both cultural and theological commitments. Reading and applying the Bible is never simply a matter of "doing what the text says." It is always a process in which we bring our own theological commitments with us as a guide. In this concluding section we will explore what it might mean to integrate women into the cruciform narrative of our Christian communities.

The Economy of the Cross

The big picture of the Christian story is that God has bound himself to humanity, through the nation of Israel, for the purpose of bringing the world from the failure of old creation into the glory of new creation. This, of course, is the story that Christianity shares in common with Judaism. What distinguishes the story of Jesus is that the means God chooses is a crucified Messiah whose kingdom-inaugurating activity was one of upending the economy of the world.

The implications of this surprisingly cruciform kingdom are consistently worked out in the words of Jesus and of Paul: to follow a crucified Messiah is to commit oneself to self-giving love as the way of life. Moreover, both Jesus and Paul extend the application to the power dynamics and social hierarchies of the world. To follow a crucified

Messiah is to confess that those who are mighty by the standards of the world are not the ultimate insiders but are likely to be the consummate outsiders in the kingdom of God. Conversely, to be enfolded into the kingdom of the crucified Messiah is to be given the status of consummate insider, even if one was previously at the margins of society.

> Consider your own calling, my brothers and sisters: that there were not many wise according to the flesh, not many mighty, not many of noble birth. But God has chosen the foolish things of the world in order to shame the wise, and God has chosen the weak things of the world in order to shame the strong, and God has chosen the ill-born things of the world and the despised—the things that are not in order to nullify the things that are. (1 Cor. 1:26–28)

The way God shows that the world's wisdom is foolish is by demonstrating that the economy of God's kingdom is the inverse of the economy of the world. It is not what one brings from the world to the church that gives one value in the church, but that God has made one who had nothing to bring from the world a member of this body of Christ. God has performed such an inversion so that no one may boast before him (1 Cor. 1:29).

But here's the point we too often skip past even when we affirm this much: if the "getting into" the kingdom of God is not based on socially constructed hierarchies, then bringing such hierarchies with us into the church is a denial of the gospel itself. Much of the Corinthian correspondence is spent advancing just this argument about life in Christian community. The means by which we enter (God's grace in uniting us by the Spirit to the body of the crucified Christ) is the sole grounds by which we differentiate among ourselves in the body (by the Spirit pouring out the gifts of God and thereby differentiating among the equal members of Christ's crucified body).

This is the gospel story that, I believe, calls us to make good on what we catch glimpses of in the New Testament. When we read of women as coworkers, as a deacon, as an apostle; when we read of women speaking and praying in public worship; when we read of women transcending social mores in order to follow Jesus in his itinerant ministry or sit at his feet like a disciple; when we read of women being entrusted with the task of bearing witness to the resurrection—in each of these moments we are catching glimpses of a new creation that has no hierarchical distinction between male and female. It is not a vision that is worked out consistently in the first-century culture in which the New Testament writings grew up, but it is one that fits within the plot of a story that turns all social hierarchies on their head as God comes to rule the world through a crucified Messiah.

This is the first reason I believe that the inclusive, more egalitarian voice of the New Testament demands our allegiance in our contemporary settings: it does better justice to the gospel story. In particular, the more inclusive elements of the New Testament do better justice to the holistic vision of new creation that makes God's blessings known "far as the curse is found."

Overcoming the Fall

One of the besetting problems with 1 Timothy 2, as I read it, is that the prohibition on women's speech gives the last word to the curse of the fall rather than to the redemption of Christ. When the consequences of Adam and Eve's disobedience are meted out in Genesis 3, God tells the woman that her pain will be greatly multiplied in childbearing, and that her desire will be for her husband and he will rule over her (Gen. 3:16). With the redemptive economy of the cross as our lens for reading the story of Scripture, and of the world, we see that the man ruling over the woman is not the "order of creation" but the effect of the fall. To bring this subordination of women into the church as a norm for all times and places undermines the scope and power of Christ's redemptive work and of our own calling to make the church the living story of the new creation.

Giving No Offense

There is another angle to assess this evidence from. The household codes, the instructions governing women's participation in worship in 1 Corinthians 11, and perhaps also the instructions in 1 Timothy 2, are clearly designed to walk the line between having a distinctive Christian witness and not giving offense in first-century Mediterranean culture. There are, perhaps, nods toward a cruciform ethic transforming the mores of social hierarchy, but this comes from redefining what it means to be in the position of power rather than exploding the power dynamic entirely. These passages seem to be answering the question, What does it mean to follow Christ *given* this set of social constructs?

This, then, raises the intriguing question of what it means to follow Christ in a society with a very different set of "givens." How do we live out the story of Christ where fundamental equality of gender, rather than fundamental superiority of maleness, is the working assumption of our culture? A couple of ideas suggest themselves.

First, promoting the subordination of women to men would have precisely the opposite effect in our world when compared to the ancient world. If the household codes are written to promote Christ while avoiding the giving of unnecessary offense in the ancient world, then to follow the letter of the codes will undermine their express purpose because promoting such social hierarchy is deeply offensive in the modern West.

Second, however, as we set aside the patriarchy of the past we must cultivate an awareness of our own potential pitfalls. The writing of household codes into the Jesus narrative that we see on the pages of the New Testament serves as a warning to us that we are ever susceptible of wrongly baptizing our society's standards into the name of Christ without recognizing that baptism into Christ always brings with it death to the old and resurrection to the new. Therefore, while affirming an essentially egalitarian position on gender, we must also be willing to take seriously that it, too, might possess the power to undermine the new creation narrative.

In articulating a position of fundamental equality, we must not lose sight of the good news that the New Testament contains when speaking of Christian leadership. That is to say, fully embracing women in the ministries of the church is not an opening for women also to participate in the power game that defines the rulers of the earth and has, far too often, typified the rulers of the church. When we speak of equality in the church, we are not simply affirming, along with the world, that every position of leadership should be open to men and women equally, but that the leadership that is so open to all involves reblazing the trail of Calvary. This is an equal call to becoming the least and servant of all, and, at the same time, it is an equal call to all to participate in submission to such leadership that models for us self-giving love. In fact, a truly cruciform egalitarianism will be most clearly displayed in a community in which "be submissive to one another in the fear of Christ" (Eph. 5:21) becomes a higher and more sought-after goal than attaining to the positions of power.

I am acutely aware of the danger of saying that our culture is now getting right something that most cultures, and the church in particular, have gotten wrong for thousands of years. But I would argue that at times it is not only possible but necessary to say that our culture gets something right that the ancients got wrong. Indeed, it is no accident that the US Declaration of Independence from the British Crown includes the statement "We hold these truths to be self-evident, that all men are created equal." The theology that had so long undergirded kingship and a ruling class was precisely the claim that people are *not* created equal: some men are created with greater gifts of rule, some with less; men are created with greater gifts of rule, women with less. To say "all people are created equal" is to declare that we are, as a people, appealing to our creation by God as testimony that the social hierarchies, which established not only kingship but also male hegemony more generally, are invalid valuations of humanity. To say that our time and place is getting something right that the ancients and others of our theological forebears got wrong is not chronological snobbery. In this case, our cultural setting has the power to help open our eyes to an aspect of the gospel many of us had missed before.[13]

Neither Paul nor Jesus is an egalitarian, up to the task of pleasing those of us who would like to see the Bible unequivocally enjoin the full inclusion of women as coequal members and leaders in the church and in the world as a whole. But both indicate that women in the early church were not restricted by social expectations of subservience in either learning or teaching, either following or leading. And Paul, as much as Jesus, articulates a gospel that sows the seeds for the flowering of a fully inclusive church. His arguments in the Corinthian correspondence, that the replication of social hierarchies within the church is a denial of the gospel itself, can be modeled by the church only when our communion lives out a story in which there is no longer Jew or Greek, slave or free, male and female, but we are all one in Christ Jesus.

7

Liberty and Justice for All?

> No, no, we are not satisfied, and we will not be satisfied until justice rolls down like waters and righteousness like a mighty stream.
>
> —Martin Luther King Jr.,
> "I Have a Dream"[1]

The "scientific research" that went into the writing of this book included an exchange with my brother, a campus minister, that went something like this:

"So, who are your students who are into Jesus but not so fond of Paul?"

"It's my students who are really into justice," he replied. "The students whose gospel is Jesus proclaiming liberty to the captives don't have much time for Paul."

This line of alienation from Paul stems from at least two factors. One of these is a growing appreciation of the robust, biblical picture of justice that places care for the poor and release for the captives squarely within the mission of God. The increasing awareness of and respect for ministries such as International Justice Mission reflects this renewed understanding of the social breadth of the gospel. Moreover, the New Testament passages driving the resurgence of justice theology are largely derived from the ministry of Jesus, especially his inaugural sermon in Luke 4 (we will look at this in more detail below).

Claiming that there is a revival of interest in justice is not to say that Protestant Christianity, whose theology leans heavily on interpretation of Paul, has been devoid of the topic. However, *justice* has often carried a very different connotation in Protestant, especially evangelical, circles. In a system of theology that functions, at its core, as a way to ensure that the law of God is upheld, *justice* carries connotations of "getting what we deserve" or "Christ getting what we deserve" so that the strict demands of legal justice can be upheld in the justification of sinners. I hope that we have already seen enough of Paul's theology, and his theology of justification in particular, to create space for a reinterpretation of what justice might mean to Paul. But the larger question remains: Is there a driving concern for social justice in Paul's letters?

Related to this is the cautious approach some take with Paul due to the way he was used by those who wanted biblical grounds to legitimate the enslavement of Africans. Howard Thurman, born in 1900, relates what has become a classic story in this regard. Home for summer vacation from college, he asked his grandmother why she would not allow him to read any of the Pauline letters.

> "During the days of slavery," she said, "the master's minister would occasionally hold services for the slaves. Old man McGhee was so mean that he would not let a Negro minister preach to his slaves. Always the white minister used as his text something from Paul. At least three or four times a year he used as a text: 'Slaves, be obedient to them that are your masters . . . , as unto Christ.' Then he would go on to show how it was God's will that we were slaves and how, if we were good and happy slaves, God would bless us. I promised my Maker that if I ever learned to read and if freedom ever came, I would not read that part of the Bible."[2]

Paul, so it seems, has not merely been silent on the issue of justice; he has been complicit in some of the gravest miscarriages of justice in the modern Western world.

The issues we take up in this chapter are closely related to those in the prior chapter on women. The problems tend to focus on the same types of texts (household codes), and the gospel dynamic of upending the world's hierarchies is going to be a significant component in the process of resolving the biblical tensions. But Paul has another card to play in this discussion as well. The liberating and unifying claims of his justification theology will unmask the uses to which Paul was put in legitimating slavery as nothing less than antigospel.

The Good News of Freedom

When in Luke's Gospel Jesus stands in the synagogue and reads from the Isaiah scroll, he proclaims a gospel whose very heartbeat is what we would call "social justice." Luke recounts the scene as follows:

> He unrolled the scroll and found the place where it was written:
> "The Spirit of the Lord is upon me,
> because he has anointed me
> to bring good news to the poor.
> He has sent me to proclaim release to the captives
> and recovery of sight to the blind,
> to let the oppressed go free,
> to proclaim the year of the Lord's favor."
>
> And he rolled up the scroll, gave it back to the attendant, and sat down. The eyes of all in the synagogue were fixed on him. Then he began to say to them, "Today this Scripture has been fulfilled in your hearing." (Luke 4:17–21 NRSV)

The passage in Isaiah Jesus reads from reflects the Old Testament tradition of a Year of Jubilee—a time when debts were canceled, when economically expedient decisions to borrow money or sell land would be undone, when slaves would be freed in a restorative year of celebration. Isaiah 61 is likely picking up on the geopolitical realities of Israel's continuing servitude to other nations. The Year of Jubilee, so Isaiah hopes, will become Israel's national story as God reverses its enslavement and the spiritual blindness that brought it about. In the ministry of Jesus, these two strands are woven together. The hopes that Jesus fulfills are nothing less than the hopes of Israel that a Davidic king would rule the descendants of Abraham—and this reign is one that literally brings sight to the blind and hearing to the deaf as well as a reversal of fortune for the socially marginalized and impoverished. The "good news" as Jesus proclaims it is well captured in modern discussions of "social justice."

But there is also a surprise in store for Jesus's audience. If we were to continue reading the chapter of Isaiah that Jesus reads from in the synagogue, we would discover how Israel was to receive its "good news." The day of its salvation, according to the prophet, was to be

> the day of vengeance of our God. . . .
> Strangers shall stand and feed your flocks,
> foreigners shall till your land and dress your vines;
> but you shall be called priests of the Lord. (Isa. 61:2, 5–6 NRSV)

Isaiah's vision seems to have been one in which Israel is glorified by means of the subjugation of the nations. But Jesus has a different narrative in mind.

Immediately after the crowd praises his gracious words, Jesus goes on to tell them of how the ancient prophet Elijah helped not the widows of Israel but instead a gentile woman of Sidon, and how his successor, Elisha, cured not the lepers in Israel but only Naaman the Syrian (Luke 4:26–27). The people's reaction turns from adoration to rage, and they attempt to kill Jesus.

What accounts for their sudden turn? The scandalous implication of Jesus's good news is that God's promises to Israel will come as a blessing through Israel for the sake of the nations' glory rather than coming to bless the people of Israel at the cost of the nations' humiliation. Although Israel was politically and militarily subject to Rome, the Jews were the insiders in the plans and promises of God. Without downplaying Israel's central role in the story, the narrative of Jesus as it unfolds over the two-volume work of Luke-Acts insists that gentiles, the consummate outsiders in Israel's drama, are brought in to stand on equal footing as participants in the promises of Israel.

The two parts of the sermon are inseparable. Social justice addresses a whole swath of problems caused by failures in the physical world together with disparities in the distribution of power and wealth. When Jesus comes to inaugurate the day of the Lord's favor, and does so by driving back forces of societal exclusion, spiritual enslavement, physical brokenness, and material lack, he is demonstrating that a "gospel" of Israel's liberation from Rome is too small a message to bear the stamp of the God who is the Maker of heaven and earth. The agenda of Jesus's God is to beat back forces much more powerful than Rome. The God of Israel would see even Rome freed from its captivity, even Rome's blind eyes enlightened.

When plotting the narrative of the gospel story, we frequently return to the observation that it turns the economy of the world on its head. In the case of social justice, the gospel story even displaces the nation-state as the ultimate arbiter of peace and justice. This means, in the first-century context, that the exaltation of Israel at the expense of Rome would be a perpetuation of the injustice already rampant on the earth—only now with a different perpetrator in charge.

To include the gentiles in the solution to the problem by also making them recipients of the deliverance that God has in store rewrites the story of the problem that Jesus came to solve. Social justice is not about one ethnic group that needs to be exalted, even at the expense of another if necessary. Social justice is about our whole, modern, complex society modeling the peace, plenty, and order the biblical narrative depicts the world having descended from into strife, lack, and disorder. By insisting that good news comes to the gentiles, Jesus claims that justice for all lies at the heart of the gospel.

Perhaps writing ourselves into the story of Luke 4 would help us grasp the point. As followers of Jesus, we are self-proclaimed insiders. We speak of the glorious future that God has in store for us. We look forward to the consummation of the reign of the King we now serve. Thus, when we hear the words of Jesus, we hear in them promises of the deliverance that we are enjoying now and will enjoy more fully in the age to come.

But then Jesus turns the tables and says that God takes his deliverance to those outside the people. The abundance of the kingdom is sent to the renegade children who are rescued from the trash dumps.

Agents of freedom are sent to the Buddhist woman in Thailand to free her from her life as a sex slave. A Hindu family is sprung from its bonded labor in an Indian brick kiln. In such scenarios we discover that as long as we focus on ourselves, even as the blessed people of God, our gospel is too small. The vindication of the church, even, is not a large enough category for depicting the good news that God has in store. Because the gospel is about social justice, it cannot be contained within one tightly delimited people, and because the gospel bursts the borders of particular peoples, it repeatedly shows itself to be an inherently social gospel.

If we are to make the link between Jesus and Paul, we are going to have to learn to hold the two parts of Jesus's sermon together: the good news is both the declaration that God's liberating work of justice is powerfully at work in Jesus and the insistence that God's reign is extending beyond the borders of Israel in order to embrace gentiles.

How, then, do Paul's letters relate to these concerns?

Paul and Racial Equality

One, and Free

Starting with the second issue, we saw above in our discussion of church unity that Paul was the foremost champion of full inclusion of non-Jews in the early church. What the ministry of Jesus could only anticipate became fully realized in Paul's ministry. Gentiles across the Mediterranean were confessing that Israel's King is, in fact, Lord of the entire cosmos. As we explored in our discussion of justification by faith, Paul's passionate, even at times angry, letter of Galatians is an extended demonstration of why gentiles cannot be treated as second-class citizens within the church.

The good news proclaims liberty, and those who receive the good news are to walk in light of the freedom they have been called to. Therefore, to subject gentiles to the yoke of the Jewish law is a denial of the gospel itself (Gal. 4–5). For Paul, the gospel announces a freedom that brings to an end Jewish claims of ethnic and religious superiority and inaugurates communities in which no group has to become like the other in order to be fully included in the people of God.

In short, Paul's proclamation of "justification by faith" has a horizontal as well as a vertical dimension.[3] Ethnicity is wrapped up in practices that delineate people groups. The struggle Paul faces when confronting the question of whether to circumcise the non-Jew Titus (Gal. 2:1–4), and when Cephas refuses to eat with gentiles (Gal. 2:11–14), is that the family harmony has been broken. The Jewish members of the family are insisting that the gentiles have to become like them to truly be embraced. Within early Judaism, these defining practices included circumcision, Sabbath keeping, and food laws. When justification comes up in Paul, we find him attempting to clear space for gentiles to be fully included in the people of God without adopting these Jewish ethnic markers.

At the same time, we must not overlook that Paul repeatedly asserts that there is ample space for Jews to participate in the Christian story without abandoning their own unique identity. Paul's letters repeat the slogan "in Christ neither circumcision nor uncircumcision means anything" three times (1 Cor. 7:19; Gal. 5:6; 6:15). The gospel says that we become part of God's family by being united by faith and the Spirit to the crucified and risen Christ. The New Testament repeatedly depicts this becoming true of both circumcised Jews and uncircumcised gentiles. Therefore, requiring gentiles to take on another's racial and ethnic identity in order to enjoy full participation in the people of God, for them to be regarded as equals, is nothing other than a rejection of "the truth of the gospel" (Gal. 2:5, 14). And the same might be said for Jews: they need not renounce their Judaism in order to faithfully play the story of Christ. Creating other standards of full participation, or introducing inequalities based on other measures of value, refutes this gospel. Gentiles do not have to become Jews in order to become part of the people of God. And, we might add, neither must Jews become gentiles.

With such a horizontal argument about the implications of the gospel, Paul's letter to Galatia eviscerates the social hierarchies that have marred Christian witness. When the gospel has been scripted into an overarching story of one race's or one nationality's inherent superiority, rather than standing as a larger story poised to transform those smaller narratives of inequality, it has, in fact, denied itself.

Moving from Paul to the racially based slavery, subjugation, and segregation that mars the stories of North America and Europe, I see the argument going something like this: if the laws and regulations that God gave to Israel cannot become markers of inherent superiority within the church without contradicting the gospel, then neither can American stories of cultural or industrial development, white stories of racial superiority, or capitalist stories of economic necessity. In short, every line of argument (whether implicit or explicit) that the church accepted as undergirding the necessity or divine sanction of slavery tacitly denies the gospel that Paul proclaimed.

Carrying this a bit further, Paul's refusal to allow his churches to be swallowed up by a distinctively Jewish identity points toward an embrace of cultural and racial difference as a defining marker of the body of Christ. Judaism provides a beautiful social location to embody the gospel in, while requiring all Christians to occupy that space denies the gospel. Bringing it closer to home for many readers of this book, not only is it a renunciation of the gospel to uphold one race's claims of inherent superiority, it also contradicts the gospel to require that all Christianity be cast in the mold of white, Western Christianity. This is, of course, a challenge for missionaries bringing the gospel to cultures overseas, but presuppositions of cultural and racial superiority haunt us at home as well, often in the guise of correct theology and worship practice. Many of our churches, seminaries, denominations, and parachurch organizations continue to tacitly communicate that one has to become white (and Western and modern) in order to become fully part of the people of God.

But Paul's gospel will have none of this. The church, in which there is no longer a relational disparity where Jew is greater than Greek, free is greater than slave, and male is greater than female, cannot countenance, either, white as greater than black (or brown or yellow or red).

The narrative of the gospel is God's people set free. This is a defining reality of the people of God: "It was for freedom that Christ set us free" (Gal. 5:1). Although in this letter Paul is most concerned that the Galatians themselves do not turn from the gospel to enact a different sort of purportedly saving story, we have an additional consideration to weigh. What does it mean to make the gospel of freedom known to the ends of the earth? To ask this question is to come to the place where we are confronted with a mandate to be agents of the justice of God in the world.

Counterevidence

These racial implications form the gospel-story framework that we take with us as we turn now to listen to the counterevidence from Paul's letters: some of their statements about slavery. It is worth pointing out that in Paul's day claims of ethnic and racial superiority were not the primary arguments made in favor of slavery. Those issues are tangled together in our more recent story but not, typically, in the biblical discussions or in the broader Greco-Roman world.

As we found in our discussion of women in the previous chapter, so also with the issue of slavery, much of the biblical testimony comes from household codes. The passage Howard Thurman's grandmother referred to comes from Ephesians 6, and a similar passage is found in Colossians 3. As usual, the instructions found here come in pairs, one set of statements aimed at the subject member of the relationship, the other set aimed at the "superior." The passage from Ephesians reads like this:

> Slaves, obey those who are your lords according to the flesh with fear and trembling, in the sincerity of your hearts, as to Christ—not with "eye service" as those who seek to please people, but as Christ's slaves, doing the will of God from your innermost being. Offer your slave-service with enthusiasm, as to the Lord and not to people, knowing that each person, whatever good thing that person might do, will receive it as a reward from the Lord, whether slave or free. And you lords, do the same things to them and leave aside threatening, knowing that both their Lord and yours is in heaven and with him there is no partiality. (Eph. 6:5–9)

As with the issues of women and men, so in the case of masters and slaves there is a both/and here. On the one hand, the instructions assume a social structure that is not shared by our society, a hierarchical arrangement of persons in which one is master and the other servant. The instructions not only assume such a structure but also regulate the structure rather than offering a way out of it. On the other hand, the relationship is regulated by the gospel story in a way that recontextualizes both roles. In doing so, it declares that these earthly relationships are not ultimate and sows the seeds for exploding the presumed hierarchy.

The danger of recontextualizing these relationships within a religious narrative is that God can become the power behind the subjugation of slaves. As the story told by Thurman's grandmother highlights, the promise of heavenly reward for well-behaved slaves is a powerful force for the status quo. In such a reading, the Lord Jesus seems to stand just over the shoulder of the lord slaveholder, lending cosmic authority to the slave owner's claims.

However, in Ephesians 6 the opposite is true as well. If the Lord Jesus is visible over the shoulder of the lord slaveholder, he stands just as squarely behind the slave, receiving the treatment meted out by the earthly master. At the end, we discover that God is unimpressed with earthly assessments of status. The Master of All shows no partiality.

Although this passage does not call for an opening up of the full freedom of the gospel to those who are enslaved, it does plot a trajectory for the transformation of the institution of slavery within the church. It does not lend divine imprimatur to the master's whip; it calls for masters and slaves, united to one another in Christ's body, to begin recognizing Jesus in the face of one another.

Realizing the Freedom We Have

Paul brings the issue of slavery and freedom into his conversations about the gospel in more places than these household codes. In 1 Corinthians 7:17–24 Paul is working through the implications of God's calling people into Christ: What does this mean for people confronted with the possibility of changing their status in the world? On the one hand, Paul wants to say that any station in life is a viable place to flourish as God's child. "No longer Jew nor Greek" means that both Jews and gentiles can fully serve God without becoming the other. "No longer slave or free" means that both slaves and free people can fully serve God without becoming the other. On the other hand, even though Paul sees the gospel transcending such earthly divisions, he does not refuse to draw out the profound implications of the gospel for people in slavery.

Paul asks his readers, "Were you called while a slave?" And though he says, "Don't worry about it," he is nonetheless compelled to add, "But if you are able to become free, much more should you do that!" (1 Cor. 7:21). This affirmation that it is truly better to become free is all the more striking because it comes in the middle of a paragraph whose main point is "don't change your station." Perhaps driven in part by an expectation that Jesus would soon return, Paul was encouraging his readers in every station of life to recognize that they could fully serve God in whatever place they were when called into the divine family. But even though he is mounting an argument against pursuing a change in social status, the gospel dynamic of freedom compels him to urge Christians to realize as much earthly freedom as they can. Why should someone who is a slave pursue freedom? "For (because!) the person who was called while a slave is the Lord's freedman" (1 Cor. 7:22).

Although we might be tempted to make the argument that being "spiritually freed" means that earthly freedom is entirely insignificant, Paul makes precisely the opposite claim. It is because the gospel proclaims liberty to the captive that those who are enslaved on earth should pursue and be given full liberty. And so Paul concludes, "You were bought with a price (i.e., the price of Christ who died for us); do not become slaves of people" (1 Cor. 7:23).

This brings us back to the suggestion we made concerning "freedom" in Galatians. If we are freed people, we are called to realize that freedom in every aspect of our lives. Fidelity to the Christian narrative is not had when people are living enslaved. This is true for the church itself, and it is true for the entirety of the new creation that Jesus is Lord over. We limit the scope of Jesus's restorative reign if we do not stand against slavery as antithetical to the story God is calling the whole creation to live into.

The gospel story that Paul tells not only unravels the narrative of racial superiority that undergirded the African slave trade, it also unravels the story of slavery itself. To confirm that Christ is the Lord of all people is simultaneously to claim that human lordship over a slave is an infringement on what is God's. The freedom that Paul proclaims in the gospel is not merely a freedom from the guilt of sin, nor is it merely a freedom from the enslaving power of sin. It is both of these. But Paul insists that the spiritual dynamics of his gospel must play out in the lives of Christian communities as well. To perpetuate slavery in a place defined by the gospel of liberty is to live a story that contradicts the gospel narrative. We have all been bought with a price to be bondslaves of Christ and are therefore not to be slaves of people.

Paul and Social Justice

This brings us right up to the brink of that first leg of Jesus's sermon in Luke 4. What does all this have to do with concerns about social justice? When we are speaking about freedom, are we simply dredging up the debates of the past about whether Africans should be slaves to people of European descent? By no means. We are brought into our own day and age as well, in which the slave trade is just as active as ever, especially with women being trafficked as sex slaves. Broaden the scope slightly from sex slavery per se to other forms of commercial sexual exploitation, including prostitution and pornography, and we are looking at an estimated ten million women and children ensnared. If Paul's gospel is not good news to these powerless victims, one might well contend that it is not good news at all, with no power to bring about salvation.

Living into a Cosmic Narrative

This is one reason that it is absolutely critical that we take hold of two central dynamics of Paul's gospel narrative. First, we must remember that Paul's story is one of new creation, a cosmic story in which the entire world is remade—including a disarming of the enslaving powers and the enthronement of a King who is Master of all masters, all despots, all presidents, all pimps. Second, we need to recognize that the power of the story is realized in communities that chronicle the gospel account in their actions, communities that make their little stories faithful retellings of the master narrative that defines them. This is exactly what we see Paul doing in 1 Corinthians 7. The community that is formed when God buys people to himself in Christ (1 Cor. 7:23) is called to realize its freedom from earthly masters whenever possible. And so we, called to extend the gospel story as we are sent on the mission of God, rightly embody this message when we enable others to be free of earthly masters and thereby at liberty to serve God alone. The "justice" of Paul's gospel is not merely the "justice" of our reckoning before the throne of a cosmic law court but a justly ordered new creation that is, even now, breaking into the present evil age. It is the justice spoken of the by the prophet Amos and invoked by Martin Luther King Jr., justice that must "flow like torrents of water, and righteousness like an ever-flowing stream" (Amos 5:24).

As we walked through Paul's gospel story in the first few chapters of this book, we saw that his gospel is not merely the drama about how a sinful individual can stand before a holy God. Such individual stories function within redemptive communities that, themselves, are part of a newly ordered cosmos. Paul may be misconstrued as an enemy of social justice only to the extent that these corporate dynamics are ignored and that we refuse to apply the gospel dynamics of liberty and equality in the worlds that God has placed us in. This is a challenge for the evangelical church, a call for us to rearticulate the gospel and the identity of the church such that we embrace a redemptive calling that extends throughout the whole created order.

As I have followed church-related news recently, I have seen an overly spiritualized and individualized "gospel" flare up in pointed antithesis to the reading of Paul I'm advocating here. In one news item, a nationally broadcast conservative talk-show host warned people that social justice "is a perversion of the gospel." In another, the racist history of the Southern Presbyterian Church was defended on the grounds of "the spirituality of the church," which makes interference in matters of national law none of the church's business.

In both of these theologies, the gospel is too small. In neither of these theologies is Paul's gospel story, or Jesus's gospel story, being told or enacted.

When Jesus's ministry is read through the lens of his sermon in Luke 4, the social justice edge becomes clear to see: good news to the poor is inseparable from giving sight to the blind and freedom to the captives and the oppressed. His ministry is marked by a concern for the powerless and outcast, as we saw above in our chapter on the kingdom of God. These are the concerns of social justice, in a nutshell. Paul's commitment to a ministry of the cross draws him to advocate similar practices within the church.

One Equal Body

As Paul sees the gospel taking root in his churches, he interprets the establishment of these communities as living narrations of the story of Christ crucified. Such a theology, such a narrative, will always be a story of God's hand of blessing coming to the outsiders, the downtrodden, and the dead in order to embrace them as insiders, lift them up, and raise them to new life. These are the spiritual dynamics of God's transformation of individuals, and they are therefore to be the social dynamics that define the lives of communities comprised of those God calls to himself.

In striving to have our minds transformed by the gospel narrative, we keep coming back to 1 Corinthians. The letter is a marvelous test case for us, largely because the community was getting the gospel so wrong in its life together that Paul had to give it a full-scale re-orientation from numerous angles. One such angle was the church's practice of according status and privilege based on social standing. The inequalities of the social order were being reproduced in the church, leading Paul to protest that the Corinthians had failed to understand the gospel story.

When rebuking the Corinthians for various divisions, Paul has to remind them that when they were called there were "not many wise according to human standing, not many mighty, not many born into privilege" (1 Cor. 1:26). The point here is that God's calling a person to Christ is itself the source of all wisdom, what allows a person to know true might by the power of the Spirit, the honored place of being a member of God's family. The creation of an alternative community in Christ turns the economy of this world on its head. And the church is to function with and be agents of extending this new equality into the world.

We see Paul's insistence on the church embodying this world-subverting narrative when he comes to discuss the Lord's Supper in 1 Corinthians 11. The Lord's Supper celebration is to be a commemoration of Jesus's death, but it is also a proclamation that the church is itself the one body of the crucified Christ. Therefore, a church that continues to act as though the surrounding culture's assessments of worth are legitimate markers of status and belonging has denied the gospel it professes to proclaim. By perpetuating divisions in the church, the Corinthians who gather to eat are not eating the Lord's Supper anymore (1 Cor. 11:20). They have falsified the meal through their actions.

In particular, the Corinthians were dividing themselves along economic lines that, in our Western cultures as well, tend to either buy people special status or relegate them to subservient positions: "Do you despise the church of God and shame those who have nothing?" The "haves" were feasting and getting drunk while the "have-nots" were going hungry. This, says Paul, is a repudiation of the gospel.

Giving as Justice

Stepping somewhat closer to the sorts of justice concerns that would call us not only to treat one another well but also to actively engage in transformative action, 2 Corinthians 8–9 erects a rich theology of giving on the foundation of the self-giving love of Jesus. These chapters encourage the Corinthians to participate in what became a hallmark of the latter part of Paul's missionary career: collecting money from the gentile churches to take to the impoverished people of Jerusalem. In these chapters we find the gospel narrative of Jesus sustaining a vision of Christian action that meets the physical needs of those in want.

While Protestant Christianity has most often put the term *grace* (Greek: *charis*) into play as God's acceptance of sinners, Paul in these two chapters puts the word to use ten times (which is more than we find in the entire letter to Galatians) as he speaks of God's, Christ's, and people's giving. The gospel of grace is a gospel that calls on us to give. Giving to people in need renarrates the gospel story God has called us to.

Before walking through the passage itself, I want us to put back on the table the sermon of Jesus from Luke 4. There, the issue of social justice and the gospel's boundary-bursting power were inextricably linked. Throughout Paul's discussion of giving, we find the same dynamic at play. Only this time, it is the gentiles who are being summoned to give to the other. The collection Paul is taking up is for impoverished Jews in Jerusalem. Giving is a way of living out the multiracial character of the gospel. As we examine the narrative dynamics of giving in 2 Corinthians 8–9, we do well to interrogate how such a call to give across ethnic lines might provide stage direction for faithful enacting of the Christian drama in our various twenty-first-century contexts.

In keeping with the gospel story as a narrative of Jesus, who gave his life so that we might live, Paul summons the Corinthians to consider their own giving in light of Jesus's self-emptying. Giving is an enactment of the gospel narrative of Jesus the Son. Paul summarizes the Jesus story thus: "You know the *grace* of our Lord Jesus Christ, that for your sake he became impoverished, even though he was rich, in order that you might be made rich through his poverty" (2 Cor. 8:9). He offers this short retelling of the gospel story because he wants the Corinthians to have a picture of what love looks like. Participating in this collection for the poor is showing proof of their genuine love (v. 8), a love modeled and embodied in the self-giving, enriching grace of Jesus. Giving to the poor is the Corinthians' own act of grace, embodying the gospel of grace itself: "see to it that you abound in this grace also" (v. 7).

The story of grace and giving is also a story of trust in the provision of God. More than this, it entails a recognition that the reason God pours out blessings on his people is so that this people can, in turn, extend God's grace to the world. We see this in a few ways in 2 Corinthians 8–9. First, to be a person inspired to give to the poor is to be a recipient of God's grace, an actor living out the gospel of Christ. Not only does Christ become poor so that many may become rich, but also the grace of God comes so that Christians who are persecuted and deeply impoverished become rich and lavish in the act of giving (8:1–4).

A second place we can look to see the horizontal purposes in God's gifts to his children is in 9:6–13. Again deploying the language of grace, Paul says that God is able to make grace abound to his people in order that they might always have enough for the purpose of being able to abound in good works for other people (2 Cor. 9:8). God gives to us so that we might give to others, especially to those who are poor or otherwise in need.

Paul cites a psalm to demonstrate what faithful living under God looks like, a psalm that reflects on a righteous person by saying,

"He scattered abroad, he gave to the poor, his righteousness endures forever" (2 Cor. 9:9, citing Ps. 112:9). Why can God's people have confidence to scatter their goods abroad, to give their resources to the poor? Because, Paul insists, "God will supply and multiply your seed for sowing" (2 Cor. 9:10). Grace is not merely a gift from God to place us, spiritually, in a right relationship with God. Grace is also God's giving abundantly of the world's resources to his children so that they, in turn, can be instruments of God's generous grace in God's world. Grace has an inherently missional quality that summons us to become conduits. We must extend our abundance to those in need. This is the reason God gave it to us in the first place.

We begin to see here how recognizing a social gospel in Paul requires, first of all, getting our gospel straight. Too often in Protestant churches the categories of grace and righteousness are so tightly wound up with our limited ideas of the gospel, and our understanding of that gospel is so focused on individuals, that we fail to see that God's grace to us binds us in social obligation to one another. The purpose of grace is not for us to hoard as individuals—either spiritually or materially—but for us to freely give. And the coming of righteousness is not the arrival of a static quality or standing before God but a dynamic gift that grows when God works through the grace of his people. That faithful person who scatters and gives to the poor has a "righteousness [that] endures forever" (2 Cor. 9:9). And, Paul says, such righteousness grows as God is at work in the works of the believer to bring it to fruition: God will "increase the harvest of your righteousness" as you give generously, with the result that God is praised (2 Cor. 9:10–11).

In fact, to meet the needs of the poor is nothing less than obeying the gospel that the Corinthians confess (2 Cor. 9:13). Using their abundance of material possessions is not merely an add-on to the gospel, an optional extra. For those who have received of the abundance of grace and God's gift of righteousness, giving to the poor is the only way to be faithful in a world in need of material grace and the transforming ramifications of the righteousness of God. Living out the gospel of gift and grace is itself a grace that comes from God and therefore brings praise to God. It has been said that mission exists because the worship of God does not.[4] If this is so, then the heart of the mission of the church is to give to the poor because the end of this cycle of giving ultimately returns to God in the form of praise and thanksgiving. If the "grace" flows downhill from God, the final return is a fullness that overflows to God in praise and thanksgiving. Because such service proves that people marked by the gospel of God are faithful to that confession, the outcome is people glorifying God (2 Cor. 9:12–15).

From first to last, giving to the poor is an expression of the gospel narrative because it participates in the rectification of the inequalities of the world; therefore, giving to the poor is nothing less than the indescribable gift of God (2 Cor. 9:15). This is the heart of social justice.

Social justice is built on the premise that God is not bound to the economy of the world's zero-sum game but instead enacts an alternative economy of abundance. And this is one reason social justice cannot be maintained within the walls of a particular people. The God who is Creator of the earth has enthroned Jesus as Lord over it all. In 2 Corinthians this means that the gospel call to give takes the resources of the gentile Christians and places them in the hands of Jews in Jerusalem. And it means that the gentiles share in the blessings of the kingdom because God has acted to send his blessings out from Israel into the world. With our giving, we who are Christ's are called to show the span of the love of God, the extent of Christ's reign, and the breadth of the new humanity that God would receive worship from.

Liberty and Justice for All

In Martin Luther King Jr.'s famous "I Have a Dream" speech, we find an easy movement between biblical imagery of equality and freedom, foundational American documents such as the Declaration of Independence, and the hopes and plight of African Americans in the mid-twentieth century. It is a speech that slides freely between issues of racial identity, freedom, and justice. As it does so, it creates the implicit argument that full equality of blacks and whites in America is one picture of a groaning creation that is nonetheless drawing closer to the biblical picture of a rightly ordered world. By evoking the biblical imagery and situating it in his calls for a world of racial equality, full freedom, and justice, King proclaimed that the gospel indicatives of racial equality, freedom, and justice are simultaneously the gospel imperatives that God's children must obey. Is this what the good news looks like in Jesus and in Paul?

Indeed it is. In Jesus's story, social justice is much clearer. The proclamation to, and embrace of, the socially marginalized and the promise of freedom to the captive are dynamics of Jesus's ministry that embody a liberating gospel narrative. When the kingdom of God subverts the kingdom of this world, it does so by God's approbation and exaltation of the least-expected members of society. It comes by the bringing of justice to the powerless, the enthroning of the poor, the freeing of the prisoner. And as we saw in the climax to Jesus's sermon in Luke 4, the embrace of the outsider includes the surprising inclusion of the gentiles as part of the victory God is working to win from within the story of Israel. To walk the way of Jesus is to participate in this world-subverting economy of the kingdom of God.

Because Jesus was working within a region of Jews who were, by and large, already considered insiders in the people of God, the accent in his own ministry fell largely on the more stereotypical social justice dynamic from Luke 4. It would be up to his followers to make good on the world-embracing implications of his message. For Paul, by contrast, the entirety of his ministry was among gentiles, so the issues of equality and freedom are more continually in the fore than those we might tend to deem broader questions of social justice. However, both the passage from Luke 4 and our study of Paul's letters show us that these issues of equality and justice are finally two sides of the same coin that is the currency of the gospel.

For both Paul and Jesus, the gospel is one of freedom. And so for both, God's agents on the earth are both to proclaim freedom from spiritual bondage and to work for freedom from bondage to the powers of the world. For both, God's people are formed by faithful response to Jesus, and so God's people are to fight against inequalities based on race or social standing.

It is because the gospel story declares that there are no longer the antitheses that constrained and defined people as Jew and Greek, slave and free, male and female, that King can conclude his famous speech with words that echo not only an African American spiritual but also the letters of Paul:

> When we allow freedom to ring, when we let it ring from every village and every hamlet, from every state and every city, we will be able to speed up that day when all of God's children, black men and white men, Jews and Gentiles, Protestants and Catholics, will be able to join hands and sing in the words of the old Negro spiritual, "Free at last! free at last! thank God Almighty, we are free at last!"[5]

The good news Paul proclaims, no less than that announced by Jesus, beckons us to participate in so hastening the day when freedom and justice flourish on the earth—signaling the reign of the crucified Messiah.

8

Sex in the Plot of God's Stories

> The more perilously the protagonist's situation is drawn the more remarkable will the redemption appear. A tepid plot inscribes a lukewarm God.
>
> —Gary A. Anderson, *The Genesis of Perfection*[1]

Sex is woven into the Bible's story of humanity from the very beginning. In the creation narrative of Genesis 1, God creates male and female, blessing them with the command to be fruitful and multiply and fill the earth (v. 28). In the creation story of Genesis 2 the sexual overtones are even stronger. With the creation of the woman, Adam says, "This at last is bone of my bones and flesh of my flesh." And the narrator comments that this arrival of the woman out of Adam's flesh and bone indicates the goal of the man-woman relationship, to reunite in one flesh: "Therefore a man leaves his father and his mother and clings to his wife, and they become one flesh" (Gen. 2:24 NRSV). In the Genesis story, this is the resolution of creation's first problem.

God had created the man first and then observed, "It is not good for the man to be alone," so that the creation of woman as helper and sexual partner stands as the Creator's first intervention on behalf of the beloved human creature.

Folks not knowing any better might anticipate that a holy book beginning with such robust affirmations of human sexual activity would meet with a generally favorable reception in our sex-charged culture. However, the unfolding story plots what sexual expression should look like in ways that are significantly more limiting than what many people want, experience, and believe to be viable expressions of Christian faith. And so we are confronted, for instance, with the issue my friend raised over lunch: How do we square the "do not judge" Jesus with the "homosexual-condemning" Paul? We have already opened up a different vista for the "do not judge" Jesus, but what about sexuality? What sort of indicators do we have about what faithful sex looks like within the story of God's renewal of creation?

Homosexuality is, of course, the lightning rod in today's debates about Christian sexuality. In my estimation, however, before we can take up the homosexuality issue we need to sketch a much larger framework for the role of sex in the Christian story. For Jesus, how does the coming reign of God lend a distinctive stamp to what sex is and how it should be both faithfully received as a gift and then in turn given to another? And for Paul, what does sex have to do with the new creation that comes through the crucified and risen Christ?

Sex in the Kingdom of God

Marriage and Creation

What did Jesus have to say about sex, and what does this tell us about sex in the kingdom of God? In Mark 10, when Jesus is asked about divorce he replies by invoking the creation story of sexual oneness. The setup, as Mark tells the story, is that the Pharisees were testing Jesus about divorce law. Jews in the first century all saw that the Old Testament law provided some plausible reasons for divorce, though they differed over what grounds were in keeping with the law. Perhaps it is not insignificant here that the Pharisees ask, specifically, whether it is lawful for a man to divorce his wife and not the other way around (Mark 10:2).

Jesus's answer, affirming the permanence of marriage, may in part be addressing the fact that the legal debate is wholly centered on the man's freedom to do as he wishes with his wife with little concern for the life the woman would be left with. In a patriarchal society, a divorced woman was in an exceedingly vulnerable position. Without the protection and provision of the man whose house she had joined, and with the stigma of the divorce itself, she could easily find herself in a desperate financial situation as a social outcast.

Jesus puts the question back to the Pharisees by asking what Moses commanded. And while they cite a command about giving a bill of divorce, Jesus draws them to an earlier, more foundational command of Moses (the presumed author of Genesis through Deuteronomy). The provision of the possibility of divorce was a concession to hard hearts, Jesus claims. The more telling moment of the narrative demonstrates that a physically joined man and woman are made one flesh by God. Jesus cites Genesis 2:24, which is the first "command" concerning marriage, a comment by the narrator on the story of Eve's creation: "For this reason a man shall leave his father and mother and be joined to his wife, and the two will become one flesh" (cited in Mark 10:8). Jesus draws the conclusion that this oneness is not merely a physical happening but an act of God: "What God has joined together let no human being separate" (Mark 10:9).

In this interchange we see three strands of sexual expression woven together: sex, marriage, and lifelong fidelity. This is the most basic framework of sex within the Christian story. The idea that humanity is somehow fulfilling its physical destiny through sexual union underlies the Genesis narrative: the woman came out of Adam's flesh, and the man and the woman become one flesh again through sex. The Genesis text Jesus cites is, at root, about sexual oneness. The passage also contains an indication of something like marriage. Though ideas about marriage and weddings have varied culture by culture over the millennia, the creation narrative contains the comment that the act of sexual oneness comes with the establishment of a new house, a new family, to become husband and wife. Moreover, the assumption Jesus and his contemporaries both make is that the undoing of this sexually united couple would require a bill of divorce. In the Christian story, sex takes place within marriage. Finally, this is a lifelong partnership. In the joining of two people sexually, God unites them as one flesh, not to be separated.

Jesus's Story of Sex within Our Own

This Christian picture has begun to stand increasingly in contrast to the norms of Western culture. Studies cited by the Kinsey Institute indicate that well over half of all teenagers have had sex by age eighteen and that most of these have had more than one partner.[2] Ours is a world in which sex is often far removed from hopes of oneness (lifelong or otherwise) and frequently engaged in outside of what is assumed will be a lifelong relationship. Moreover, divorce is increasingly commonplace, with the claim frequently being advanced that the divorce rate in the United States sits somewhere close to 50 percent. The point of drawing in these statistics is not to demonize or point fingers but to help establish the context in which many of us are being called to stage the Christian drama. What does the Christian story look like when played well in this arena?

First, if we are to extend the narrative of Jesus into our world we must make every effort to ensure that we are actively and lovingly calling all types of sinners into the community rather than demanding that people give evidence of living the Christian story before being welcomed in. That is to say: we must not reverse our story, and as twenty-first-century insiders place ourselves in the role of the first-century insiders who rebuked Jesus for receiving all the wrong people to himself. Avoiding the role of the arrogant insider is likely to happen only when we are actively cultivating relationships with people outside the community who are not interested in having their lives scripted into Christian roles. The church must become the place where divorced men and women know acceptance and belonging, not to mention help and support. The church must become the place where the sexually promiscuous experience a committed form of love and embrace that prove to be the authentic expressions of acceptance of which serial sexual encounters are only cheap parodies.

Second, we can't surrender that such coming to Jesus, like all coming to Jesus, is for forgiveness of sins. We must not act like sexual sins are in a special heightened category, but neither can we act as though the category of sin does not apply here. Too often, the contemporary church allows its members' and ministers' experience of sexual promiscuity or marital failure to change the Christian story of sex and marriage. Pastors are using their own divorces to create theologies in which God calls people into marriages for a season and then calls them out again; instead, in the Christian narrative we should be proclaiming the good news that God extends forgiveness to the parties of divorce even where they have failed to keep the vows that they made in his name. Christian churches must also acknowledge that in both marriage and divorce there are often victims who need to be consoled and delivered as well as sinners who need rebuke and forgiveness. The gospel of grace and of salvation in Jesus is undermined to the extent that we will not name and ask forgiveness for our sexual and marital sins. Similarly with the issue of sex outside of marriage: the huge numbers of people who do not live up to the ideal of chastity outside marriage and fidelity within it should not function as the interpretive lens that transforms our understanding of where sex fits into the story of the kingdom of God. Instead, here is an opportunity for us to proclaim that even our sexuality is marred by both the guilt and the power of sin—and that in Christ Jesus we can know both forgiveness and freedom.

Finally, we need to start acting like we actually believe that the Christian story line of sexual oneness in lifelong marriage is a better plot than the one on offer in the world around us. This, it seems to me, is the steepest climb facing followers of Jesus. The seductive images of sexual freedom, the deeply engrained voice constantly telling us that we deserve more and better than we already have, the lure of particular relationships that offer us feelings of significance and security—each of these bears fruit in a church that seems unable to convince itself that the sex promoted in the world around us offers a less satisfying course than the path of chastity and fidelity. Here is our challenge: Can our theological imaginations be so transformed that we can start believing that the Christian story of sex is beautiful and depict it as such?

Speaking recently on the issue of faith and globalization, theologian Miroslav Volf addressed one significant way that the major religions of the world all speak with one voice in the face of globalization. Globalization has as a major driving force the idea that the good life consists in the fulfillment of our desires, our experiential satisfaction. Together, however, the religions of the world stand and insist that life is more than pleasure.[3] This is not to deny the importance of pleasure but to insist that all pursuits of pleasure must be properly fitted within a larger overarching framework. In the case of sex, the Christian story describes that place as the lifelong marriage relationship. And when it comes to the hot topic of homosexuality, any plea for a Christian engagement in such sexual practice will also have to fit within this rubric of a committed, lifelong relationship of oneness.

Looking at the biblical landscape, including some Old Testament pictures of God as the husband of Israel and the imagery of adultery and prostitution that the prophets employ to speak of Israel's faithlessness to God, I am struck by the abiding theme of faithfulness as a component piece to biblical pictures of marriage. When we put this together with the cross as the defining image of the Christian story, it seems that the church has something unique and beautiful to offer our culture about both marriage and sex: there is life to be found along the way of giving up our own desires in faithful service to the person we will marry or have already married.

The Coming Kingdom and Christian Hearts

If Jesus's account of marriage seems to draw on creation with surprisingly little room for transformation in light of the coming kingdom of God, it may be because his vision of the eternal kingdom does not include sex. When Sadducees (religious leaders who did not believe in resurrection) question Jesus about resurrection of the dead, they set up a story that draws marriage into question (Mark 12:18–27). In this riddle, seven brothers each take the same woman in turn, in hopes of giving her children, but she ultimately dies childless. So then, whose wife will she be in the resurrection? Jesus answers that in the resurrection people do not marry but are like the angels in heaven. Sexual expression within marriage seems like a penultimate expression of our humanness, one no longer necessary once we are no longer defined by first creation. This is an important warning to us, that none of us place our sexuality (in whatever ways it may be whole or broken) too near to the heart of our identity. Sex is an important part of our life on the earth, but not the most important thing any of us has to say about ourselves.

One final word about sex in Jesus's story of the dominion of God is that Jesus ups the ante on the Ten Commandments' prohibition of adultery. As he does at several points in the Sermon on the Mount, Jesus takes a prohibition against a given action and declares that even the corresponding state of the heart it grows from is sinful. Just as anger is tantamount to murder, so too lust is tantamount to adultery (Matt. 5:27–28). This passage is an important reminder that our sexuality, including our sexual desires, is very much within God's purview when we want to learn what a faithful Christian life looks like. Not only are sexual actions that violate the marriage covenant sinful, but so too are the heart dispositions of lust that lead to such consummating actions. This should caution us when we come across arguments that suggest that our own impulses and desires are reliable guides to expressing ourselves sexually.

A critical stage on the path to spiritually healthy sex lies along the way of naming, confessing, and turning from misguided desires. We must be willing to come to God for forgiveness from sexual sins, healing from sexual brokenness, and freedom from sexual enslavement.

In Paul's letters we see a number of points of agreement with Jesus and also a few more ways of thinking about sex that form a distinctly Christian complement to the basically Judeo-Christian creation framework we find in the Gospels. With both of these on the table, we can put together a robust picture of where sex falls within the plot of God's story, a framework within which our further reflections will have to make sense whatever we say about particular issues such as same-sex relationships.

Looking at sex in Jesus's proclamation of the kingdom of God, we are reminded that Jesus came not merely to include but also to forgive. As the church has grown more gracious about divorce, more lenient about premarital sex, less concerned about extramarital sex, and more accepting of homosexual sex, it has begun to surrender that part of the good news that proclaims to us the extent of God's gracious forgiveness. As proclaimers of the message, we are giving up the powerful tool of acknowledging ourselves to be, in the area of sexuality, in ever-present need of God's grace and mercy.

Sex and the New Creation

Jesus's Framework and Union with Christ

Paul's letters reflect the same Jewish presuppositions that inform Jesus's words: assumptions about sex occurring within a husband-wife relationship and indications that sexual immorality entails sex not within this confine. We also see Paul advocating the lifelong permanency of marriage, though he makes some allowance for divorce.

In 1 Corinthians 7, Paul begins answering questions that the Corinthians posed to him in a letter. He begins by affirming a valuable place for celibacy ("It is good for a man not to touch a woman," 1 Cor. 7:1), but then proceeds to speak of the importance of sex within the marriage relationship. Paul describes sex as a marital duty that each partner owes to the other and considers it a mistake that members of the congregation would indefinitely abstain from sexual relations (1 Cor. 7:2–6). Marriage is an important divine provision for the expression of our sexual desires. First Timothy 4:1–3 also includes marriage as one of the good gifts God has given to be shared in by those who know and believe the good news.

But while 1 Corinthians 7 affirms marriage as the arena for sex within the Christian story, and while it argues in no uncertain terms for the indispensability of sex within that relationship, the passage is far from a celebration of either sex or marriage. First, Paul views sex as a concession to human weakness rather than a celebrated component of our human flourishing. He sees his own way, of celibacy, as the preferred course, with marriage provided for those who cannot do the better thing. God has allotted marriage for those who would burn with desire if they did not have such a sexual outlet (1 Cor. 7:6–7). Here, at any rate, it does not seem that Paul is interested in creating the sort of robust role for marriage and sex within the new creation that he pursues with other ethical issues.

In fact, Paul's reservations about marriage in this particular passage stem from his conviction that Jesus's return to bring this age to a close is imminent. He therefore advocates that people not look to change their station, not look to get married if they are single, not look to get divorced if married, because "the time has been shortened" (1 Cor. 7:29). In such a context, it is better to be unfettered by concerns of the marriage relationship, to be completely free to please only the Lord (1 Cor. 7:32–35). As he gives this advice, however, he distances his authoritative teaching as an apostle from the opinion he expresses about whether to get married: "I have no command from the Lord, but give an opinion as one who is trustworthy by the Lord's mercy" (1 Cor. 7:25). Paul advises us to take his opinion about the limited value of marriage with a grain of salt, and we do well to take him up on his offer in light of the mistakenness of his impression about the nearness of Jesus's return.

But where Paul does give more authoritative instructions, the passage works within the framework that Jesus advocates in Mark: sex is presumed to occur within marriage, sex is an important part of marriage, and a marriage relationship is presumed to be an enduring one that God's people should not seek to terminate. This last point is made several times in the passage, as Paul states the general advice that no believer should initiate divorce with his or her spouse, but makes allowance for divorce should an unbelieving spouse leave (1 Cor. 7:10–17). Moreover, when he gives his advice about believers not initiating divorce, he claims that he is passing on Jesus's instructions (1 Cor. 7:10). Paul is self-consciously placing his instruction within the framework affirmed by Jesus.

Old Creation and New Union

Turning to Ephesians 5, we find an extended metaphor of marriage as imaging Christ's relationship to the church. The passage references the Genesis 2 creation-marriage text, as Jesus does in Mark 10. The repetition of Genesis 2 in both Jesus's teaching and Paul's in Ephesians underscores its continuing importance as a script for how sex fits into the plot of God's story. And there is more to be said in light of Jesus's saving work as well. The physical union spoken of in Genesis 2 provides a point of contact for Paul's idea of spiritual union with

Christ. Paul's convictions about how we are saved, by being united with Jesus, add depth to how we are to understand the significance of marital oneness in the Christian story.

In Ephesians 5, the oneness that Genesis speaks of, and that Jesus affirms, is likened to the oneness that the church experiences in union with Christ. The two relationships therefore become images of each other: marriage a picture of union with Christ, and union with Christ a picture of marriage. In particular, the cruciform gospel narrative shapes the love that the husband and wife are to express to each other within the marriage relationship. What Christ was and is for the church, what the church is to be for the world, and what Christians are supposed to be in community with one another is what husbands and wives are to model in their relationship as well. The Christian definition of love as self-giving for the life of the other finds uniquely apt expression in the well-lived marriage union.

Thus, without in any way undermining first creation, new creation in Christ lends a distinctively Christian cast to an otherwise Judeo-Christian story of marital oneness.

The ultimate criterion for us, as we strive to faithfully extend the Jesus story into the present, is not first creation but new creation. In this case, tracing the trajectory through Jesus and Paul, we find that old creation is simultaneously affirmed and transformed. Marriage is about a man leaving his parents and being joined (sexually and otherwise) to his wife and thus creating a one-flesh union, but this one-flesh union now pictures not merely the return of man and woman to their one-flesh origin (as in Genesis) but also the return of humanity to its holy oneness with the Creator God; it images our return to the family of God through union with God's firstborn Son.

Sexual Sin and Union with Christ

For Paul, as for Jesus, inappropriate sexual expression is one of a number of stereotypical sins that mark those who are failing to live in accordance with the life of holiness that God requires of God's people. Sexual sins are often found in "vice lists," catalogs of sins that characterize lives lived out of step with God's desires. Thus, when Jesus is talking about sins that spring from the heart in Mark 7, he talks about not only evil thoughts, murder, stealing, and pride, but also adultery in particular and sexual immorality more generally (Mark 7:21–22). Similarly Paul, in 1 Corinthians 6, lists activities that give evidence of a person's failure to take hold of the coming kingdom of God. There he includes not only idolatry, stealing, and covetousness but also sexual sins of adultery and fornication (vv. 9–10). We will return to the words that possibly denote homosexual activity in the next chapter.

Here, I simply want to point out that there are consequences for accepting the framework that both Paul and Jesus hold for sexual expression within the story of God. If faithful sexual expression occurs within a lifelong marriage relationship of faithful oneness, then our engagements in sexual expressions that occur outside this framework make us culpable before God. Not only the breaking of our commitment to fidelity within marriage (adultery) but also sexual activity without that marriage commitment (fornication) indicate both our human brokenness with its concomitant need for healing and our human sinfulness with its concomitant need for forgiveness. With the same position found not only in Jesus and Paul but also in Acts (15:29; 21:25), the Pastoral Epistles (1 Tim. 1:10), Hebrews (12:16; 13:4), and Revelation (throughout), the church must own up to its responsibility to declare that God does, in fact, care quite deeply about what we do with our bodies, whether out in the open or behind closed bedroom doors.

No attempt to speak for God on matters of sex can claim that God has no interest in this aspect of the bodily life that God created and gave to humanity for its own good. Moreover, no attempt to speak as the community of Jesus's followers can finally deny that inappropriate sexual expression is sin that points us toward our need for repentance and forgiveness.

We have had an opportunity to explore how letters bearing Paul's name contain both the general framework of sexual oneness within lifelong marriage and the more specifically Christian framework of sexual and marital oneness as a picture of Christ's union with the church. Similarly, in talking about sexual sins we have not only the generalized condemnations of adultery and sexual immorality but also a specific line of discussion that draws out the ramifications of sexual infidelity for our union with Christ.

In 1 Corinthians 6:12–20, Paul seeks to dispel the notion that what we might do with our bodies is irrelevant to our salvation in Christ. Quite to the contrary: the bodily resurrection of Jesus becomes a divine statement that the body is no mere container for the "spirit" that "really matters." Our bodies matter to God. God will raise them up again. And he has Spiritually joined us to the risen body of Jesus. Bodies, and our bodies' union with other bodies, are part of God's saving story. Bodies are not incidental; "the Lord is for the body": the resurrected Lord Jesus is raised to rule the world by means of the embodied church that serves as the manifestation of his risen body on the earth. What Paul says about sexual immorality is comprehensible only within the context of this inherently embodied understanding of salvation.

Our bodies, Paul says, have a purpose. That purpose is known through our union with the bodily raised Jesus. Our bodies are given to us not for the purpose of sexual immorality, but for the purpose of being joined to and serving the resurrected Lord (1 Cor. 6:13). Just as sexual oneness with a spouse serves as a prohibition against being sexually joined to anyone other than the one we have been united to, so oneness with Christ serves as a prohibition against other, illicit unions. To be joined in sexual immorality (specifically, in this case, to be joined to a prostitute) is to amputate a portion of Christ's body and make it the member of the other body we've joined ourselves to sexually (1 Cor. 6:15–17).

Here we discover that one-flesh union is something that happens not only within the context of marriage but any time one has a sexual relationship. The reason sex must occur within the framework of fidelity to one lifelong partner is that all sexual unions create one new flesh out of the two. As Paul works it out here, such an encounter with a prostitute (or, likely, anyone outside the body of Christ) entails sinning against Christ's body by taking our bodies away from him and joining them to another person. Similarly, sex outside the oneness of marriage takes people away from the union that is theirs (or that is to be theirs) with their spouses by making them one with another.

Because sex creates a one-flesh union, all sexual sin is sin "against one's own body" (1 Cor. 6:18–20). What we choose to do with our bodies we also cause Christ and the Spirit to be entailed in. This sheds some light on Paul's later word that those who marry are to be married "in the Lord" (1 Cor. 7:39): the assumption must be that when one joins one's body to the body of another, both bodies will already be joined to the body of Christ. Barring this, the marriage bond has the power to remove a member from the body of Christ.

Sex in the Christian Story

The discussion of union with Christ underscores the importance of articulating a place for sex within the Christian story. The powerful currents of our cultural tides would pull the church into a very different framework for understanding sexuality. Tying this framework to not only an ancient creation story but also our saving union with Christ raises the stakes considerably. If the Christian life is defined as a life lived under the lordship of the King of God's kingdom, or if it is defined as participating in the new creation through our union with that creation's first New Creature, then we must plot sex also within those stories.

The Christian claim is audacious. It is a story of life along the way of the cross, a narrative that claims we can find our life only by losing it. Too often, Christians have believed the competing narrative that speaks of finding greater security, a greater sense of significance, a greater amount of pleasure, or even greater love, through sex outside the lifelong bond. We have not lived as though the Christian story really offers a more compelling vision of reality than the alternatives that confront us. We need to get this story straight because it is tightly connected with the gospel. We are an embodied people. We are a people created to be joined to another body. We are a people meant to be given security through such a lasting physical, sexual union. And we are a people meant to be given eternal security through lasting union with the physical body of the resurrected Christ.

As we turn now to take up the issue of homosexuality, we must insist with equal clarity that any would-be Christian position must make good on the demand to be a truly Christian narration of the story of sex.

9

Homosexuality under the Reign of Christ

> Love love is gonna lead you by the hand
> into a white and soundless place.
> Now we see things as in a mirror dimly
> then we shall see each other face to face.
>
> —The Mountain Goats
> "Love Love Love"[1]

The Bible as a whole does not have much to say about homosexuality. Jesus says nothing about it. (We will reflect more on the significance of this below.) From the Old Testament there is, of course, Leviticus 20:13, which calls male homosexual intercourse an "abomination." But to my conservative friends I say that it will never do to appeal to this passage as a foundational argument against homosexual unions in the current-day church. To do so ignores the way that this particular manifestation of Old Testament law is part of a larger framework that most Christians no longer regard as binding. Few will stand by the notion that a couple should be excluded from the people of God if they have sex while the woman is menstruating (Lev. 20:18), for example. If it is replied that the labeling of homosexual intercourse as an abomination is the key, then we are forced to wrestle with how Deuteronomy 14:3 uses precisely the same Hebrew word to refer to the eating of unclean food—dietary laws that the church has confessed since the first century to have been removed in Christ. Christians regularly claim that the laws in Leviticus no longer provide us with the standards for demarcating who is faithfully living in obedience to God—and such interpretive moves are surely correct. We cannot, then, cherry-pick verses that support particular positions we wish to continue advocating. We will have to assess homosexual actions from a later point in the narrative.

Paul: Homosexuality as Anticreation

There are three or four passages where homosexuality is in view in the New Testament: Romans 1:18–27, 1 Corinthians 6:9–10, and perhaps 1 Timothy 1:8–11 and Jude 7. We can see from this list that Paul is, in fact, the main voice when it comes to the New Testament teaching on homosexuality.

Anticreation in Romans 1

Paul comes closest to situating homosexuality within a larger theological frame of reference in Romans 1:26–27. In the flow of the passage, people first suppress the knowledge of God; God responds to this by giving people over to idolatry; and as a result of this further denial of God, God gives people over to homosexual practice: women desiring each other and men desiring each other (Rom. 1:18–27). In other words, in Romans 1 homosexuality is depicted not as a sin awaiting future wrath but as a manifestation of God's present-day wrath against an idolatrous world.

The next important dynamic to recognize in this passage is that it tells a narrative of the undoing of creation. Romans 1:20 indicates that God is known through the creation itself. Then, in echo of the Adam and Eve fall narrative in Genesis 3, Romans 1:22 speaks of humanity becoming foolish in its attempt to become wise (compare Gen. 3:6, "When she saw that the fruit was desirable . . . to make one wise"). Such folly bears fruit in the worshiping of idols in the forms of various creatures—a list of created animals that echoes the creation story in Genesis 1. The order of creation is inverted when people serve the creatures they were created to rule rather than God, who gave humanity the creatures to rule on God's behalf. This idolatrous worship of creatures leads to God handing people over to the shame of unnatural inclinations in homosexual desires and actions (Rom. 1:26–27).

The disordering that begins when people refuse to do the most natural thing in the world (recognize and worship the God to whom nature testifies) culminates in the reversal of natural sexual desires and, more generally, disordered minds that approve the things that should not be done (Rom. 1:26–28). In this anticreation narrative, homosexual activity is one element of the nadir humanity descends to as it bears the consequences of denying the Creator God.

A third element of Paul's argument is crucial for us to bear in mind. Paul is echoing a typical Jewish denunciation of gentiles. An argument that runs very much the same is found in the Jewish writing *The Wisdom of Solomon*. There too we discover that homosexuality, and sexual immorality more generally, is a result of idolatry that, itself, stems from rejecting the Creator God.

But the crucial difference between *Wisdom* and Romans is that *Wisdom* sets the table with these sins in order to then turn to praise God for how different the Jewish people are as the objects of God's favor. In Romans, it seems that chapter 1 is the setup for a very different interpretation of Israel's story. Romans 1 sets a trap that's sprung in chapter 2. The point is not "this is how evil *they* are, so now we can rejoice about how righteous *we* are"; instead, Paul turns the tables: "Therefore you are without excuse, every one of you who passes judgment, because in those things for which you condemn another you also condemn yourself—for you yourself practice the same things!" (Rom. 2:1).

One of the implications of this rhetorical trap is that we read the passage wrongly if we take the condemnations of chapter 1 as grounds for a sense of moral superiority. The point of the passage in context is that people who would feel morally superior (law-keeping Jews) to those whom Paul describes in chapter 1 (sinful gentiles) actually fall under the same verdict of condemnation that they themselves issue. Many of us miss the point by reading Romans 1 as a cause for a smug sense of moral superiority.

At the same time, it would be a mistake to allow the rhetoric of the passage to obscure its claim. The point is not that the Jews were judgmental and therefore those who practice the sins in chapter 1 should not be seen as sinful after all. Instead, the point is that Paul's fellow

Jews are judgmental and should not be because they are equally guilty. The point is not that there is nothing to fear in a coming judgment but that we all exist under the peril described. In the more extended argument of Romans 1:18–3:20, the point is to show that everyone is guilty of sin and in need of the rectifying death of Jesus to enable us to be part of God's family.

Thus, while the rhetoric minimizes the leverage one can find in Romans 1:26–27 for a holier-than-thou sense of moral superiority, it does so not by exonerating homosexual activity as not really sinful after all but by claiming that all are guilty of such sins and therefore in need of God's grace and forgiveness.[2]

The point is that the sins that Jews would recognize as causing the gentiles to fall short of God's glory are similar to the sins they are culpable of: All sin and fall short of the glory of God (Rom. 3:23; compare Rom. 1:21, 23). All are alike in the dock of anticreation, failing to glorify God and give thanks—a situation that all need rectified by the new creation inaugurated in the death and resurrection of Jesus. In such a narrative of God's creation-restoring work through Christ, homosexuality sits as one element of the larger canvas of the disordered world that needs to be set to rights. The picture of Genesis 2 is not restored merely when people preserve their sexual activity for the one person they will be faithful to for life; it is restored when a man leaves his house to be joined to a woman as his wife.

Both Male Partners in 1 Corinthians 6?

Paul is consistent in his condemnation of homosexual activity. In 1 Corinthians 6, both partners in male homosexual activity seem to be implicated in Paul's list of the unrighteous who will not inherit the kingdom of God: "Neither fornicators nor idolaters nor adulterers nor 'effeminate' nor 'homosexuals' nor thieves nor covetous nor drunkards . . . will inherit the kingdom of God" (1 Cor. 6:9). The terms in quotation marks are often taken to refer to the two male partners in male homosexual activity. I'll start with the second.

The Greek word *arsenokoites*, often rendered "homosexuals" in our English Bibles, is regularly taken in contemporary scholarship to mean the active partner in male homosexual intercourse. Dale Martin has written a popular rebuttal of this, indicating that nobody actually knows what the word meant, and that the context clues from other usages favor something more along the lines of abuse of power.[3] Martin's argument, however, skips by two important pieces of evidence. First, notwithstanding the other sorts of sins (such as economic exploitation) in the company of which the term might appear in other ancient vice lists, in Paul's vice list in 1 Corinthians 6 the word is found precisely where we anticipate finding sexual sins. Another important lacuna in Martin's study is that he does not deal with the cognate word, *arrenokoites*, of which the biblical word is a variant.[4] It seems the word has basically two meanings. In one group of texts it seems to mean something along the lines of conspiring against another person (the abuse-of-power meaning that Martin cites), and in another group of texts it clearly does concern sex and quite possibly male homosexual relations. If I may venture a vulgar comparison, it seems that the range of meanings for *arsenokoites* is roughly equivalent to our phrase "someone who screws someone else." The word carries sexual connotations, likely a homosexual connotation in Greek, but also a range of meanings for those who wrong others in various ways.

The first word, *malakos*, is sometimes translated "effeminate" (KJV, NASB) or "male prostitutes" (NRSV, NIV 1984). This word normally means "soft," or "effeminate," and has been taken in tandem with *arsenokoites* to indicate the passive partner in a male homosexual encounter. Martin is concerned with the translation of this word as well. He makes a convincing case that the word does not mean "male prostitutes"; however, his study does not eliminate being on the receiving end of a male homosexual encounter as one meaning of the word. Instead, Martin's study includes a host of other ancient notions of "effeminate" characteristics as possible connotations in addition to its meaning in the realm of male homosexual relationships. As he concludes one leg of his study, "all penetrated men were *malakoi*, but not all *malakoi* were penetrated men."[5]

All this suggests that the common reading of the passage today is viable: Paul condemns both partners in male homosexual activity in 1 Corinthians 6:9. Martin offers some counterevidence, but in the end suggests that, yes, the Bible does condemn homosexuality but for reasons that we should reject in our own day and age. The depictions of homosexual activity that fall under such headings as "effeminate" derive from a general disregard of women, such that calling someone effeminate is an insult. Such sexism, Martin argues, should not be the basis of our own ethical assessments. And surely he is right about that.

The story, however, is larger than the historical derivations of a couple of Greek words. In Paul's understanding of the narrative that arcs from first creation to new creation, the primal story of male-female marriage is an inseparable part of the framework of God's provision for human sexual expression.

By placing his condemnation of homosexuality in this list of those who "will not inherit the kingdom of God," Paul makes the claim that homosexual practice is not a faithful way to enact the story between inauguration of new creation and its consummation. As we will discuss in more detail below, this is one major way that the issue of homosexuality is qualitatively different from the issue of women in church leadership. Whereas homosexual activity regularly appears on lists of ways that one might show oneself to be straying from the path that leads to inheriting the kingdom, neither being a woman nor leading as a woman ever appears in such contexts.

In the Christian life that Paul advocates, we strive to take hold of the cross as a way of life in order to bring the fruits of new creation to bear on the present. A life defined by these vices indicates that one is disqualified from new creation by virtue of living according to the flesh of the old creation rather than according to the Spirit of the new. This fits the picture he paints in Romans 1, where homosexuality is a sign of the world gone wrong, a world that God is setting to rights by the work of Christ through the power of the Spirit.

We must return now to Jesus.

The Silence of Jesus

One of the most striking pieces of data for many who study the issue of homosexuality is that Jesus is silent about such practice. We have seen that Jesus comments on other aspects of human sexuality and that these comments make it clear that how we express ourselves sexually is a crucial component of our faithful life within the kingdom of

God. But on the issue of homosexual expressions he says nothing. What are we to make of this?

Silence of Consent?

As the old saying goes, "Those who are silent are presumed to consent." But making an argument from the silence of the Bible is notoriously difficult, with the result that such arguments tend to carry little weight to any besides those who offer them. Often, those advocating for an embracing posture toward homosexuality draw attention to Jesus's silence on the issue as a significant contrast to Paul's condemnations. By failing to condemn the practice, so this line of reasoning goes, Jesus either tacitly endorses it or at least leaves wide open the possibility that faithful discipleship might include homosexual practice. On this reading of the evidence, the old maxim leads us to assert that Jesus's silence allows one to presume his consent to homosexual practice.

It seems to me, however, that Jesus's silence makes precisely the opposite point. Both Jesus and Paul were Jews. The major difference between their ministries, as we have had cause to remark on throughout our study, is that Jesus ministered primarily within the bounds of the Jewish people whereas Paul took the message to the nations. This difference in context accounts for Paul's need to articulate what Jesus could take for granted. Among Jewish people, the assumption is that homosexuality is a perversion of God's order of creation. The creation narrative that undergirds Jesus's and Paul's positive framework for sex within lifelong marriage is the same creation narrative that grounds the condemnations of homosexuality in Jewish law. Jesus's Jewish contemporaries shared this biblical foundation. I do believe that the old maxim about silence creating an assumption of consent is helpful here. But we have to recognize that the opinion among Jesus's contemporaries in the face of which he was silent and to which he thereby gave his tacit consent was the idea that homosexual practice is a violation of the divine intention for sexual expression.

Put differently, much of what we know about Jesus and Jesus's teachings we know because his actions and words put him in conflict with his contemporaries. He ate with the wrong people, allowed the wrong people to touch him, stretched and/or broke the rules concerning the

Sabbath by healing and allowing his disciples to harvest grain. When Jesus disagreed with the traditional interpretations of the law, he provocatively did things to indicate this and directly taught so as to draw attention to it—and such deviations from the norm drive the conflicts we see in the Gospels that ultimately leave Jesus hanging on a cross. The silence of Jesus on the issue of homosexuality is powerful, because if he had opposed the Jewish law on this point we surely would have heard about it.

Inclusive Social Justice?

But if Jesus is silent on the issue directly, there are other dynamics of his ministry that seem to open the door for full inclusion of practicing homosexuals within the community of his followers. One common argument toward this end is that homosexuals are the modern-day lepers: social outcasts whom Jesus will receive to himself despite the rejection such people experience even at the hands of the people of God. Another is that full inclusion of homosexuals is a demand of the social justice that was demonstrated in the last chapter to be a hallmark of Jesus's ministry. Let's look at each in turn.

The "modern-day leper" argument is one that does not well serve the cause of those who wish to see homosexuals more fully included in the church. In our discussion of Jesus's ministry as one of inclusion, we saw that Jesus's embrace is a transforming embrace, one that accepts all the wrong people, to be sure, but also one that cleanses, heals, and forgives. In other words, the people who gather around Jesus are embraced not because they are good enough already, but because they recognize their need for transformation and forgiveness. And so with the issue of leprosy itself, the texts play much more into the hands of those who do not see homosexual practice as a viable option in the church: such outcasts can come to Jesus and find mercy, forgiveness, healing, and transformation so that they can be part of God's healed and restored people. The lepers are never simply embraced as they are restored to community. Their leprosy is healed. I am not here advocating that this application of the leprosy passages to the issue of homosexuality is the way they should be read in all our churches today. I am, rather, highlighting why the argument that homosexuals are "modern-day lepers" does not serve the cause of full inclusion of practicing homosexuals.

What, then, about issues of justice more generally conceived? A recent online editorial from the Religion News Service echoed popular sentiment with its assessment that modern-day debates about homosexuality mirror the church's debates, and splits, over issues of slavery in the nineteenth century. On the one hand, there are those claiming the moral high ground of equality and justice—even if it means discounting some of what the Bible says—and on the other hand, there are those claiming that the Bible speaks clearly and therefore refusing to acknowledge the viability of the more inclusive position. Moreover, this ecclesiastical debate mirrors a debate about justice taking place in the culture and politics more generally.[6]

Such arguments carry a powerful appeal. Christians who are able to see both that grave injustice was perpetrated in the African slave trade and that the Bible was an instrument of that injustice are wary of making the same mistake again. But there are striking differences between the debates that must not be discounted. First, from beginning to end the Bible deals with homosexuality as something that makes us culpable before God. The same cannot be said with respect to issues of racial or gender difference. In other words, debates about homosexuality that arise around issues such as ordination are in a different category from those surrounding full inclusion of women in ministry—being a woman is never condemned as sinful, never listed in a vice list. We need to keep the category of sin operative in our discussions of sexuality in the church, and we have to acknowledge that the Bible's placement of homosexuality into this category makes it a unique case when compared with (other) justice issues.

Another important difference between homosexuality and issues of slavery or women in church leadership is that the New Testament's depiction of homosexuality stands as a voice crying out in opposition to its surrounding culture. In these other cases, by contrast, Scripture seems to be reflecting broader cultural mores, perhaps unreflectively. The broader acceptance of homosexuality in our own day and age does not, of itself, place us in a fundamentally different position from the ancient Mediterranean world in which the biblical strictures against homosexuality were written. The churches that are moving to embrace homosexuality often seem unwilling to articulate any sexual ethic that stands in opposition to the prevailing culture. But the New Testament picture of heterosexual lifelong fidelity and oneness has always stood as a countermovement to the prevailing winds of its day.

Finally, homosexuality is different from these justice issues in that there is no biblical countervoice. Whereas in the issue of women in leadership there are both indications and counterindications, and in the issue of slavery there is a gospel dynamic of freedom that undercuts the institution as a whole and also direct evidence of just such an application of the gospel to the world, with homosexuality the Bible speaks with one consistent voice in both Testaments. Thus, in stark contrast to the slavery debates, in which each side could take a piece of biblical evidence about the particular issue and apply it to its cause, there is no direct biblical evidence that can be so wielded by those who would advocate a more affirming stance toward homosexual practice in the church.[7]

Where Do We Go from Here?

Arguing for Homosexual Practice

The direct biblical evidence is not well poised to support the argument that practicing homosexuals should be affirmed in their lifestyle as living in a manner congruous with the Christian story. The Bible's countercultural voice seems well disposed to play the same role in our world as it did in the ancient: articulating a vision for sexual expression that calls all of us to die to what we may prefer to do, believing that, in such obedient death to instant gratification, wandering hearts, and desires for partners that are embraced to our own harm, God offers us new life.

Is there, then, no argument to be made in affirmation of homosexual practice? For all that the biblical evidence weighs against it, I do believe that a case can be made. Here is what such a line of reasoning would need to consist of, as I see it, to faithfully participate in the biblical narrative.

First, advocates of Christian homosexual practice must be willing to articulate not a sweeping endorsement of all homosexual engagement but instead one that is framed within the biblical standard of lifetime loyalty to one partner who is also in Christ. This means that a number of denominations that are currently wrestling with the issue of homosexuality are going to have to backtrack from the concessions they made in the wake of the mid-twentieth-century's "sexual revolution," and return to the call for abstinence outside marriage and a diligent perseverance of the marriages that members of the church have entered into. If there is going to be a Christian affirmation of homosexuality, it must take place within a more robust biblical theology of sexuality than many churches are currently endor ing.

Second, advocates of Christian homosexual practice will have to find more compelling ways to plot homosexual partnerships within the narrative of God's story. One such avenue might be to take into consideration some of the narrative dynamics by which the new creation is impinging on the old. I will often describe the Christian life as a matter of grabbing hold of the future and bringing it to bear on the present. But if this is the case, then the hints that the coming kingdom of God will not be a matter of marrying and giving in marriage (Mark 12:25), that in this new world order there is no longer, as in the first, "male and female" (Gal. 3:28), may provide an avenue for reconsidering the finality of the biblical depiction of heterosexual marriage as the only viable Christian option.

But if one were to articulate a position of homosexual practice within a more generally acceptable framework of sexuality, and if one were to cultivate a nuanced theology that gave weight to the overarching biblical narrative while arguing against the particular strictures we encounter there, how would we finally be able to determine that this was a viable Christian depiction of God's intentions for sexual expression? It would, in the end, require the church as a whole to experience and/or recognize the inclusion of practicing homosexuals within its number to be an affirming work of the Spirit of God.[8] There is precedent for the church's overturning of the biblical requirements for full inclusion and affirmation within God's people: the idea that gentiles did not have to be circumcised to become part of the people of God flies in the face of a huge swath of Old Testament teaching. But the Spirit of God gave divine testimony to God's approval of these gentiles without their becoming circumcised Jews—testimony that had to be given time and again, and even then was not received without a fight (see Acts 10–11, 15, and all of Galatians).

Indeed, if there is anything genuinely new about our situation in the twenty-first century when it comes to the question of homosexuality, it is not that our culture has more of a place for it than the prejudiced ancients, and it is not even that recent science suggests that we are predisposed to certain sexual preferences. The real difference is that there are Christians who are both striving to faithfully follow God and simultaneously living within committed homosexual relationships. This is part of the current-day experience of the church, and one that must be carefully weighed when we consider whether homosexuality is, as Scripture seems to indicate, a deviation from what is acceptable before God or whether it is, as its advocates would claim, a new work of the Spirit in a surprising extension of the mission of God.

Love Your Neighbor as Yourself

In the first draft of this chapter, I went straight into the conclusion. But I realized that such a move failed to tell the full story. A Christian culture dominated by believing the right things about Jesus too often forgets that believing in Christ and walking in love are inseparable. In this case, followers of Jesus have too often forgotten that articulating a position on homosexuality does not in itself answer the questions: What does it mean for me to love my homosexual neighbor as myself? What does it look like for me to do unto my homosexual neighbor as I would have done to myself? Here again I look to the traditionalists and beckon them to a more faithful embodiment of the gospel. If the faithful Christian practice of committed homosexuals provides the strongest argument in favor of the church's blessing of homosexual unions, the rancorous, destructive, and otherwise unloving behavior of the traditionalists is one of the strongest indications that they are not on the side of God.

By this point in our examination of the storied nature of the Christian life we have seen enough to know that theology that produces bad behavior loses its claim to be giving faithful stage direction to the Christian drama. If the conviction that engaging in homosexual intercourse is sinful bears only the fruit visible in "God Hates Fags" signs and rallying support for ballot measures that seek to eliminate civil equality between homosexual couples and their heterosexual counterparts, then it has failed as a dramatization of the story of Jesus.

To work out the idea of loving our homosexual neighbor, we need to look at two interrelated questions. First, do these neighbors of ours really qualify as those we are called to love in the name of Jesus? And second, if so, what does such love look like?

On the question of whether they qualify, Luke tells a marvelous parable that preempts any impulse we might have to write homosexuals out of our embodiment of the story. Indeed, the story seems particularly well suited to addressing the issue of homosexuality, because the setup consists not only of Jesus's instruction to love our neighbor as ourselves but also of a religiously impeccable person's attempt to limit the scope of that love.

Jesus tells the parable of the good Samaritan in order to respond to a scribe. Scribes are experts in the legal traditions of Israel. And this particular scribe has just been commended by Jesus for saying that the way to eternal life is to love God with heart, soul, strength, and mind, and to love one's neighbor as oneself (Luke 10:25–28). But then the scribe presses further: who, exactly, is my neighbor? And here's where the story begins to turn, not merely because Jesus gives a somewhat surprising answer, but because there is a perfectly good answer already embedded in the command to love one's neighbor. "Love your neighbor as yourself" is a quote from Leviticus 19:18. The phrase before it is, "You shall not hold a grudge against any one of your people" (literally, "the sons of your people"). Will Jesus uphold the limited scope of the command as it focuses on the people of God?

Jesus turns the scribe's expectation on its head in two ways. First, Jesus appeals not to another passage of Scripture but instead to his own story as the authoritative source of knowledge about who a neighbor is. And, second, the story itself illustrates not love within the approved people of God, but love that erupts outside the borders of the community of faith—even while the people of God are dutifully keeping the law. We will never understand the full implications of the parable of the good Samaritan until we recognize that it depicts the religious insiders avoiding love for the sake of keeping the law that God gave to Israel.

The story is a familiar one: a man is robbed on a highway and left for dead. Passing by, a priest and a Levite both leave the man where he lies. Why would they do this? Because they were scrupulous in their obedience toward God. The man is described as "left for dead," which means that as far as anyone could see by looking at him, he was dead. Death in the Jewish and biblical traditions conveys what came to be called "corpse impurity." And here's the thing about corpse impurity: the biblical law forbids priests from contracting corpse impurity from anyone other than their nearest relatives, and the high priest was not even allowed to contract impurity by coming near to his dead father or mother (Lev. 21:1–15). So when Jesus tells the story about priests and temple-serving Levites walking on the far side of the road, he is telling a story of people who were fulfilling their duty to follow the law of God.

In the end, it is the outsider, the Samaritan, who helps the half-dead man, surrendering his own money and promising to pay whatever the cost of nursing him back to health might be (Luke 10:33–35). And so a story that was prompted by the question, "What must I do to inherit eternal life?" ends with the religious outsider standing as the one who has shown mercy and who has thereby fulfilled the great command to "love your neighbor as yourself." While the priest and the Levite were scrupulously keeping God's law, the Samaritan was showing himself to be a neighbor to the man in need.

No clearer story could be told to show us that our predilection for keeping our love to ourselves runs counter to the way of Jesus. When we restrict our love to those who roughly fall within the boundaries of those who are living lives pleasing to God, or when we use biblical regulations as reasons for excluding ourselves from the duty of providing for a person in need, we violate the command to love our neighbor as ourselves. We may even be showing ourselves disqualified for the eternal life that comes to those who love God and love neighbor.

Put differently for our present discussion: the homosexual is the Christian's neighbor, and Christians' duty is to love homosexuals as ourselves. If the result of our biblical convictions is that we stand on the streets with "God Hates Fags" signs, we are not holding a Christian position but are using a Christian idea to prop up our rebellion against the life that Jesus calls us to.

What, then, might it look like to love our homosexual neighbors? I would suggest a few things here for the day and time I am writing in, though hopefully the particular things will embody ways of thinking Christianly that can be applied to other contexts in which the question, What does love look like? is confronting God's people.

Recently the issue of homosexual marriage has been a hot topic in the United States. The issue of state-sanctioned marriage versus state-approved civil partnerships is complex. But there are a few issues that surround the debate that Christians should be asking themselves using this grid: What does it look like to do to my homosexual neighbor what I would want done to me? And, as we answer this question, we should feel ourselves compelled to stand on the front lines in securing the result. Here are some issues I wrestle with:

> *If I arrived at a hospital unconscious, would I want my life partner to be admitted to my bedside? If my partner were taken to the hospital in this state, would I want to be admitted?* If the answer to these questions is yes, then we as Christians should be actively ensuring that our homosexual neighbors are afforded such access to their partners in the hospital.
>
> *If the people I loved and trusted counseled me against marrying a certain person, would I want them to have the power to stop that marriage against my will and against the will of my would-be partner?* If the answer to that question is no, then we as Christians should seek to have removed the power that outsiders might have to keep consenting adults from being united in something like marriage.
>
> *If partners decide that one is going to work and one is going to stay home, do I want the employer or insurance company to have the power to keep the stay-at-home partner off the employed partner's insurance plan? If my wife's employer (in my case, the State of California) found out that her husband works in a field that discriminates on the basis of religious conviction—which is antithetical to their state-mandated religiously inclusive stance—should they be allowed to withhold survivor benefits or insurance benefits based on these differences?* If the answer to these questions is no, then we have an obligation under the reign of Christ to see to it that our homosexual neighbors are not eliminated from such partner benefits for their differing convictions and lifestyles.

One thing that scholars sometimes point out is that Jesus's Golden Rule ("Do unto others as you would have them do unto you" [Matt. 7:12]) is paralleled in other great traditions. To an extent this is true. Often, however, we find in other traditions the admonition that we avoid the negative: "*Don't* do unto others what you *wouldn't* want them to do to you." I think this difference is important. As I see it,

Jesus's positive command compels us to positive action where we might otherwise simply refrain from acting negatively. In other words, it is not a sufficiently faithful enactment of the Christian story to refrain from going out with the "God Hates Fags" sign. Abstaining from such action is refraining from doing unto others what I would not have them do to me. But it is not yet doing what I would like to have done for me. It is incumbent on us to show the homosexuals in our communities that we will work tirelessly for them to have what we would never stand to be deprived of ourselves.

And this brings me to one final biblical story, the story of the centurion who comes to ask Jesus for his servant's healing (Matt. 8:5–13). One thing that strikes me about this story is that it is not simply the story about an outsider with faith. Behind such a picture of the faithful outsider stands a Jesus to whom an outsider could come, knowing that Jesus would respond favorably. And here are the questions I have for the church as we strive to faithfully narrate the story of Jesus in the twenty-first century: Have we loved and served the people around us, have we worked for their good, with sufficient passion that someone who is not part of our community would come to us and ask for help? Do we show the world that our deepest concern is to spread abroad the love of God? Or have we allowed the cosmic story of the kingdom of God to become a quaint, domesticated skit put on by the children only at our own family reunions?

Concluding Thoughts

Clearly, the issues taken up in this chapter are contentious in the current-day life of the church. Part of what I hope to accomplish here is a plotting of not only a position but also a way of thinking about sexuality within the narrative of God's work to redeem the world for himself in Christ. A major concern I have as I listen to the debate unfold around me is the insufficiently Christian way people are advocating for certain positions.

To the liberals I say that it will never do to cordon off God from certain areas of our lives or to simply baptize our impulses or past actions. At a conference I recently attended, a world-renowned theologian quipped, when asked about homosexuality, that he did not think God was concerned about what we did behind the closed doors of our bedrooms. The notion that we can close a door and thereby exclude ourselves from the concerns of God is antithetical to the biblical narrative of the God who created us as embodied souls, who draws us into loving relationship with himself as the God who gave us our bodies as well as our souls, who demonstrates his commitment to the body in the raising of Jesus from the dead, and who summons us to live the gospel narrative by yielding both body and heart to the way of Jesus. Claiming that God has no concern about sex stands in sharpest antithesis to the biblical narrative. Indeed, it seems to me that if the pro-homosexuality argument is going to work within the church, it will have to argue the opposite point from that asserted by this theologian. If homosexuality is a viable path of faithful discipleship, it must be because God wants the very best for us, even behind our closed bedroom doors.

I find similarly insufficient the idea that having a desire means that God is okay with our acting on it. We have seen throughout our journey through the narratives of Jesus and Paul that the gospel story calls us to repentance for our orientation toward grasping after power. We have seen that it calls us to repentance for our orientation toward running roughshod over the environment. We have seen that it calls us to repentance for wanting to veer far from the recognition that we are a people who need to be called repeatedly to repentance and judgment. We have seen that it warns us about the sinful lusts of our hearts.

But on the other side of the argument, we must not be lulled into thinking that we hold our positions simply because we live in obedience to the Bible. Some of the biblical strictures against homosexual relations are embedded within Old Testament legal codes that we no longer identify as binding for the life of the church. Indeed, this debate takes us into the very heart of our commitment to the Bible. What, in fact, is the Bible, and what are we to do with it? The Bible is not a rule book but a story of God's plan of redemption. We affirm and oppose various actions as being either more or less fitting to the biblical narrative. While the position against homosexuality clearly has the better of the biblical argument, that might not mean that the church has thereby received the last word that God has to say on the subject.

And, perhaps more important, I want to say to those who stand on the traditional side of this position that how we hold our theology is as important as its content. We deny the gospel if our conviction that someone is theologically incorrect causes us to act as though we are excused from loving him or her as ourselves. The story of Jesus brokers no such compromise, not even in the name of truth, or, perhaps we should say, *especially* not in the name of truth.

And so, while certain cultural currents warrant voicing a warning to those who might downplay the gravity of sexual sin, the warning is equally apt for those of us who might downplay the gravity of our failure to love our neighbor as ourselves. Ours is no tepid story of a lukewarm God, and the redemption that takes hold of us is nothing less than life out of death. Many of us need as much rescuing from our failure to relentlessly pursue the good of our neighbor as our neighbors need rescuing from their failure to submit their sexual desires to the reign of Christ.

In the realm of sex as much as any other, the Bible testifies that all of us, whatever our sexual identity, are full of disordered desires that point us toward our need for the twin redemptive work of both forgiveness from guilt and liberation from bondage. We must exercise extreme caution in claiming that our own array of experiences demonstrates the creative hand of God at work rather than our need for that re-creating hand to bring us the grace of forgiveness and new life. And we must be eager to extend the same grace and transforming embrace that ushered us into the kingdom of God.

10

Living Interpretations

> A story is a way to say something that can't be said any other way, and it takes every word in the story to say what the meaning is.
>
> —Flannery O'Connor, *Mystery and Manners*[1]

As we come to some final reflections on Jesus and Paul, it occurs to me that someone might ask what kind of book this is. Is it a theology book? Of sorts, but not a book of systematic theology. Is it an ethics book? At times, though it is far from a rule book. Is it an introduction to Jesus and Paul? Of course, but hopefully the sort of introduction that begins a relationship more than the type that inaugurates a freshman intro course only to be forgotten at the end of the semester. This is a book of storied theology. We have walked together through the stories that Jesus and Paul inhabit in their actions, speech (in the case of Jesus), and writings (in the case of Paul)—stories that they invite us not merely to read and to analyze but also to renarrate in our own times and places.

Why have I returned to the category of story so often? Because both Jesus and Paul believe that their own lives, and the lives of Jesus's followers, are continuations of the narrative of Israel—the story to which the one true and living God has bound himself, and through which the true and living God is bringing about the reconciliation and rectification of the entire created order.

Why have I returned to the category of story so often? Because stories instruct by embodying and showing rather than simply telling. And it seems that North American evangelical Christianity suffers from "telling disease": our concept of what it means to know and believe the gospel is so tied to the *telling* of certain propositions that we have lost the vital place of *showing* what it looks like to be a faithful follower of Jesus. Or to put it in the traditional theological categories of faith and works, we're so convinced that Christianity means having faith in certain statements about Jesus that we have a hard time conceptualizing what it means to work in a manner that is pleasing to God. Or to echo the words of Jesus, we have lost the sense that the deeds of the church should be a cause for people, seeing our good works, to glorify our Father in heaven. Because our faith is a story, it is to be narrated not in the propositions of systematic theology but in the lives of faithful communities and individuals.

Why have I returned to the category of story so often? Because it highlights the fact that we as people are always interpreting the world by placing its vast array of data into overarching narratives that help us to understand and control the world we encounter every day. Researchers from academic fields as far flung as English, sociology, and neuroscience are telling us that to be human is to tell and to recognize stories. And Jesus and Paul give us the interpretive key for determining whether we are narrating properly. That key is the story of Jesus.

Christotelic Interpretation in Jesus and Paul

I apologize for using the peculiar word *Christotelic* in this section heading. Let me atone for my sin by explaining what it means and why it is helpful. The word was coined as scholars studied Paul's use of the Old Testament Scriptures. It is derived from Paul's statement in Romans 10:4 that "Christ is the end (Greek: *telos*) of the law." "Christotelic" sums up the idea that Christ and those who are united to him are the goal (another translation of *telos*) toward which the Old Testament is aiming, the destination toward which it is heading.[2] This means that the Scriptures were given for a purpose beyond themselves. They cannot simply be read and directly applied to our lives without our recognizing that they are given as part of a story that is going somewhere—and that "somewhere" is, primarily, the life, death, and resurrection of Jesus. Then, the story that finds its climax in Jesus works itself out in the life of the community formed in him. And so Richard Hays can also speak of an "ecclesiotelic" hermeneutic: a way to interpret the Scriptures that understands the goal of the Scriptures to be the formation of the people of God who are in Christ.

What I have laid out in this book is that both Jesus and Paul approach the story of God in this same way. They understand Jesus's ministry to be the climax of God's work among the people of Israel. Jesus is the promised king, God's anointed agent to bring about the fulfillment of God's promises to his people. Jesus actually creates that people around himself, extending a forgiving and transforming embrace. But more than this, Jesus's ministry reaches back behind the story of Israel as a particular people and brings about the restoration of God's purposes for the entire world (see chap. 1 above). Jesus's ministry is the beginning of the new creation itself, and his people comprise the new humanity, the renewal of the family of God (see above, chap. 2).

As we moved in our study from Jesus as inaugurator of new creation, to Jesus as first of God's family and determiner for the identity of God's people (chap. 3), and from there to our own calling to be faithful members of that family (chap. 4), we saw that the same interpretive move was required at each step. Jesus is the key to our identity and our actions. How does new creation come about? By the self-giving love and power of the crucified and resurrected Jesus. How is the family of God formed? By following Jesus along the way of the cross and receiving the commission of Jesus, the Resurrected One. What does the family of God do? It images God to the world by giving itself in the self-giving love first shown to us in Jesus. Jesus is the interpretive key not only for reading both the Scriptures and Jesus's connection to the story of Israel but also for reading our own lives as those who would follow him. Both Jesus and Paul claim through their actions and their words that the principle of interpretation that tells us we are reading the biblical story aright is the same principle of interpretation that will tell us when we are embodying the biblical story aright in our own place and time. In other words: how we read the Bible (hermeneutics), who we are (identity), and how we act (ethics) are inseparable.

Reading and Rereading Our World

The interpretive lens we use to tell the story of our Christian faith can and must carry over into our reading of our local and global stories as well. The claim of the Christian story is that God has enthroned Jesus as Lord over all things and that his reign becomes manifest in the world as God's people carry Jesus's cruciform ministry beyond the space demarcated by our Christian communities. This perspective radically reorients other ways of seeing and interpreting our world as well. It is the reality that has the power to call us out of other ways of reading our lives and the space they unfold in, and to summon us to repentance for the misspent energies that we too often exert in service of other overarching narratives. When we see that the Christian story is one that is lived as a continual narration of the life, death, and resurrection of Jesus, we also perceive that it is incumbent on us to reinterpret all of life through this lens.

Renarrating the Powers

One example of how this approach changes our perception is in the area of Christians in the so-called secular workplace. Often in Christian circles when folks talk about large spheres of power that govern our lives, such as government or corporate life, the imagery is that of small, powerless people being swept along by irresistible currents. There is, of course, a grain of truth in this: these are tremendous forces at work that we cannot control on our own. But the gospel narrative suggests that if all we see is a force no one can stand against then we have yet to have our eyes unveiled by the Christ event.

First, the Christian story is one that recognizes that the strength and rule exerted by the powers is not the ultimate power in the cosmos. Jesus is the King over all kings, the ruler of the masters of the earth. To confess that Jesus is raised from the dead is to confess that his kingdom is ultimate, and these seemingly insuperable powers are themselves swimming in a stronger current than any eddy they might create. The powers are themselves swimming in the stream of the advancing kingdom of God, and their own ability to endure, or failure to endure, will be in direct proportion to their willingness to render to God whatever glory they might possess. Contrary as it is to the way that we often experience the world, the powers of multinational corporations and superpower governments are not the ultimate powers ruling the earth—they are powers subject to a more powerful and enduring reign. This is, in fact, what the book of Revelation paints for us in vivid colors.

But there is more to the Christian narrative of the world than the power of rule itself. There is also the means by which that rule came to be. And here we have something that, if possible, is even harder for us to believe than the story of Jesus's more-powerful rule. The means by which the powers that oppose God are brought low is through their consumption of the saints who faithfully walk in the way of Jesus, saints who, in worshiping God alone, refuse to become complicit in the people-consuming, God-denying acquisition of wealth and power that typifies the rulers of the earth. Not only does Jesus come to his throne by being seemingly overpowered by the rulers of the world (Rome in his case) through his crucifixion, but also the story of the church is one in which we too overcome the powers by living out our union with Jesus in his death. Cruciformity is not just about putting to death the sinful desires of our hearts, it is also about bringing to consummation the defeat of the powers that work against all human flourishing and that strive against giving all glory to God.

Kingdom Stories of Life

If interpreting the world through the categories of Jesus's death and resurrection gives us new lenses for assessing our place in a world gone wrong, it also has the capacity for opening our eyes to the world as it shows signs of life. Here we are butting up against the place where Christians have far too often consigned God's good world to the rubbish bin of history. Once we realize that God's work in Christ is not to save us out of this world but rather to save this world through us (something confirmed, above all else, by telling a story that climaxes with the resurrection of the body), we have our eyes opened to surprising signs of life, signs of the story of God breaking through the story lines of the world that narrate life as though it were devoid of God. Then we can begin to interpret the world as a place where Christ is at work, even if there is no member of the church there to be his official spokesperson.

If we can take hold of this, it has the power to transform completely how we participate in the mission of God. Our understanding of God's mission in the world will directly correlate with what we understand to be the extent of God's redemptive activity. When we narrowly focus on individual conversion, mission is equated with bringing individuals to repentance and faith. These are good things, to be sure, but are they exactly the same as joining the mission of God in the world? If God's mission is bigger than redeeming individual souls, then ours will be as well. We can find ourselves working in the name of God as far as the curse is found.

Speaking recently at a retreat, I had it hammered home just how difficult it is for many of us to have our minds reoriented about the breadth of the kingdom of God. I had outlined a vision for God's restorative work of new creation, suggesting that the resurrection of Jesus means that God is renewing the cosmos, society, and communities, as well as individuals. But when I split the audience into groups to talk about how this might shape how they understand their calling into various parts of the world, every group came back and told me how their work, hobbies, and interests might create opportunities to share a gospel presentation. The idea that we might work with God for the renewal of the world was not a category they could accept as one that would extend the reign of God. That group as a whole reinterpreted my words as simply putting into cosmic context how they might share the story of Jesus dying for the forgiveness of our sins.

But I want people to know that we can be as much an agent of the kingdom of God in the work we are doing as we can in using that work as a springboard for sharing a "gospel presentation." This is a message that I hope hits home most clearly with folks working in the "secular" workforce. It is tragic when the outcome of learning the Christian narrative is that we get sucked deeper into Christian subcultures and drawn only to paychecks written by Christian institutions. Instead, we should find ourselves empowered to more faithfully live out our Christian callings within whatever industry or service organization we are gifted to thrive in. Such "secular" work can be our Christian calling if it reflects both thankfulness to God, the giver of the talents required, and loyalty to Christ, who is the ultimate master of our industries.

The most basic confession of the Christian life is "Jesus is Lord." This means that Jesus is master of the entire world. Though the church is the place that is most particularly called by his name, the church as we conceive of it is insufficiently broad to contain the whole of the kingdom of God. The church is not the kingdom of God on earth but is one manifestation of the reign of God, and the place where, ideally, that reign is being brought to bear on the world.

Nonetheless, where we do not see the church, we may still be able to see God at work restoring the world through the power of the Spirit of the resurrected Jesus. If hunger is a sign of the created world gone awry through misuse of natural resources and misuse of human powers of distribution, then any time the hungry are fed, the kingdom of God is coming near. If slavery is a sign of the created world gone awry through exploitation of power, then any time the enslaved are set free, the kingdom of God is coming near. If the disintegration of human relationships is a sign that the created world has gone awry through insecurities, abuse of power, failure of love, then any time communities are formed, any time a marriage is saved, any time love is operative, the kingdom of God is coming near. In each instance, the blessings of the risen King of Love are making themselves known.

There is, of course, a danger here, that we might confuse "what is happening in the world" with "what God is doing in the world," as though these two statements meant the same thing. And perhaps those from more progressive church traditions are more susceptible to that particular trap. But there is a danger in falling off the other side of the horse as well, the danger of so restricting the activities of God to the church or to issues of personal spiritual growth that we miss our calling to praise God for what God is doing in the world and our summons to participate with this broader work as a component of our own Jesus stories.

A Storied Gospel

And with that last sentence we are right up, again, on the conjunction between how we interpret the Jesus story, how we interpret the world, and how we know what we are to do. Understanding that the Jesus story is about not just Jesus becoming Lord of my heart but rather Jesus as enthroned Lord of the entire cosmos opens up a broad vista of what faithful discipleship might look like. Such a story demands that we consider not only our church attendance and Bible reading as more or less faithfully resembling the Christian story but also our spending, saving, and giving of money; our use, abuse, and sustaining of the earth and its resources; our ignoring, engaging, helping, or abusing of people who are impoverished; and our honesty, self-giving, self-serving, and avoidance in relationships with other people. In each of these areas we are confronted with the questions: Is my life, and the life of my community, faithfully embodying the Christian narrative? Am I living a cruciform life in order to thereby experience resurrection now and bring the future age of glory to bear on the present?

Both Jesus and Paul are actively interpreting their worlds, showing how various scenes they encounter are subplots in the story of God or in the counterstory that actively works against it. To live out the Christian story in our world is not only to better discern the hand of God at work (or its absence—including false claims of those who would speak and act in God's name) but also to better discern how we can see that kingdom brought more fully to fruition.

Reading and Rereading Paul

This book began with an invitation to reread Paul. To reacquaint my readers with the apostle, I have brought him into conversation with Jesus and thereby claimed that the two speak with one voice to a much greater extent than is often imagined. At the heart of this claim is that Paul, like Jesus, is telling the story of Israel's God as a narrative that includes you and me. It reaches beyond the pages of Scripture, extends past its climactic scene in Christ, and enfolds the people of God as they themselves carry it forward into new places at later times.

Of course, there are differences between Jesus and Paul. Paul is rearticulating the Jesus story for people in much different social contexts than those Jesus spoke to. In his work we catch our first glimpse of a sustained attempt to apply the gospel in the world beyond first-century Judaism. Paul's letters show significant signs of contextualization of the story—some likely intentional and some simply the unconscious actions of someone who is working in a given time and place.

Because of the need to speak and live the Word in such particular settings, we who sit two thousand years removed from Paul's life find ourselves at varying levels of understanding of and comfort with the story as he told it. Mostly, we have seen convergence between Jesus's story and Paul's, and thereby argued that these stories provide the narrative texture for our own. But we have also seen at times that our call to live out the same story requires us to leave some of the ancient expression of it behind. I argued that the elements of patriarchy and of slavery are two of the places where faithful adherence to the Jesus story pushed us beyond biblical precedent—not in order to overturn the biblical narrative but in order to more faithfully play it out in our own particular contexts. And this is the goal: to be conformed to the image of Christ not by mere repetition of the Bible but by more faithfully embodying its gospel story in our own communities.

Such contextualizing is always the interpretive task of the church—and what we as modern readers are always doing with the Bible whether we acknowledge it or not. There is no "straight" reading of the Bible that does not require adaptation for our own context. There is no "doing what the Bible says" that is not run through a grid of associated theological assumptions. There is no "adherence to the Word of God" that does not spring from within a prior understanding of what it looks like to live the life of a faithful follower of Jesus.

And so this book functions on several levels at once. It is asking us all to become more self-aware of what we bring to the table and why we read certain passages the way we do. It is asking us to listen more closely, with a first-century ear, to what Jesus and Paul have to say. And it is asking us all to reframe our understanding of both figures in light of what we have seen. With this new perspective on both figures in hand, we return to the New Testament and hear differently what Jesus and Paul have to say. Thus, we are always in a process of learning and relearning how to better read and understand both the biblical texts and our own hearts as readers of them.

This book is an invitation to return to Jesus and Paul, and to reread both afresh, listening for the stories of the God of Israel—even where those stories strike us as offensive or strange. Rereading them with ever-greater appreciation for what they were trying to accomplish in their day is a key component of learning our own defining narrative as the twenty-first-century people of God. Wrestling with the biblical account, we will discover ever afresh how to faithfully live it out in our communities.

I do not exempt myself as author of this book from the process of returning again and again to the defining stories. I anticipate that through the conversations this book generates I will be shown by other followers of Jesus various ways that my own social location, theological presuppositions, and personal history have blurred my vision—both as I have sought to perceive the biblical text itself and as I have sought to bring into focus what faithful Christian community looks like in the twenty-first century. Indeed, it would seem the height of arrogance to write a book claiming that Paul and Jesus set us on trajectories for living out a story in the future and then turn and think that I have written a definitive word for all times and places—a word more definitive than theirs!

No, this book is a piece of my own theological journey, my own story of narrating Jesus and Paul for the time and place in which I find myself. I quite often discover that being on a theological journey is much more fruitful and productive, if often more painful, than staying in place and building a large theological house. I find this to be true not only for individuals but also for the church itself, which had to move beyond Jesus to articulate a theology about Jesus, had to discern how to write gentiles into Israel's story, had to reflect deeply on the implications of claiming that a crucified Messiah is the resurrected Lord who sits enthroned over all things at God's right hand.

And so I invite you to return to the stories of Jesus, yes, but also to the letters of Paul and to find there a wise traveling companion. Find in him both a witness to how the church embodied Jesus's story in the first century and a guide for how to faithfully embody it now. Find in him a challenge to our contemporary pursuits of peace at all costs, to our strategies of self-preservation, to our baptism of consumer culture, to our transposing of the world's economy into the key of standing within the church. Find in him an interpreter of the Jesus story, one who not only tells us how the story should be read but also models for us how to embody that retelling through the life-giving cruciformity that is the story of Jesus.

Notes

Introduction

1. John D. Caputo, *What Would Jesus Deconstruct? The Good News of Postmodernism for the Church* (Grand Rapids: Baker Academic, 2007), 27.

2. This famous quote is from Rudolf Bultmann, *Theology of the New Testament*, 2nd ed., trans. K. Grobel (Waco: Baylor University Press, 2007), 33, though he uses it in a slightly different context.

3. See Caputo, *What Would Jesus Deconstruct?*, e.g., 27.

4. See Richard B. Hays, *The Faith of Jesus Christ: The Narrative Substructure of Galatians 3:1–4:11*, 2nd ed. (Grand Rapids: Eerdmans, 2002); N. T. Wright, *The New Testament and the People of God* (Minneapolis: Fortress, 1992); idem, *Jesus and the Victory of God* (Minneapolis: Fortress, 1996).

Chapter 1 Jesus Stories in the Gospels and Paul

1. Karl Barth, *Church Dogmatics 1.1: The Doctrine of the Word of God*, trans. G. W. Bromiley, ed. G. W. Bromiley and T. F. Torrance (New York: T&T Clark, 1975), 137 (quotation marks added).

2. Unless otherwise noted, all Bible translations are my own.

3. See J. R. Daniel Kirk, *Unlocking Romans: Resurrection and the Justification of God* (Grand Rapids: Eerdmans, 2008).

4. N. T. Wright, *The Climax of the Covenant: Christ and the Law in Pauline Theology* (Minneapolis: Fortress, 1992).

5. This discussion is based on Richard B. Hays, "The Conversion of the Imagination: Scripture and Eschatology in 1 Corinthians," in *The Conversion of the Imagination: Paul as Interpreter of Israel's Scripture* (Grand Rapids: Eerdmans, 2005), 1–24, esp. 3–4.

6. See ibid.
7. Ibid.
8. I say "dominion" here because the Greek word usually translated "kingdom" (and the Aramaic word Jesus is likely to have used) can mean either the sphere over which one rules or the exercise of that rule. The term *dominion* captures this dual sense.
9. Another instance occurs in John 12:28.
10. See, for example, Richard B. Hays, *The Faith of Jesus Christ: The Narrative Substructure of Galatians 3:1–4:11*, 2nd ed. (Grand Rapids: Eerdmans, 2002), and Wright, *Climax*.
11. Hays, *Faith*, 29.
12. Mark Turner, *The Literary Mind* (Oxford: Oxford University Press, 1996), v, 20.
13. Michael J. Gorman, *Reading Paul* (Eugene, OR: Cascade Books, 2008), 145–66.

Chapter 2 New Creation and the Kingdom of God

1. C. S. Lewis, *Prince Caspian* (San Francisco: Harper Collins, 1951), 69.
2. See Richard J. Middleton, *The Liberating Image: The* Imago Dei *in Genesis 1* (Grand Rapids: Brazos, 2005).
3. Scot McKnight, *A Community Called Atonement* (Nashville: Abingdon, 2007), 62 (italics original).

Chapter 3 Christianity as Community

1. John R. Franke, *Manifold Witness: The Plurality of Truth* (Nashville: Abingdon, 2009), 32.
2. Scot McKnight, *A Community Called Atonement* (Nashville: Abingdon, 2007), 23–24 (italics original).
3. Similar understanding of this vocation to be the world's light can be found in N. T. Wright, *Jesus and the Victory of God* (Minneapolis: Fortress, 1996), 309–10, 444.
4. See J. R. Daniel Kirk, *Unlocking Romans: Resurrection and the Justification of God* (Grand Rapids: Eerdmans, 2008).
5. Richard B. Hays, *Conversion of the Imagination: Paul as Interpreter of Israel's Scriptures* (Grand Rapids: Eerdmans, 2005), 9.
6. Ibid., 117.

Chapter 4 Living Out the Jesus Narrative

1. Dietrich Bonhoeffer, *The Cost of Discipleship* (New York: Touchstone, 1995), 89.
2. Richard B. Hays, *The Moral Vision of the New Testament: Community, Cross, New Creation; A Contemporary Introduction to New Testament Ethics* (San Francisco: HarperSanFrancisco, 1996), 84–85.
3. Michael J. Gorman, *Apostle of the Crucified Lord: A Theological Introduction to Paul and His Letters* (Grand Rapids: Eerdmans, 2004), 245.
4. Ibid., 237.
5. This way of putting it is from Michael J. Gorman, *Inhabiting the Cruciform God: Kenosis, Justification, and Theosis in Paul's Narrative Soteriology* (Grand Rapids: Eerdmans, 2009), 44.
6. See Samuel Wells, *Improvisation: The Drama of Christian Ethics* (Grand Rapids: Brazos, 2004), 11–31.
7. Ibid., 41 (italics original).

8. For more on the inherent connection between justification by faith and Christians' life transformation, see Gorman, *Inhabiting the Cruciform God*, 40–104.

9. Wayne A. Meeks, *The Origins of Christian Morality: The First Two Centuries* (New Haven: Yale University Press, 1993), 196–97.

Chapter 5 Judgment and Inclusion

1. Miroslav Volf, *Exclusion and Embrace: A Theological Exploration of Identity, Otherness, and Reconciliation* (Nashville: Abingdon, 1996), 23.

2. This is a favorite phrase of N. T. Wright, occurring, among other places, in *Jesus and the Victory of God* (Minneapolis: Fortress, 1996), 272, 273; *The Lord and His Prayer* (Grand Rapids: Eerdmans, 1997), 48; and *Simply Christian: Why Christianity Makes Sense* (San Francisco: HarperOne, 2010), 103.

3. N. T. Wright, *What Saint Paul Really Said: Was Paul of Tarsus the Real Founder of Christianity?* (Grand Rapids: Eerdmans, 1997), 158.

4. Richard B. Hays, *First Corinthians*, Interpretation (Louisville: Westminster John Knox, 1997), 82.

5. Ibid., 84.

6. John Franke, *Manifold Witness: The Plurality of Truth* (Nashville: Abingdon, 2009), 27.

7. "Big Tent Christianity: Being and Becoming the Church," http://transformingtheology.org/calendar/big-tent-christianity-being-and-becoming-church (accessed May 24, 2010).

8. Volf, *Exclusion and Embrace*, 36.

Chapter 6 Women in the Story of God

1. John Chrysostom was a priest and eventually an archbishop who served in the late fourth through early fifth centuries. This quote can be found in a slightly different form in *The Homilies of St. John Chrysostom*, Nicene and Post-Nicene Fathers, Series I, (14 vols.; Peabody, Mass.: Hendrickson, 1999), 11:555.

2. Paul K. Jewett, *Man as Male and Female: A Study of Sexual Relationships from a Theological Point of View* (Grand Rapids: Eerdmans, 1976), 142.

3. This interpretation of the disciples as rocky soil follows that of Mary Ann Tolbert, *Sowing the Word: Mark's World in Literary-Historical Perspective* (Minneapolis: Fortress, 1996).

4. Joel B. Green, *The Gospel of Luke*, New International Commentary on the New Testament (Grand Rapids: Eerdmans, 1997), 318.

5. Ibid., 320 (italics original).

6. Ibid., 437.

7. Eldon Jay Epp, *Junia: The First Woman Apostle* (Minneapolis: Fortress, 2005).

8. A summary of the dynamics discussed here, including extensive bibliography, can be found in Anthony Thiselton, *The First Epistle to the Corinthians*, New International Greek Testament Commentary (Grand Rapids: Eerdmans, 2000), 799–848.

9. Ibid., 828–29.

10. See Judith Gundry-Volf, "Gender and Creation in 1 Corinthians 11:2–16: A Study in Paul's Theological Method," in *Evangelium, Schriftauslegung, Kirche*,

ed. J. Adna, S. J. Hafemann, and O. Hofius (Göttingen: Vandenhoeck & Ruprecht, 1997), 151–71.

11. See, for example, Aristotle, *Politics* I:II, V.

12. N. T. Wright, "Chapel Message" (talk given at the Wheaton Theology Conference, Wheaton, IL, April 16, 2010); online, http://wetn.stratumvideo.com/TheoCon10Media/mp3/100416Wright.mp3 (accessed August 2, 2010).

13. For more along these lines, see John Stackhouse, *Finally Feminist: A Pragmatic Christian Understanding of Gender* (Grand Rapids: Baker Academic, 2005).

Chapter 7 Liberty and Justice for All?

1. Martin Luther King Jr., "I Have a Dream," available online at http://www.usconstitution.net/dream.html (accessed July 17, 2010).

2. Howard Thurman, *Jesus and the Disinherited* (1949; repr., Boston: Beacon Press, 1996), 30–31.

3. This approach to Paul has been given traction by the so-called new perspective on Paul, particularly in the works of James Dunn and N. T. Wright. At times, however, as modern scholars have spoken of the church leaving behind the need to become Jewish, they have sounded like the NT calls us to abandon all ethnic identity markers. Instead of such an ethnicity-free vision, a more robust, creation-redeeming articulation of the gospel includes a diversity of ethnicities glorifying God together.

4. John Piper, *Let the Nations Be Glad! The Supremacy of God in Missions*, 3rd ed. (Grand Rapids: Baker Academic, 2010), 15.

5. A transcription of the speech is available online at http://www.usconstitution.net/dream.html (accessed July 17, 2010).

Chapter 8 Sex in the Plot of God's Stories

1. Gary A. Anderson, *The Genesis of Perfection: Adam and Even in Jewish and Christian Imagination* (Louisville: Westminster John Knox, 2001), 182.

2. The Kinsey Institute for Research in Sex, Gender, and Reproduction, "Frequently Asked Questions to The Kinsey Institute," http://www.iub.edu/~kinsey/resources/FAQ.html (accessed July 22, 2010).

3. Miroslav Volf, "Open Forum with Miroslav Volf: Faith and Globalization" (San Francisco, July 17, 2010).

Chapter 9 Homosexuality under the Reign of Christ

1. "Love Love Love," lyrics and music by John Darnielle, 2005.

2. On reading Romans 1, several good resources exist. An article by Everett R. Kalin agrees with the main substance of the exposition given here, using it to suggest that Romans 1 should not be a barrier to homosexual ordination ("Romans 1:26–27 and Homosexuality," in *Currents in Theology and Mission* 30 [2003]: 423–32; available online at http://findarticles.com/p/articles/mi_m0MDO/is_6_30/ai_111696783/ [accessed September 27, 2010]). Richard B. Hays agrees with the main substance of the interpretation offered here and uses it in his argument against affirmation of homosexuality by the church (*The Moral Vision of the New Testament: Community, Cross, New Creation; A Contemporary Introduction to New Testament Ethics* [San Francisco: HarperSanFrancisco, 1996], 379–406). Douglas A. Campbell agrees with

the exegesis given here but assigns it to a teacher with whom Paul is disagreeing and therefore sees it as the position that stands in antithesis to Paul's own understanding of the issue (*The Deliverance of God: An Apocalyptic Rereading of Justification in Paul* [Grand Rapids: Eerdmans, 2009], e.g., 530–93).

3. Dale Martin, *Sex and the Single Savior: Gender and Sexuality in Biblical Interpretation* (Louisville: Westminster John Knox, 2006), 38–43.

4. I am indebted to my friend Justin Dombrowski for this additional research.

5. Martin, *Sex*, 45.

6. Daniel Burke, "Gay Debate Mirrors Church Dispute, Split on Slavery," Religious News Service, July 21, 2010, http://www.religionnews.com/index.php?/rnstext/gay_debate_mirrors_church_dispute_split_on_slavery/ (accessed July 24, 2010).

7. See also William J. Webb, *Slaves, Women & Homosexuals: Exploring the Hermeneutics of Cultural Analysis* (Downers Grove, IL: InterVarsity, 2001).

8. This approach is taken by Luke Timothy Johnson, *Scripture & Discernment: Decision Making in the Church* (Nashville: Abingdon, 1996), 144–48.

Chapter 10 Living Interpretations

1. Flannery O'Connor, *Mystery and Manners* (New York: Farrar, Straus & Giroux, 1969), 96.

2. Richard Hays, focusing on the church as the end result of Christ's work, used the term *ecclesiotelic*. Recognizing, however, that the church is those who are "in Christ," others later developed the term *Christotelic*, for example Peter Enns, *Inspiration and Incarnation: Evangelicals and the Problem of the Old Testament* (Grand Rapids: Baker Academic, 2005).

Scripture Index

Mark

Luke

John

Acts

Romans

1 Corinthians

2 Corinthians

Galatians

Ephesians

Philippians

Colossians

1 Thessalonians

1 Timothy

Hebrews

James

Jude

Revelation

Subject Index